CREMA ™

JOHNNIE CHRISTMAS
DANTE LUIZ

WITH RYAN FERRIER & ATLA HRAFNEY

Thanks to **Kafka's Coffee** and
Paper Crane Coffee, the wonderful Vancouver
cafes where much of *CREMA* was written.

—JOHNNIE

Thank you to my wife, **H. Pueyo**, for her
undying support and help in this project.

—DANTE

CREMA

A haunted romance
in three chapters,
brought to you by:

JOHNNIE CHRISTMAS
Script, Cover Art

DANTE LUIZ
Art

RYAN FERRIER
Letters, Logo Design

ATLA HRAFNEY
Edits

RELISH NEW BRAND EXPERIENCE
Design

DARK HORSE TEAM

MIKE RICHARDSON
President and Publisher

DANIEL CHABON
Editor

CHUCK HOWITT & KONNER KNUDSEN
Assistant Editors

MAY HIJIKURO
Designer

JASON RICKERD
Digital Art Technician

SPECIAL THANKS TO THE COMIXOLOGY ORIGINALS TEAM

NEIL HANKERSON Executive Vice President • TOM WEDDLE Chief Financial Officer
• DALE LAFOUNTAIN Chief Information Officer • TIM WIESCH Vice President of
Licensing • MATT PARKINSON Vice President of Marketing • VANESSA TODD-HOLMES
Vice President of Production and Scheduling • MARK BERNARDI Vice President
of Book Trade and Digital Sales • RANDY LAHRMAN Vice President of Product
Development • KEN LIZZI General Counsel • DAVE MARSHALL Editor in Chief
• DAVEY ESTRADA Editorial Director • CHRIS WARNER Senior Books Editor •
CARY GRAZZINI Director of Specialty Projects • LIA RIBACCHI Art Director • MATT
DRYER Director of Digital Art and Prepress • MICHAEL GOMBOS Senior Director
of Licensed Publications • KARI YADRO Director of Custom Programs • KARI
TORSON Director of International Licensing

Published by Dark Horse Books
A division of Dark Horse Comics LLC
10956 SE Main Street
Milwaukie, OR 97222

First edition: January 2022
Trade paperback ISBN: 978-1-50672-603-8

10 9 8 7 6 5 4 3 2 1
Printed in China

Comic Shop Locator Service: comicshoplocator.com

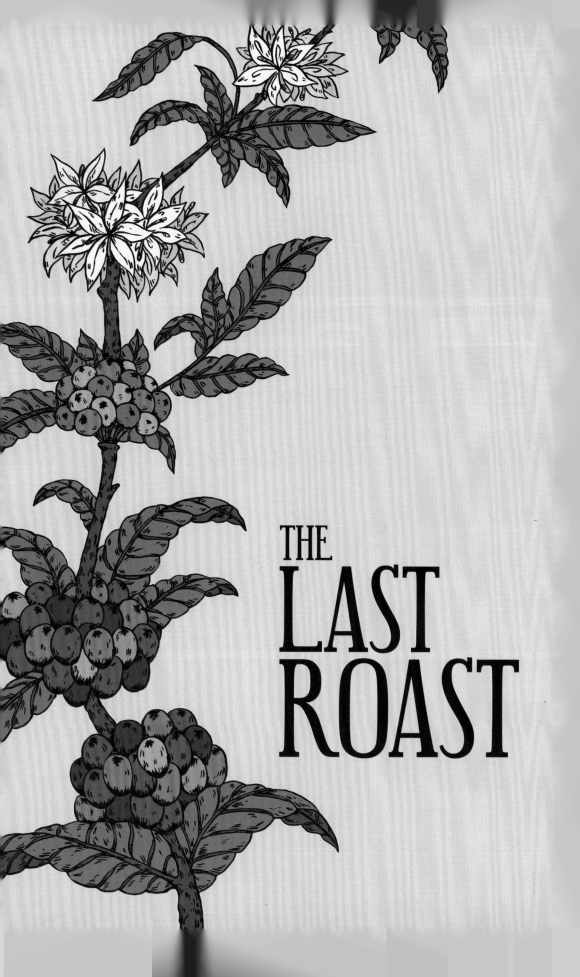

THE LAST ROAST

ESME ALWAYS FEARED SLEEP.

AS A CHILD, SHE WORRIED **MONSTERS** LURKED THERE. WAITING TO SWALLOW HER UP IN THE DARK WHERE NO ONE WOULD FIND HER. SHE'D BE LOST. *INVISIBLE.*

SO SHE MADE A PLAN TO DRINK SLEEP AWAY.

SSSHHH!

BEEP BEEEEEP

SUPER CAFEINATED

NIGHT AFTER NIGHT...

Dad's RULE

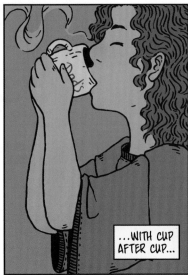

...WITH CUP AFTER CUP...

...OF **COFFEE.** **LOTS** AND LOTS OF COFFEE.

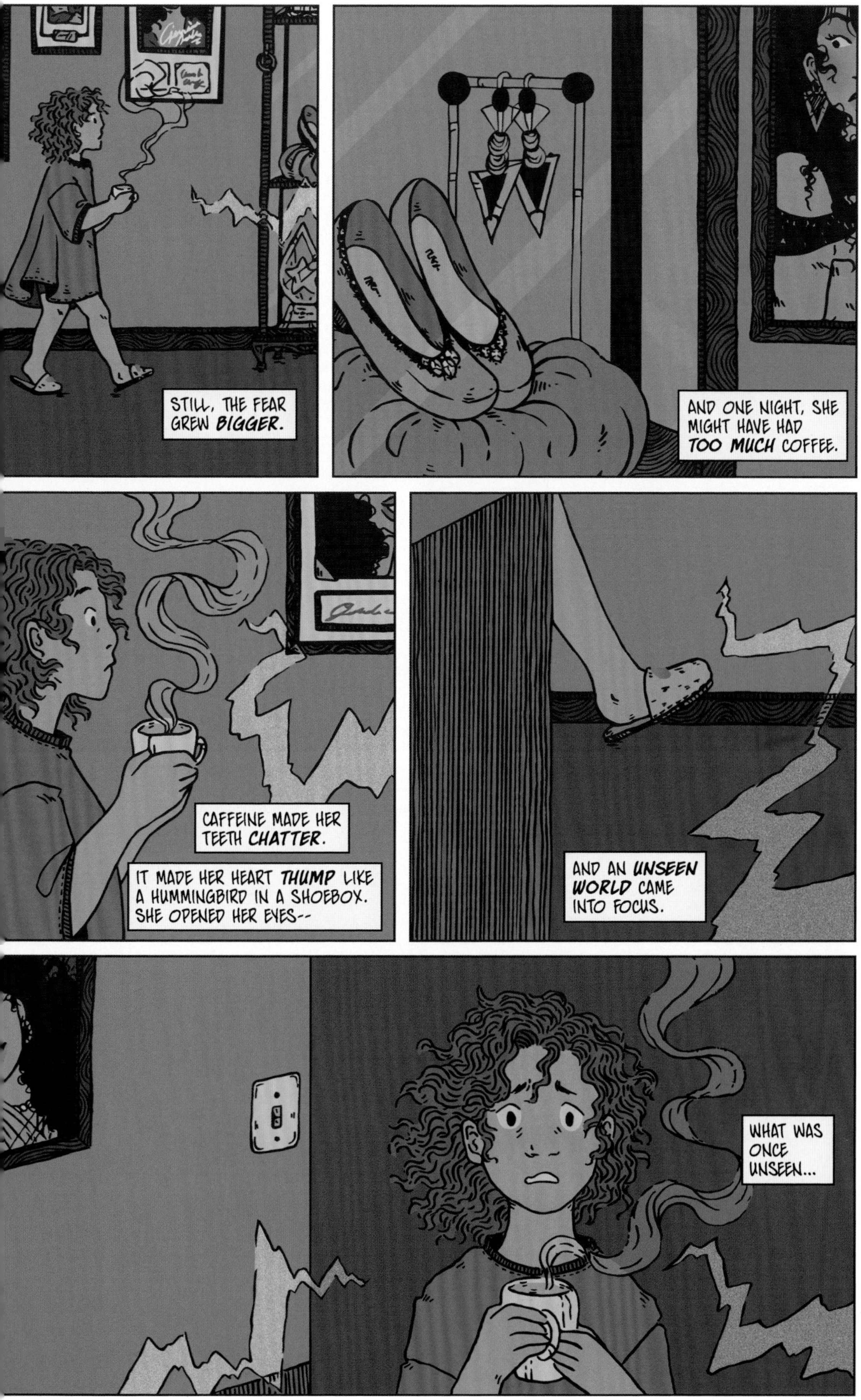
STILL, THE FEAR GREW **BIGGER**.
AND ONE NIGHT, SHE MIGHT HAVE HAD **TOO MUCH** COFFEE.
CAFFEINE MADE HER TEETH **CHATTER**.
IT MADE HER HEART **THUMP** LIKE A HUMMINGBIRD IN A SHOEBOX. SHE OPENED HER EYES--
AND AN **UNSEEN WORLD** CAME INTO FOCUS.
WHAT WAS ONCE UNSEEN...

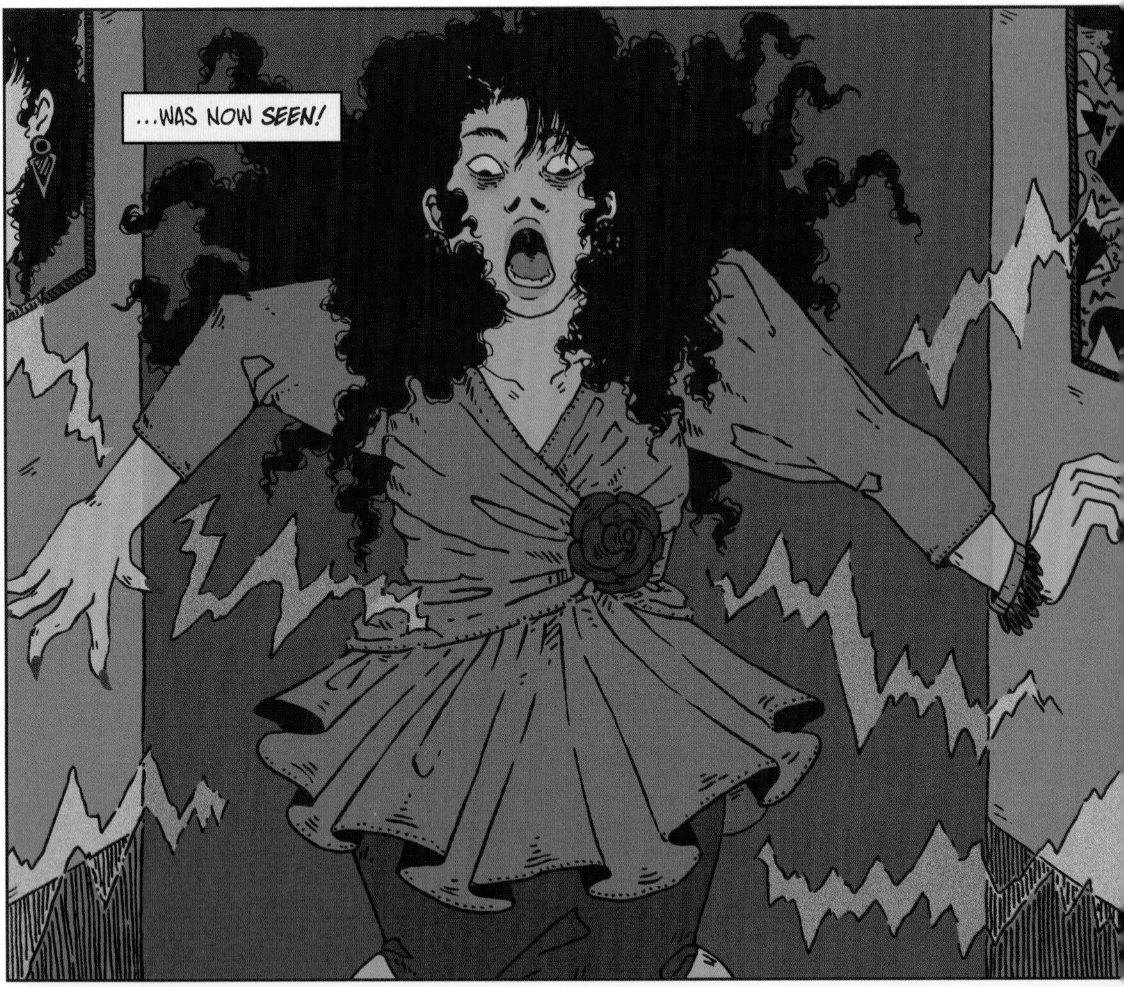
...WAS NOW SEEN!

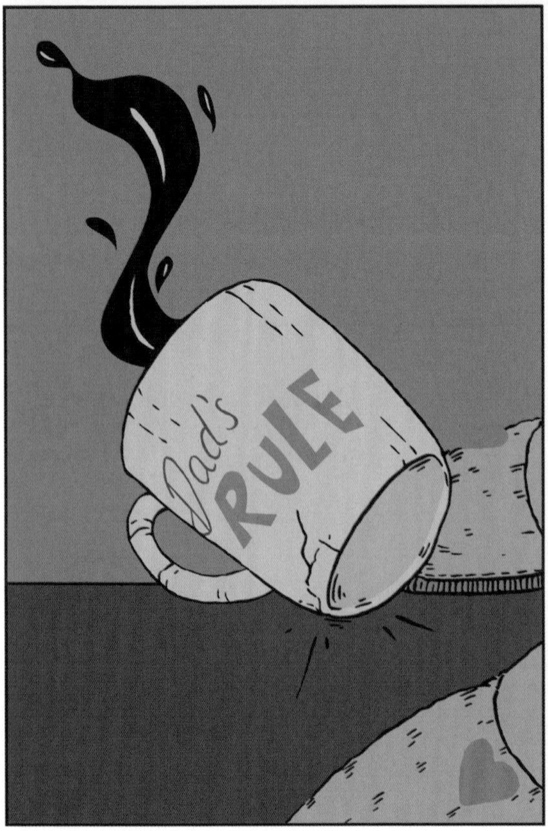
Dad's RULE

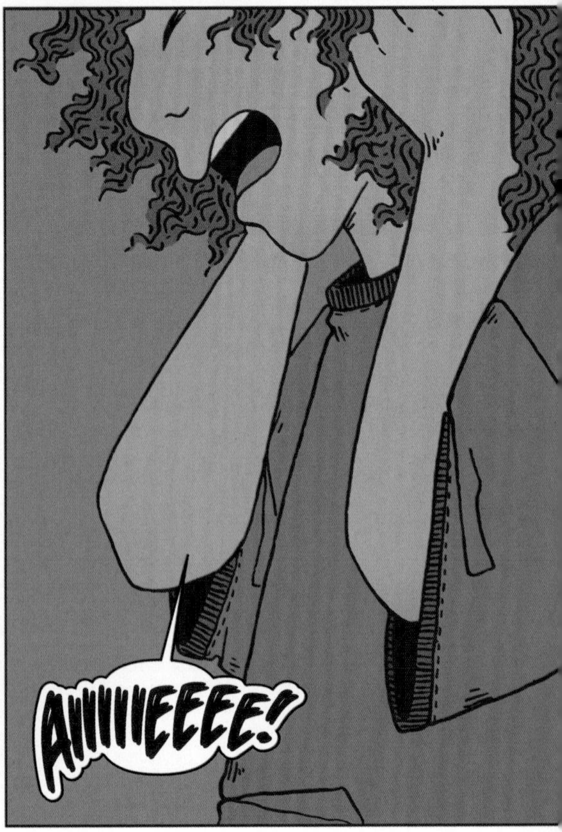
AIIIIIEEEEE!

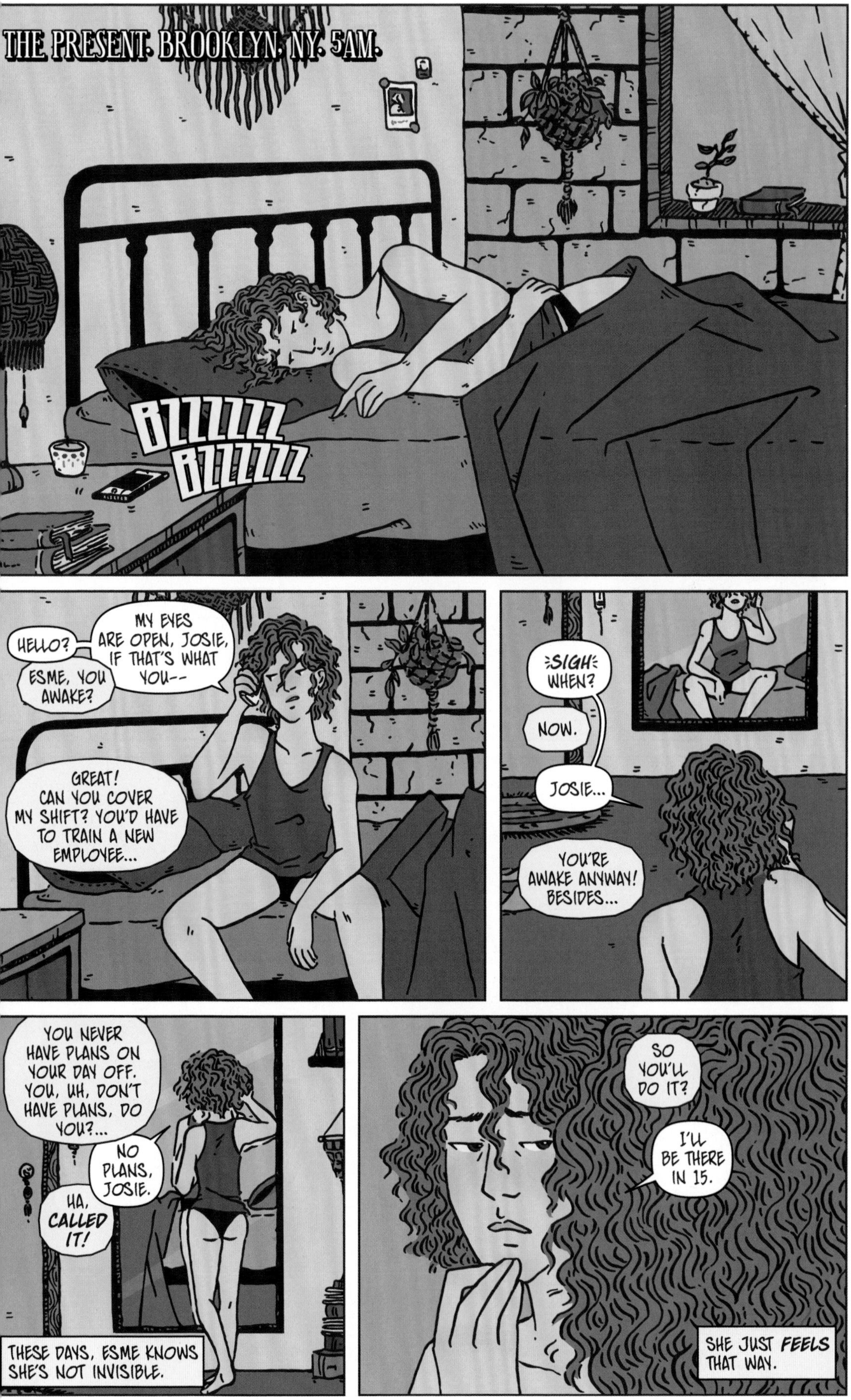
THE PRESENT. BROOKLYN, NY. 5AM.
BZZZZZZ BZZZZZZ
HELLO?
ESME, YOU AWAKE?
MY EYES ARE OPEN, JOSIE, IF THAT'S WHAT YOU--
GREAT! CAN YOU COVER MY SHIFT? YOU'D HAVE TO TRAIN A NEW EMPLOYEE...
SIGH WHEN?
NOW.
JOSIE...
YOU'RE AWAKE ANYWAY! BESIDES...
YOU NEVER HAVE PLANS ON YOUR DAY OFF. YOU, UH, DON'T HAVE PLANS, DO YOU?...
NO PLANS, JOSIE.
HA, CALLED IT!
THESE DAYS, ESME KNOWS SHE'S NOT INVISIBLE.
SO YOU'LL DO IT?
I'LL BE THERE IN 15.
SHE JUST FEELS THAT WAY.

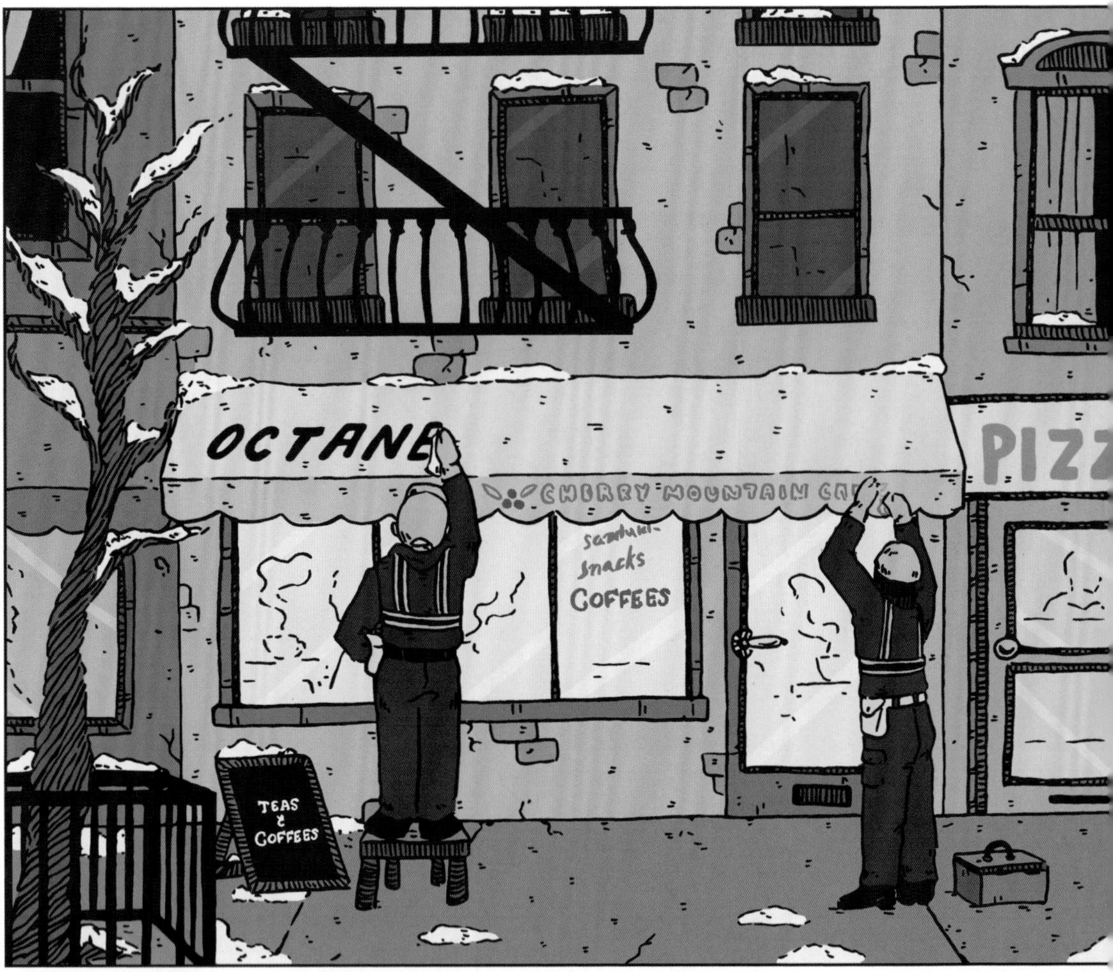
OCTANE
CHERRY MOUNTAIN
Snacks
COFFEES
TEAS & COFFEES

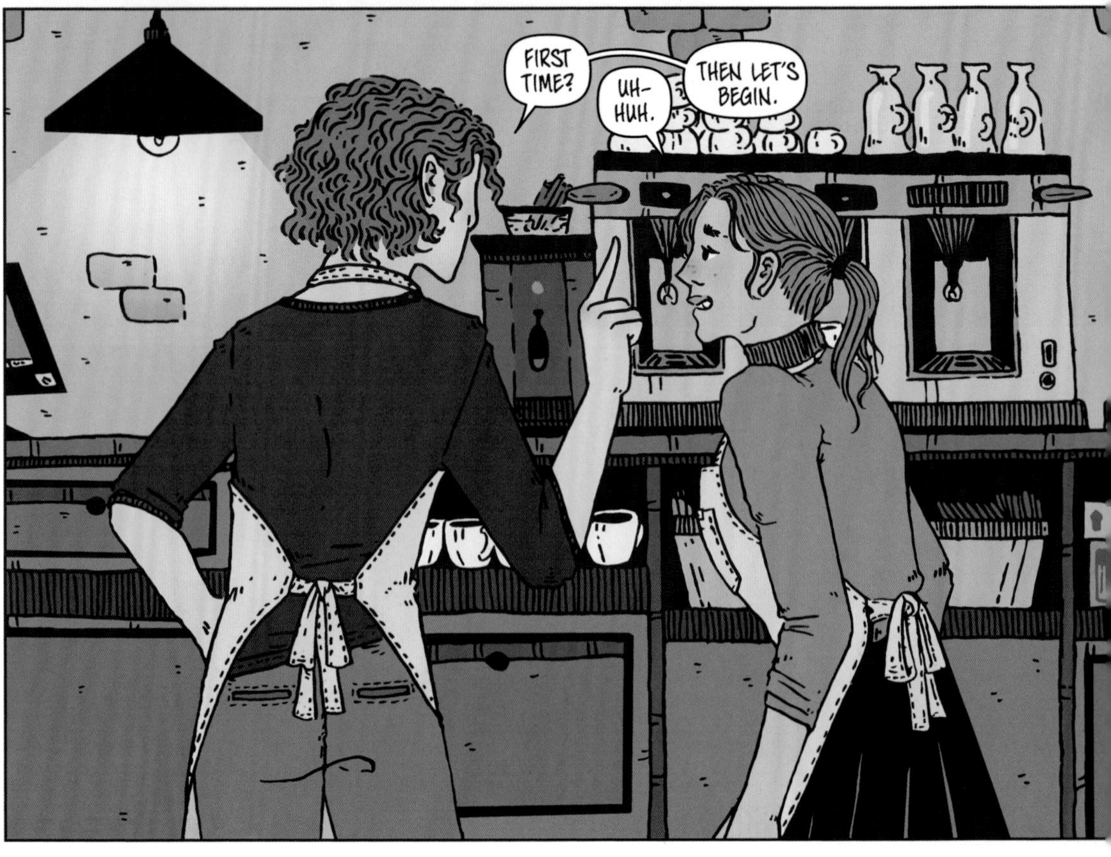
FIRST TIME?
UH-HUH.
THEN LET'S BEGIN.

A GREAT CUP STARTS WITH GREAT BEANS. AND OUR OWNERS, CHERRY MOUNTAIN FARM IN BRAZIL, MAKE THE FINEST COFFEE ON EARTH.

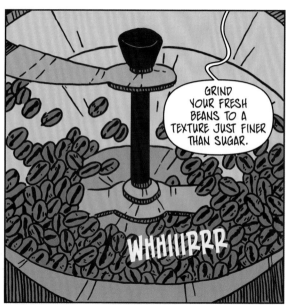

GRIND YOUR FRESH BEANS TO A TEXTURE JUST FINER THAN SUGAR.

WHHIIIRRR

LEVEL OFF THE GROUNDS AND TAMP DOWN FIRMLY.

REPLACE THE PORTAFILTER, PULL YOUR SHOT. AND BEHOLD...

...THE *CREMA*. A MOMENTARY STORM OF TEENY TINY BUBBLES. VELVETY, OILY, SWEET...

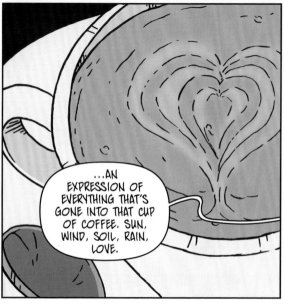

...AN EXPRESSION OF EVERYTHING THAT'S GONE INTO THAT CUP OF COFFEE. SUN, WIND, SOIL, RAIN, LOVE.

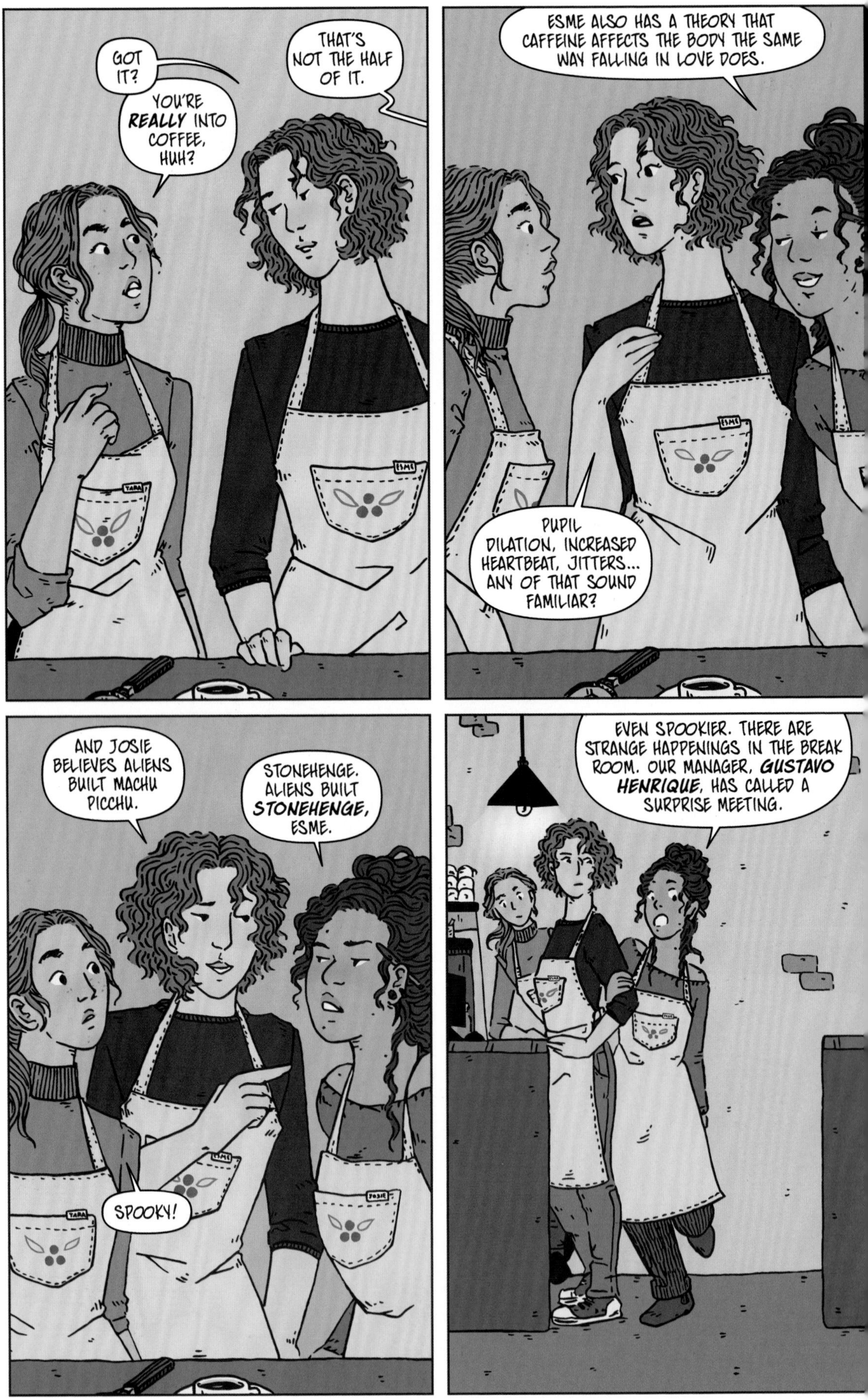
GOT IT?
YOU'RE REALLY INTO COFFEE, HUH?
THAT'S NOT THE HALF OF IT.
ESME ALSO HAS A THEORY THAT CAFFEINE AFFECTS THE BODY THE SAME WAY FALLING IN LOVE DOES.
PUPIL DILATION, INCREASED HEARTBEAT, JITTERS... ANY OF THAT SOUND FAMILIAR?
AND JOSIE BELIEVES ALIENS BUILT MACHU PICCHU.
STONEHENGE. ALIENS BUILT STONEHENGE, ESME.
SPOOKY!
EVEN SPOOKIER. THERE ARE STRANGE HAPPENINGS IN THE BREAK ROOM. OUR MANAGER, GUSTAVO HENRIQUE, HAS CALLED A SURPRISE MEETING.

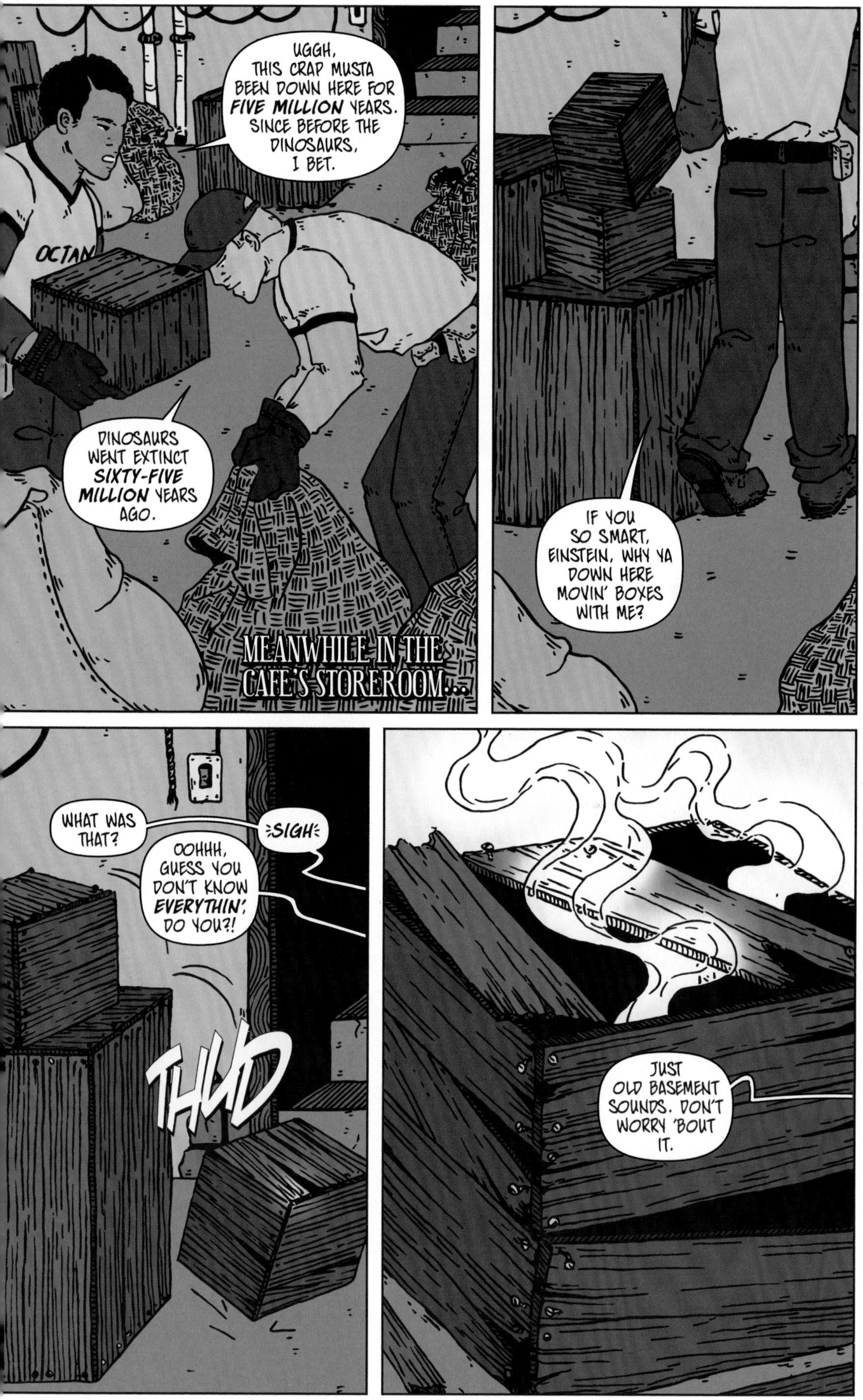
UGGH, THIS CRAP MUSTA BEEN DOWN HERE FOR FIVE MILLION YEARS. SINCE BEFORE THE DINOSAURS, I BET.
DINOSAURS WENT EXTINCT SIXTY-FIVE MILLION YEARS AGO.
OCTAN
MEANWHILE IN THE CAFE'S STOREROOM...
IF YOU SO SMART, EINSTEIN, WHY YA DOWN HERE MOVIN' BOXES WITH ME?
WHAT WAS THAT?
SIGH
OOHHH, GUESS YOU DON'T KNOW EVERYTHIN', DO YOU?!
THUD
JUST OLD BASEMENT SOUNDS. DON'T WORRY 'BOUT IT.

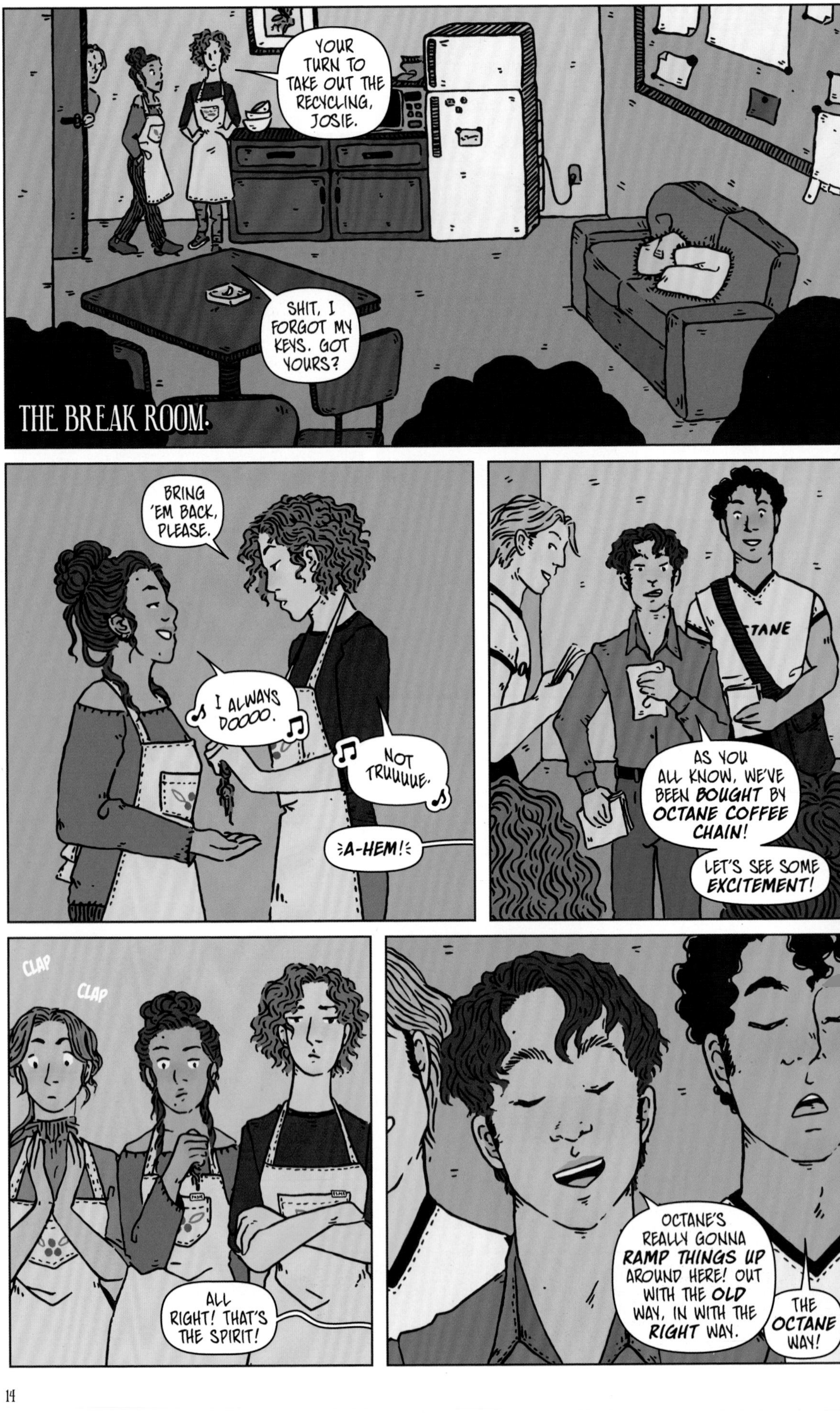
THE BREAK ROOM.
YOUR TURN TO TAKE OUT THE RECYCLING, JOSIE.
SHIT, I FORGOT MY KEYS. GOT YOURS?
BRING 'EM BACK, PLEASE.
I ALWAYS DOOOO.
NOT TRUUUUE.
A-HEM!
OCTANE
AS YOU ALL KNOW, WE'VE BEEN BOUGHT BY OCTANE COFFEE CHAIN!
LET'S SEE SOME EXCITEMENT!
CLAP
CLAP
ALL RIGHT! THAT'S THE SPIRIT!
OCTANE'S REALLY GONNA RAMP THINGS UP AROUND HERE! OUT WITH THE OLD WAY, IN WITH THE RIGHT WAY.
THE OCTANE WAY!

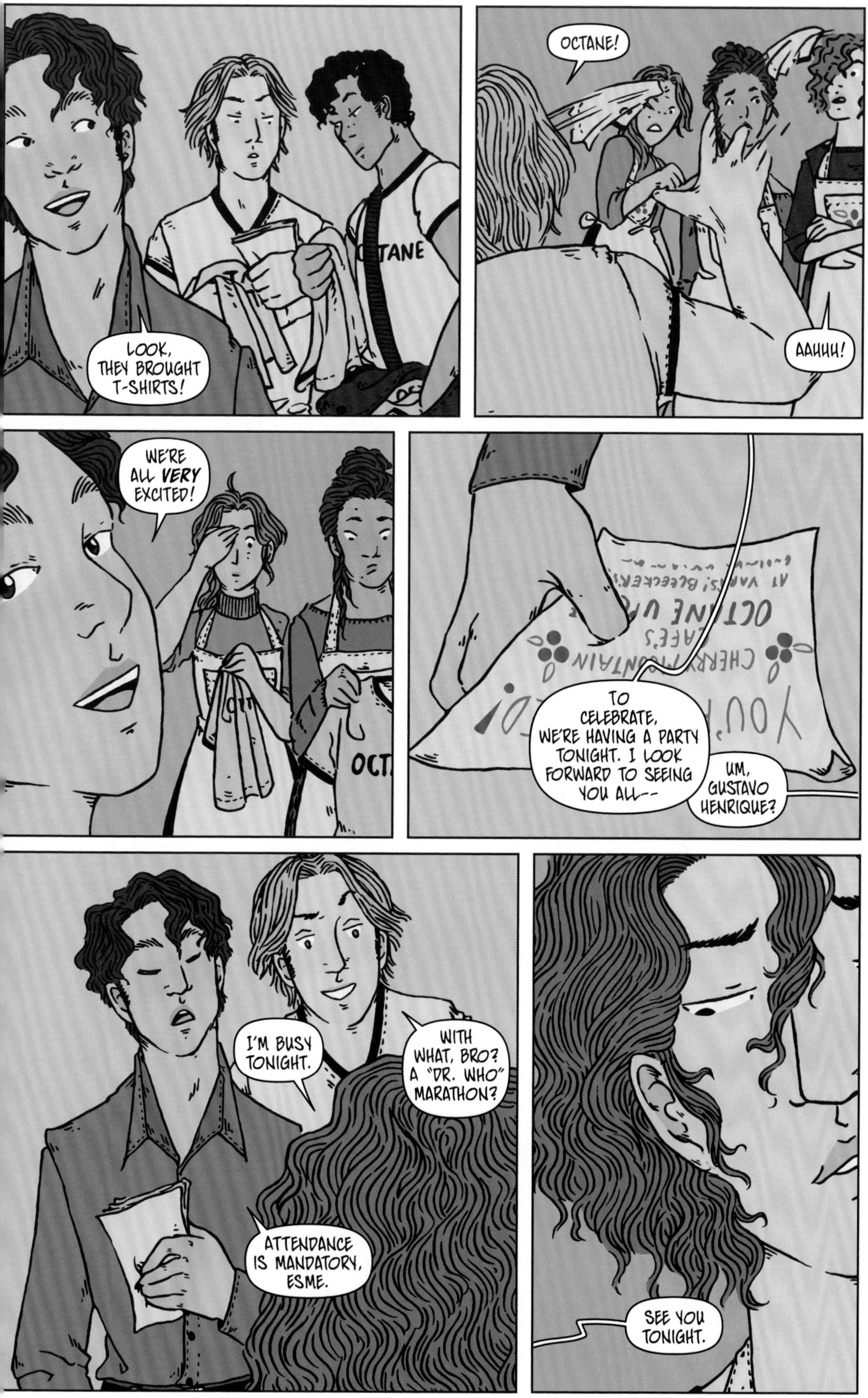
LOOK, THEY BROUGHT T-SHIRTS!
OCTANE!
AAHHH!
WE'RE ALL **VERY** EXCITED!
TO CELEBRATE, WE'RE HAVING A PARTY TONIGHT. I LOOK FORWARD TO SEEING YOU ALL--
UM, GUSTAVO HENRIQUE?
I'M BUSY TONIGHT.
WITH WHAT, BRO? A "DR. WHO" MARATHON?
ATTENDANCE IS MANDATORY, ESME.
SEE YOU TONIGHT.

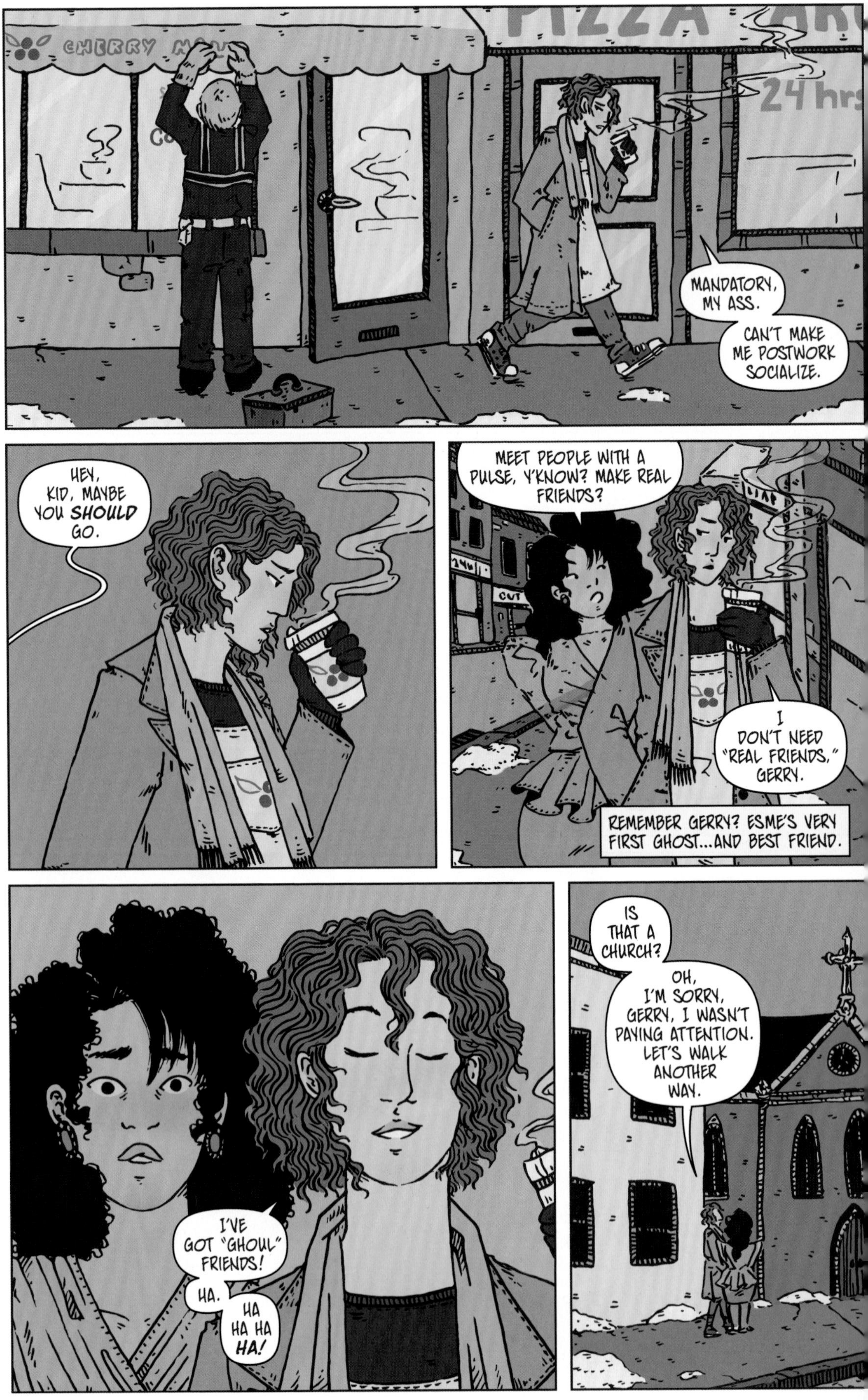
PIZZA
24 hrs
MANDATORY, MY ASS.
CAN'T MAKE ME POSTWORK SOCIALIZE.
HEY, KID, MAYBE YOU **SHOULD** GO.
MEET PEOPLE WITH A PULSE, Y'KNOW? MAKE REAL FRIENDS?
I DON'T NEED "REAL FRIENDS," GERRY.
REMEMBER GERRY? ESME'S VERY FIRST GHOST...AND BEST FRIEND.
I'VE GOT "GHOUL" FRIENDS!
HA.
HA HA HA **HA!**
IS THAT A CHURCH?
OH, I'M SORRY, GERRY, I WASN'T PAYING ATTENTION. LET'S WALK ANOTHER WAY.

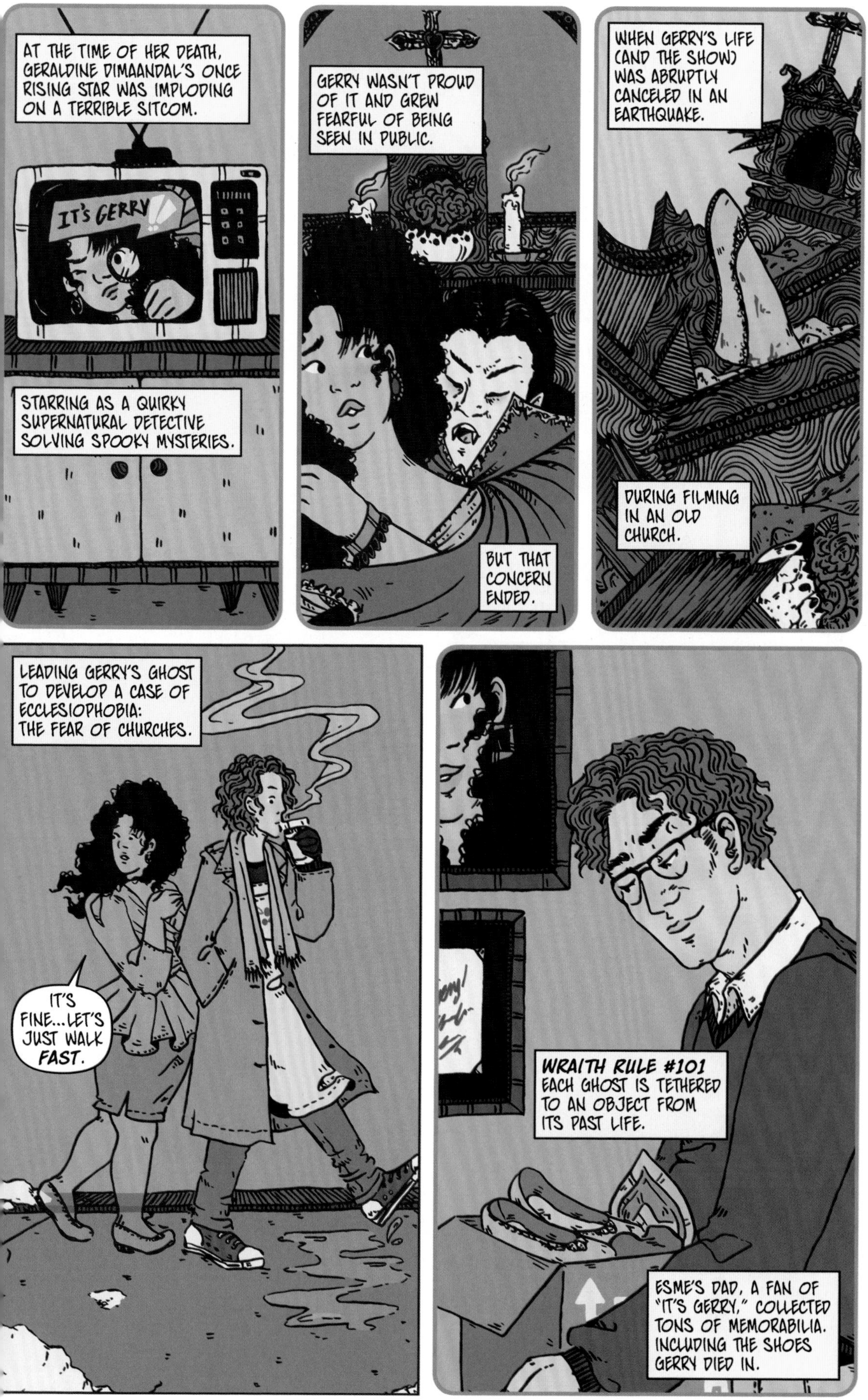
AT THE TIME OF HER DEATH, GERALDINE DIMAANDAL'S ONCE RISING STAR WAS IMPLODING ON A TERRIBLE SITCOM.
IT'S GERRY
STARRING AS A QUIRKY SUPERNATURAL DETECTIVE SOLVING SPOOKY MYSTERIES.
GERRY WASN'T PROUD OF IT AND GREW FEARFUL OF BEING SEEN IN PUBLIC.
BUT THAT CONCERN ENDED.
WHEN GERRY'S LIFE (AND THE SHOW) WAS ABRUPTLY CANCELED IN AN EARTHQUAKE.
DURING FILMING IN AN OLD CHURCH.
LEADING GERRY'S GHOST TO DEVELOP A CASE OF ECCLESIOPHOBIA: THE FEAR OF CHURCHES.
IT'S FINE...LET'S JUST WALK *FAST*.
WRAITH RULE #101 EACH GHOST IS TETHERED TO AN OBJECT FROM ITS PAST LIFE.
ESME'S DAD, A FAN OF "IT'S GERRY," COLLECTED TONS OF MEMORABILIA. INCLUDING THE SHOES GERRY DIED IN.

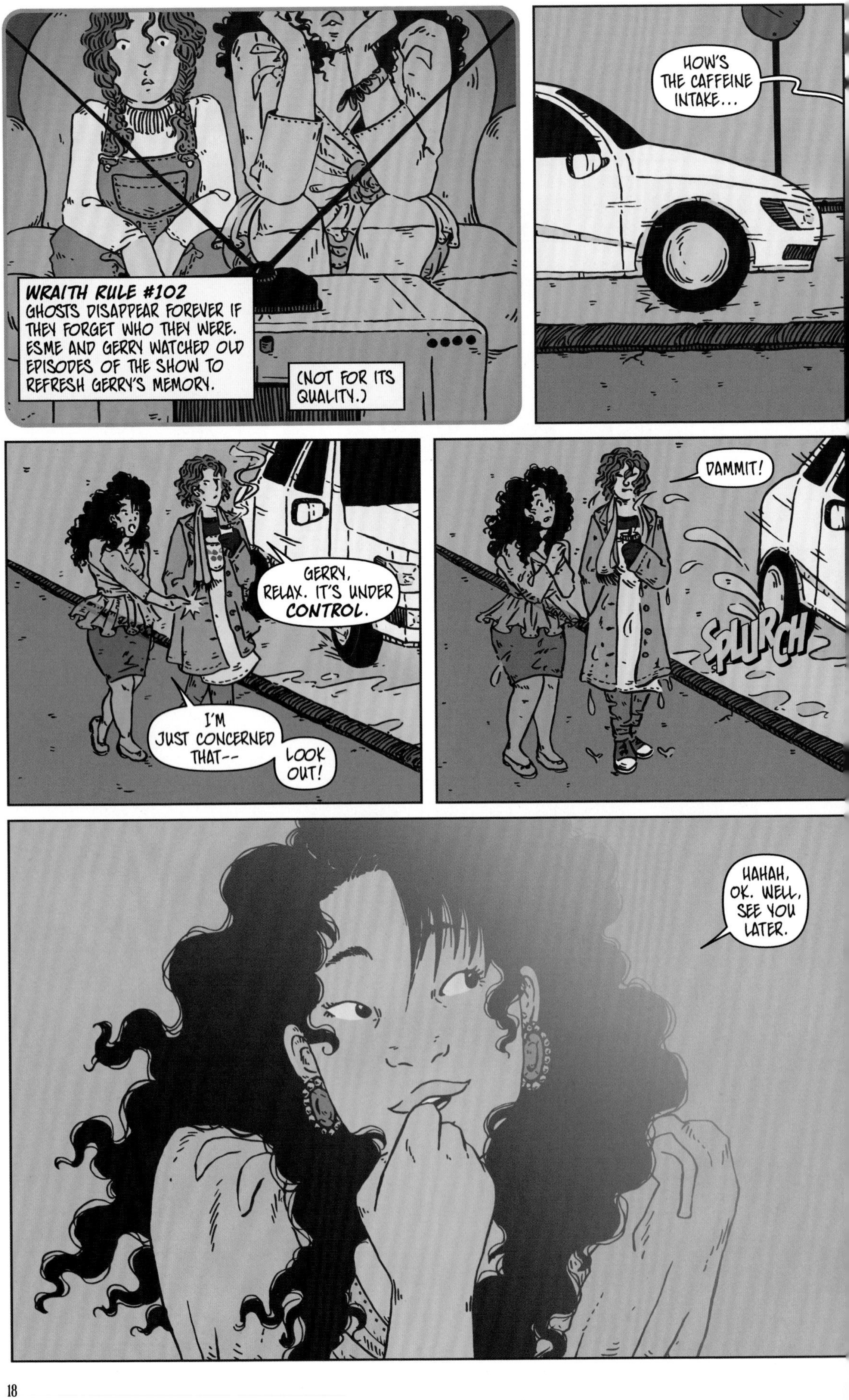
WRAITH RULE #102
GHOSTS DISAPPEAR FOREVER IF THEY FORGET WHO THEY WERE. ESME AND GERRY WATCHED OLD EPISODES OF THE SHOW TO REFRESH GERRY'S MEMORY.
(NOT FOR ITS QUALITY.)
HOW'S THE CAFFEINE INTAKE...
GERRY, RELAX. IT'S UNDER CONTROL.
I'M JUST CONCERNED THAT--
LOOK OUT!
DAMMIT!
SPLURCH
HAHAH, OK. WELL, SEE YOU LATER.

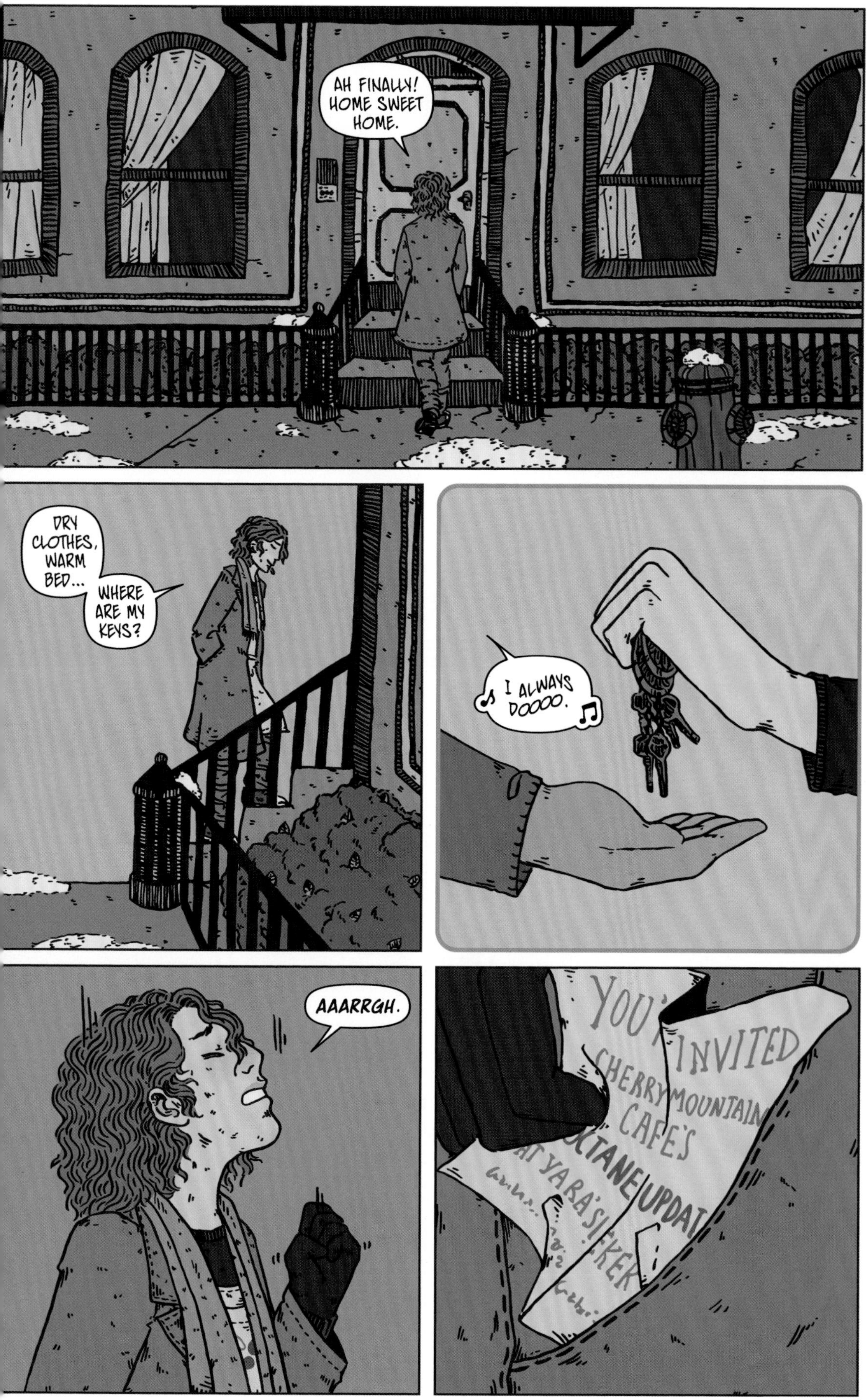
AH FINALLY! HOME SWEET HOME.
DRY CLOTHES, WARM BED...
WHERE ARE MY KEYS?
I ALWAYS DOOOO.
AAARRGH.
YOU'
INVITED
CHERRY MOUNTAIN
CAFE'S
OCTANE UPDAT

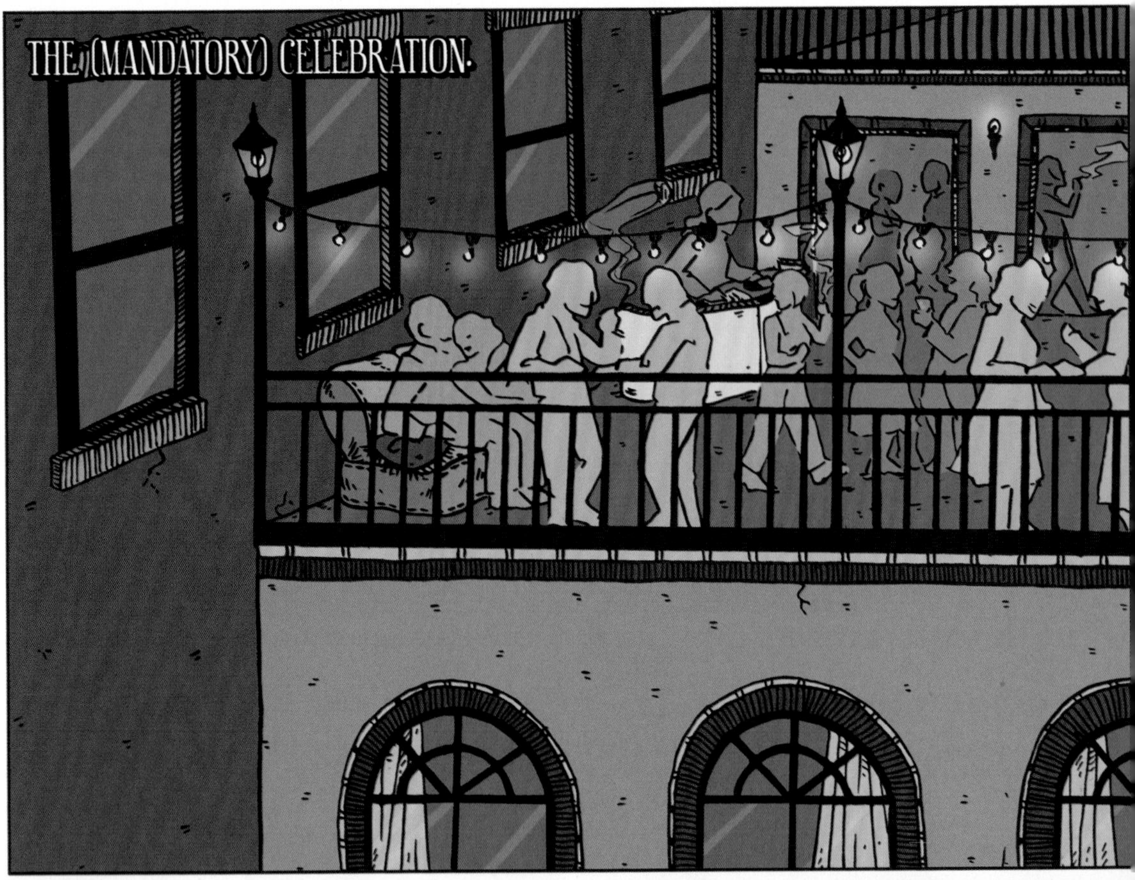
THE (MANDATORY) CELEBRATION.

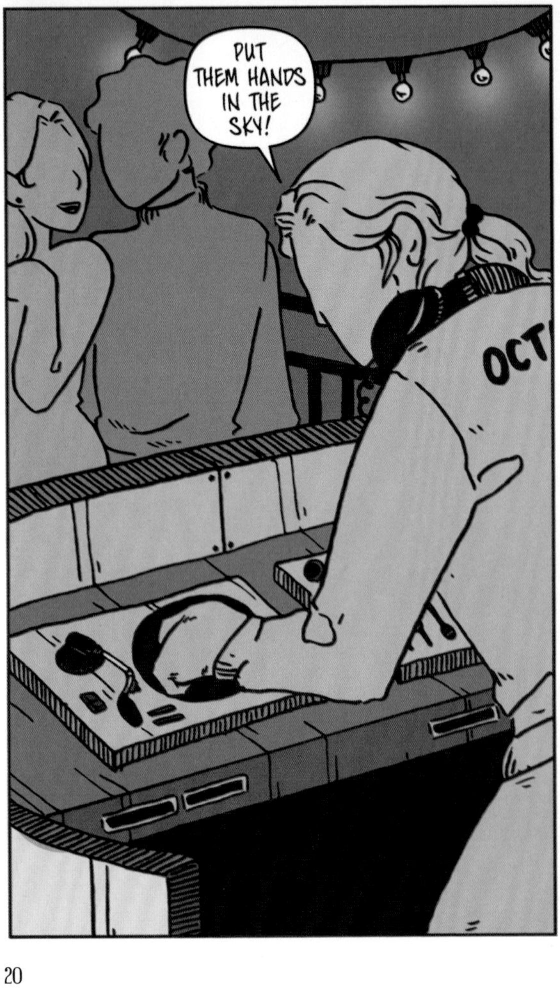
PUT THEM HANDS IN THE SKY!
OCT

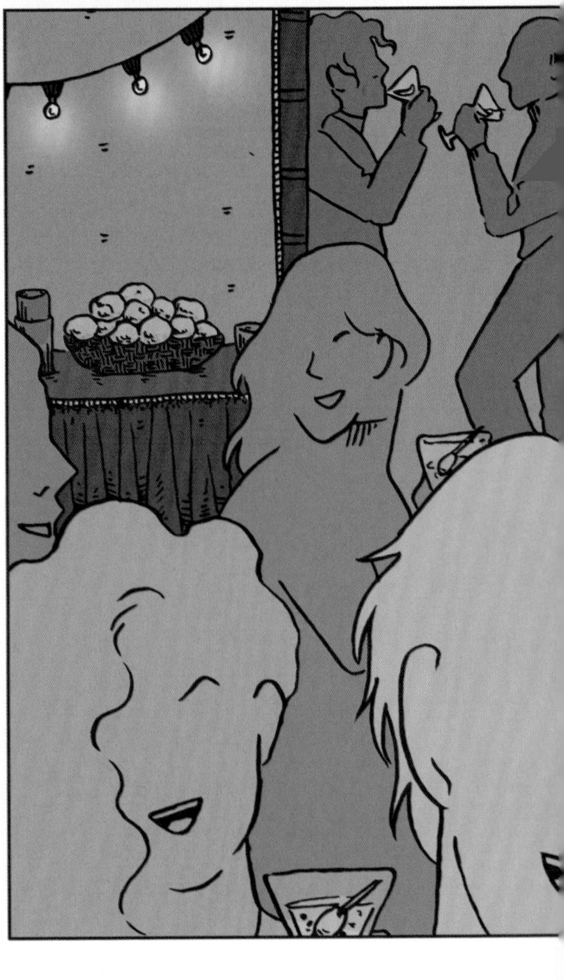

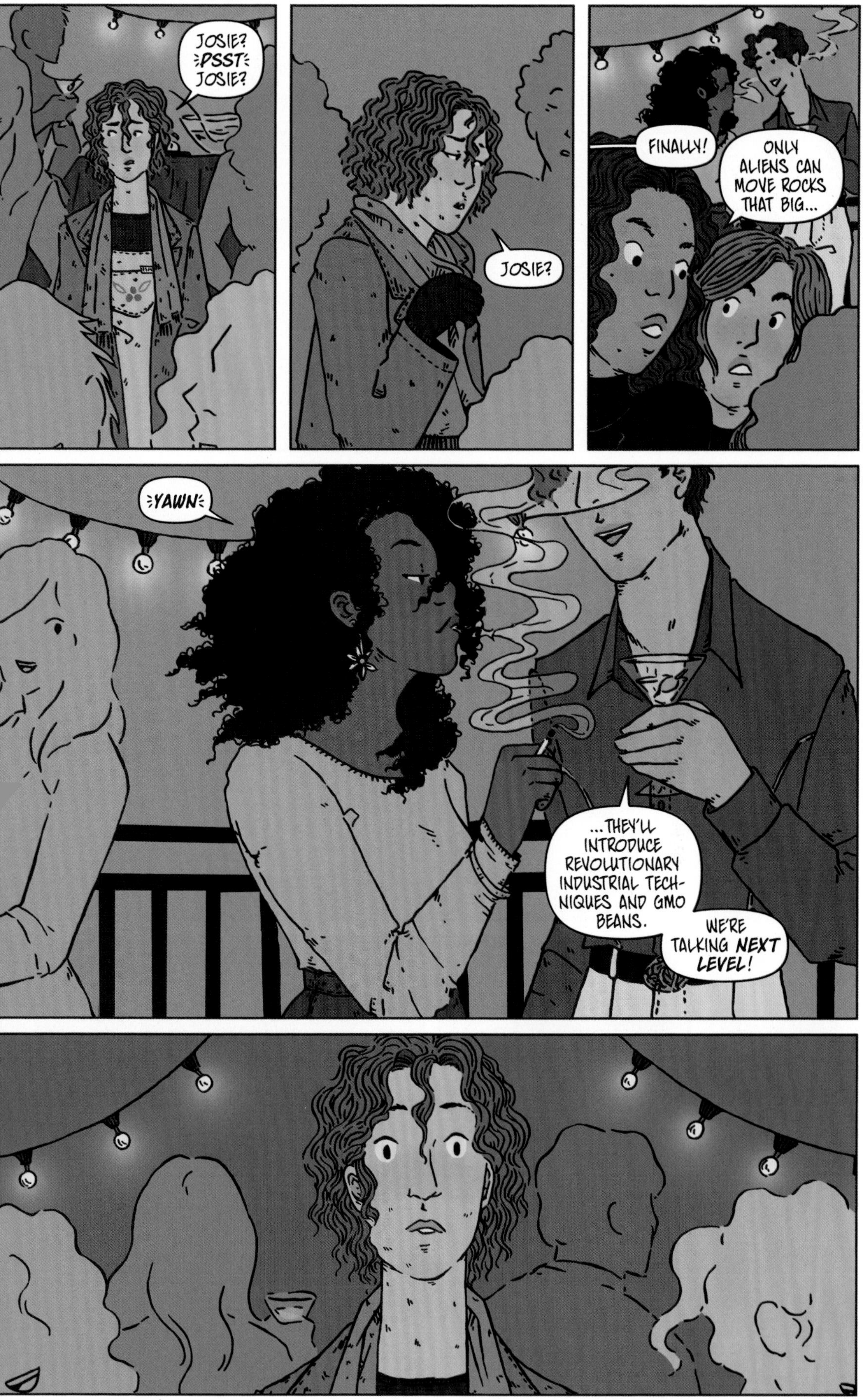
JOSIE? PSST JOSIE?
JOSIE?
FINALLY!
ONLY ALIENS CAN MOVE ROCKS THAT BIG...
YAWN
...THEY'LL INTRODUCE REVOLUTIONARY INDUSTRIAL TECH-NIQUES AND GMO BEANS.
WE'RE TALKING **NEXT LEVEL**!

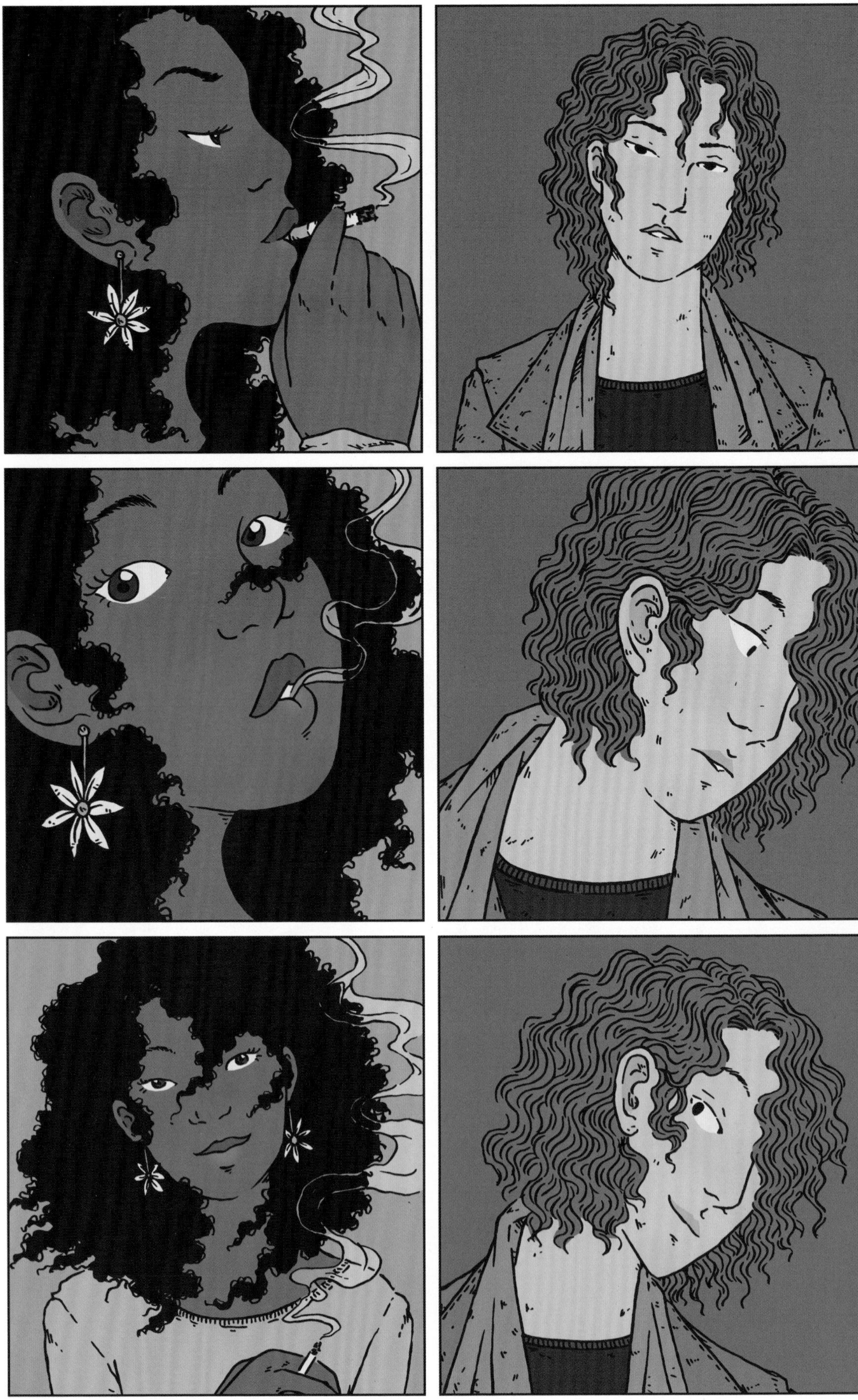

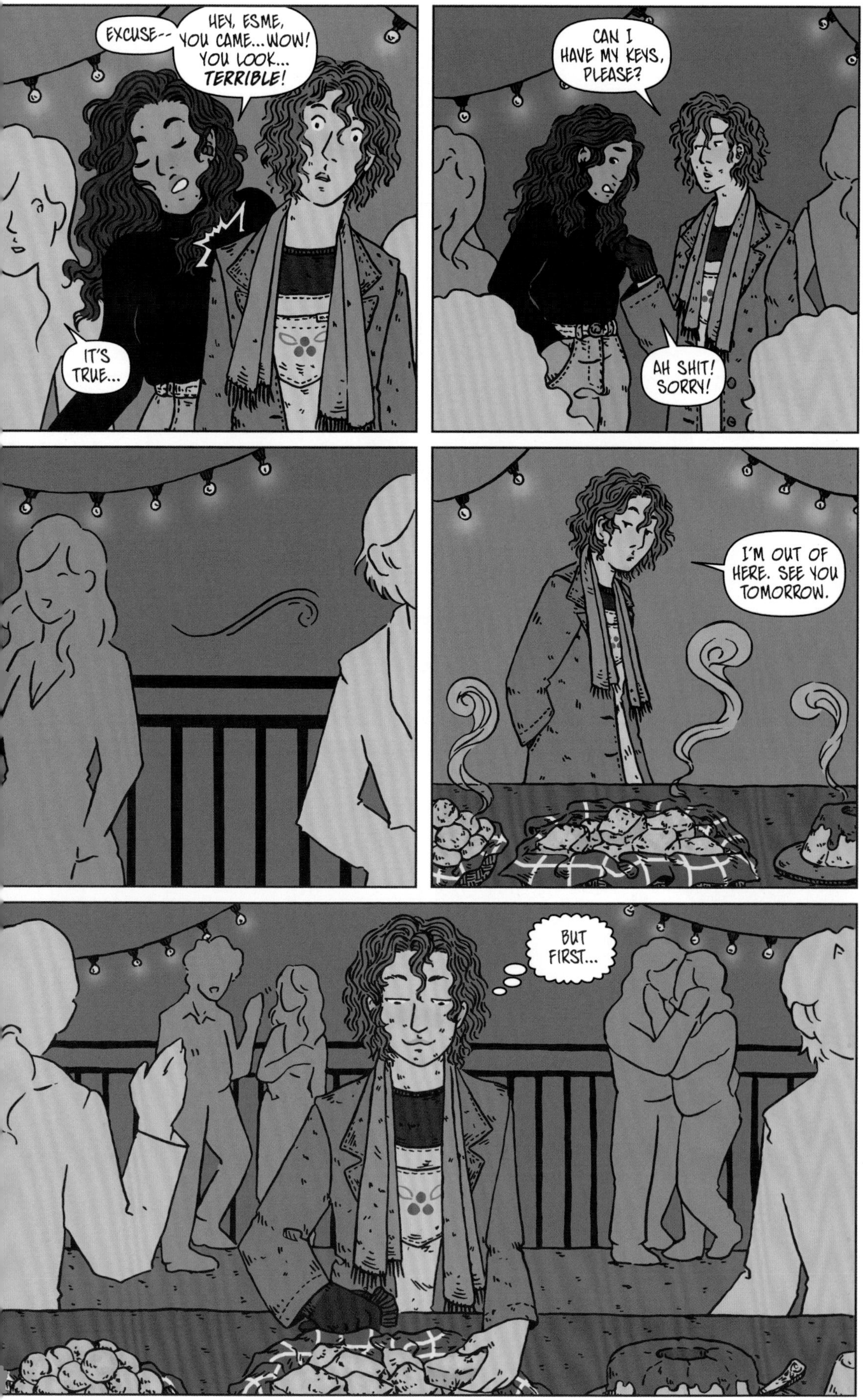
EXCUSE--
HEY, ESME, YOU CAME...WOW! YOU LOOK... TERRIBLE!
IT'S TRUE...
CAN I HAVE MY KEYS, PLEASE?
AH SHIT! SORRY!
I'M OUT OF HERE. SEE YOU TOMORROW.
BUT FIRST...

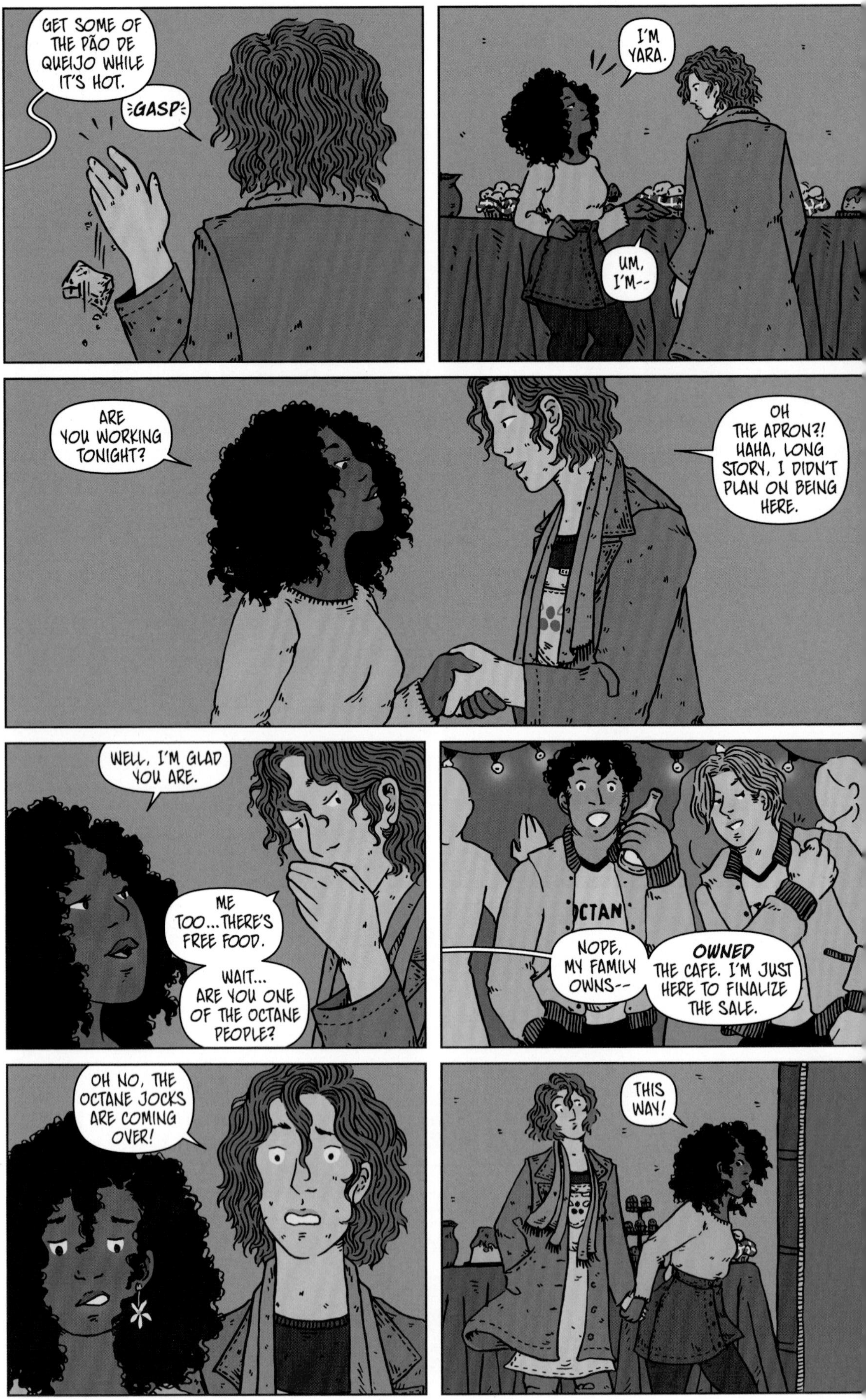

GET SOME OF THE PÃO DE QUEIJO WHILE IT'S HOT.
GASP
I'M YARA.
UM, I'M--
ARE YOU WORKING TONIGHT?
OH THE APRON?! HAHA, LONG STORY, I DIDN'T PLAN ON BEING HERE.
WELL, I'M GLAD YOU ARE.
ME TOO...THERE'S FREE FOOD.
WAIT... ARE YOU ONE OF THE OCTANE PEOPLE?
OCTAN
NOPE, MY FAMILY OWNS--
OWNED THE CAFE. I'M JUST HERE TO FINALIZE THE SALE.
OH NO, THE OCTANE JOCKS ARE COMING OVER!
THIS WAY!

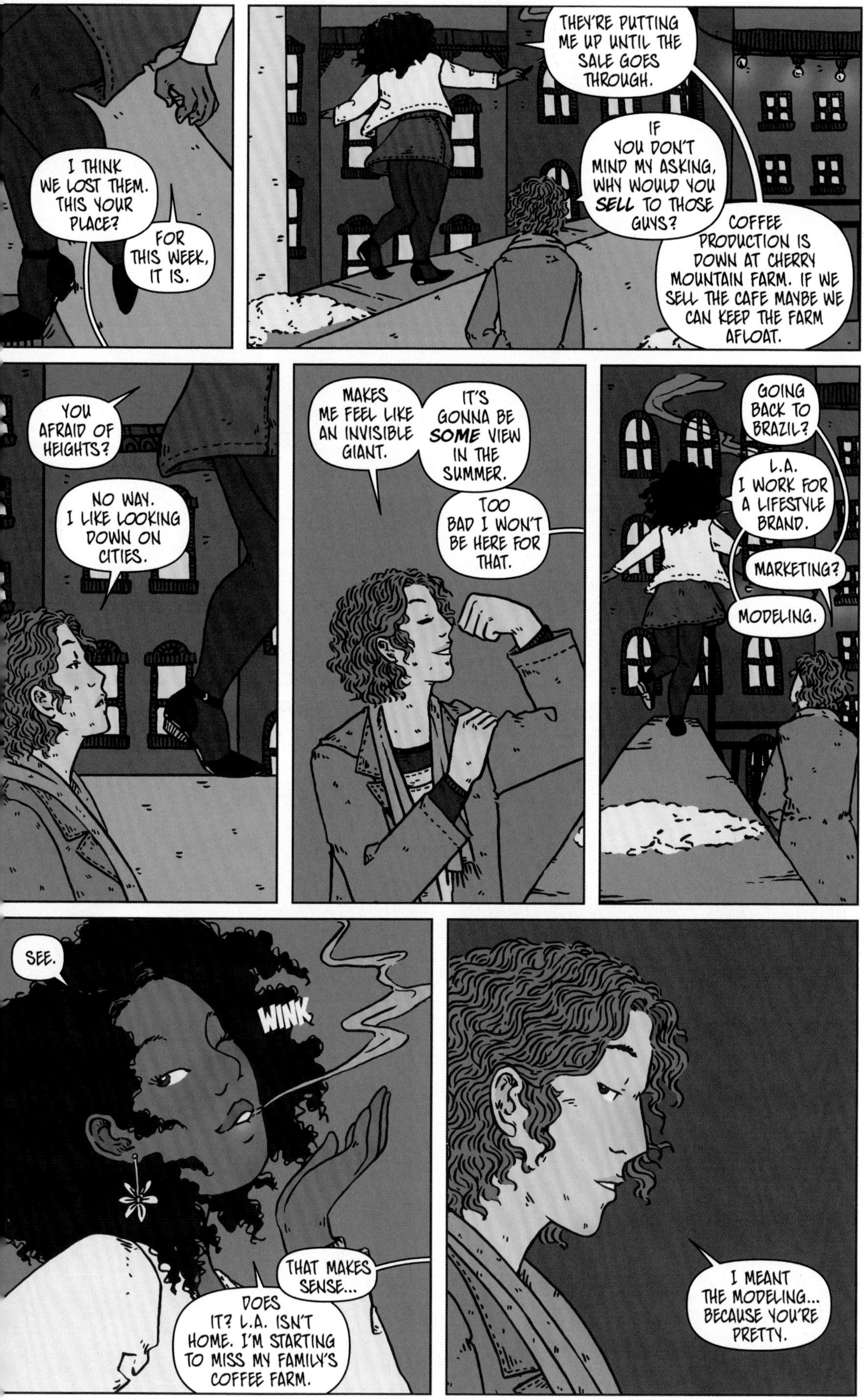
I THINK WE LOST THEM. THIS YOUR PLACE?
FOR THIS WEEK, IT IS.
THEY'RE PUTTING ME UP UNTIL THE SALE GOES THROUGH.
IF YOU DON'T MIND MY ASKING, WHY WOULD YOU SELL TO THOSE GUYS?
COFFEE PRODUCTION IS DOWN AT CHERRY MOUNTAIN FARM. IF WE SELL THE CAFE MAYBE WE CAN KEEP THE FARM AFLOAT.
YOU AFRAID OF HEIGHTS?
NO WAY. I LIKE LOOKING DOWN ON CITIES.
MAKES ME FEEL LIKE AN INVISIBLE GIANT.
IT'S GONNA BE SOME VIEW IN THE SUMMER.
TOO BAD I WON'T BE HERE FOR THAT.
GOING BACK TO BRAZIL?
L.A. I WORK FOR A LIFESTYLE BRAND.
MARKETING?
MODELING.
SEE.
WINK
THAT MAKES SENSE...
DOES IT? L.A. ISN'T HOME. I'M STARTING TO MISS MY FAMILY'S COFFEE FARM.
I MEANT THE MODELING... BECAUSE YOU'RE PRETTY.

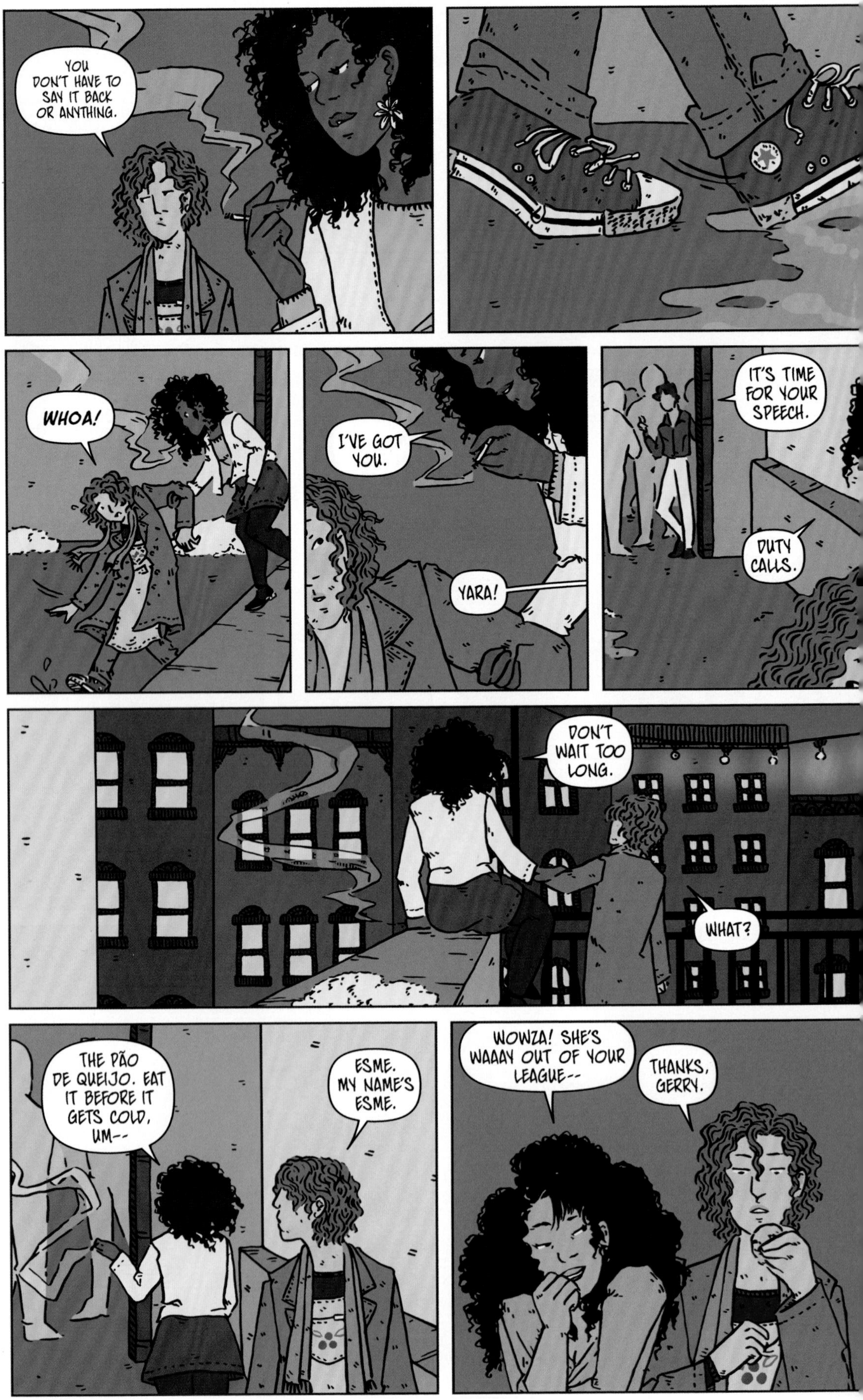
YOU DON'T HAVE TO SAY IT BACK OR ANYTHING.
WHOA!
I'VE GOT YOU.
YARA!
IT'S TIME FOR YOUR SPEECH.
DUTY CALLS.
DON'T WAIT TOO LONG.
WHAT?
THE PÃO DE QUEIJO. EAT IT BEFORE IT GETS COLD, UM--
ESME. MY NAME'S ESME.
WOWZA! SHE'S WAAAY OUT OF YOUR LEAGUE--
THANKS, GERRY.

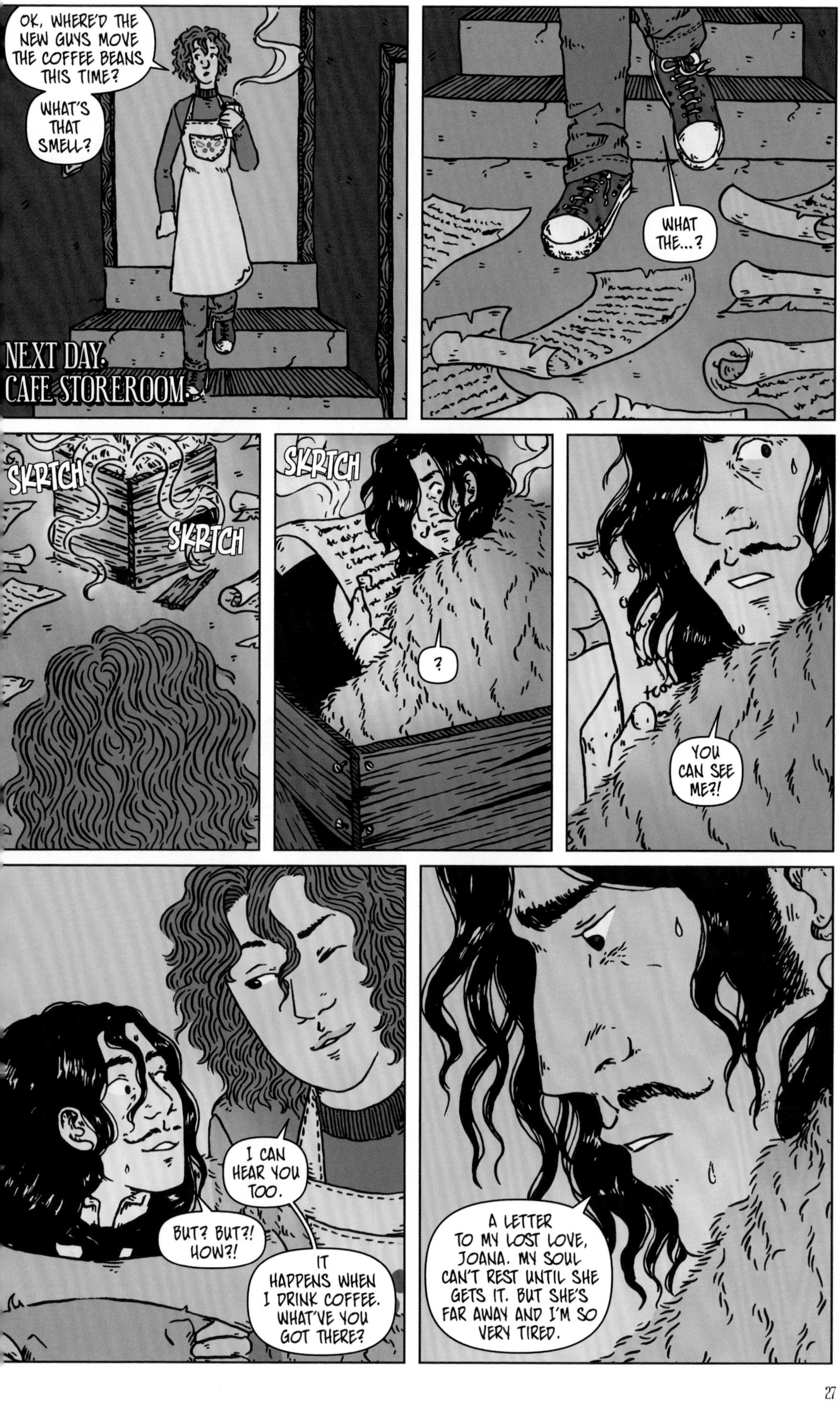
OK, WHERE'D THE NEW GUYS MOVE THE COFFEE BEANS THIS TIME?
WHAT'S THAT SMELL?
NEXT DAY. CAFE STOREROOM.
WHAT THE...?
SKRTCH
SKRTCH
SKRTCH
?
YOU CAN SEE ME?!
I CAN HEAR YOU TOO.
BUT? BUT?! HOW?!
IT HAPPENS WHEN I DRINK COFFEE. WHAT'VE YOU GOT THERE?
A LETTER TO MY LOST LOVE, JOANA. MY SOUL CAN'T REST UNTIL SHE GETS IT. BUT SHE'S FAR AWAY AND I'M SO VERY TIRED.

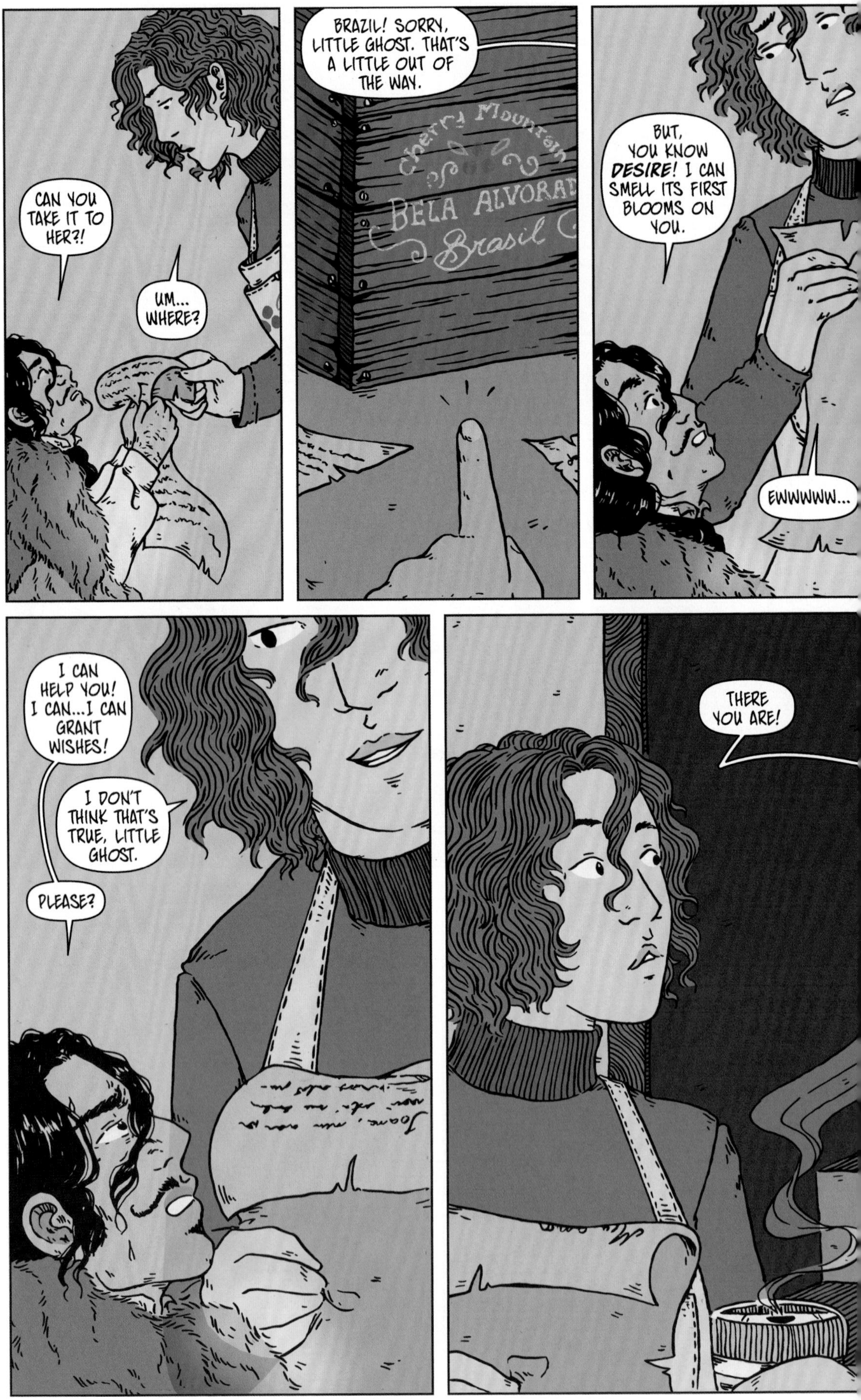

CAN YOU TAKE IT TO HER?!
UM... WHERE?
BRAZIL! SORRY, LITTLE GHOST. THAT'S A LITTLE OUT OF THE WAY.
Cherry Mountain
BELA ALVORAD
Brasil
BUT, YOU KNOW **DESIRE!** I CAN SMELL ITS FIRST BLOOMS ON YOU.
EWWWWW...
I CAN HELP YOU! I CAN...I CAN GRANT WISHES!
I DON'T THINK THAT'S TRUE, LITTLE GHOST.
PLEASE?
THERE YOU ARE!

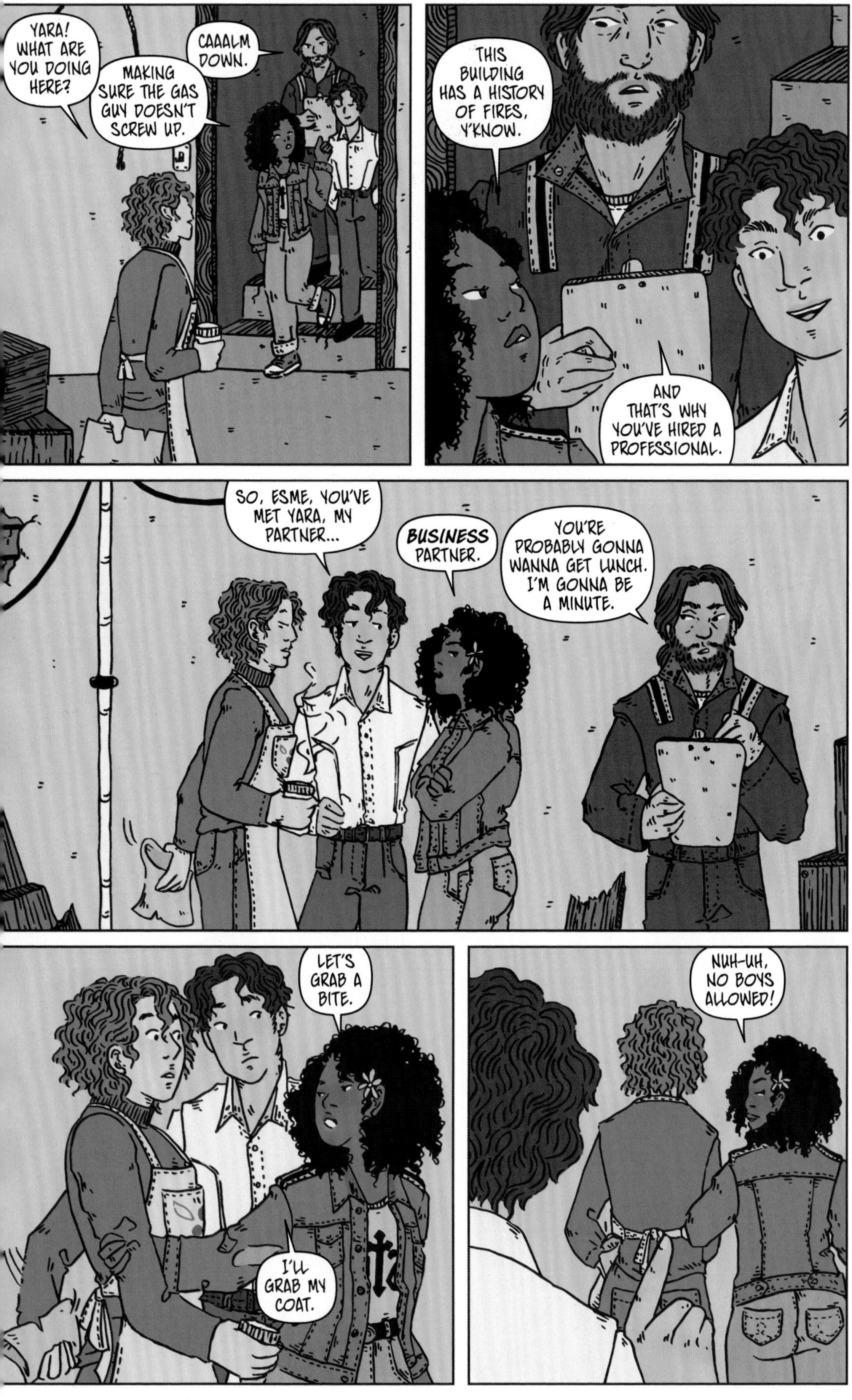

YARA! WHAT ARE YOU DOING HERE?
MAKING SURE THE GAS GUY DOESN'T SCREW UP.
CAAALM DOWN.
THIS BUILDING HAS A HISTORY OF FIRES, Y'KNOW.
AND THAT'S WHY YOU'VE HIRED A PROFESSIONAL.
SO, ESME, YOU'VE MET YARA, MY PARTNER...
BUSINESS PARTNER.
YOU'RE PROBABLY GONNA WANNA GET LUNCH. I'M GONNA BE A MINUTE.
LET'S GRAB A BITE.
I'LL GRAB MY COAT.
NUH-UH, NO BOYS ALLOWED!

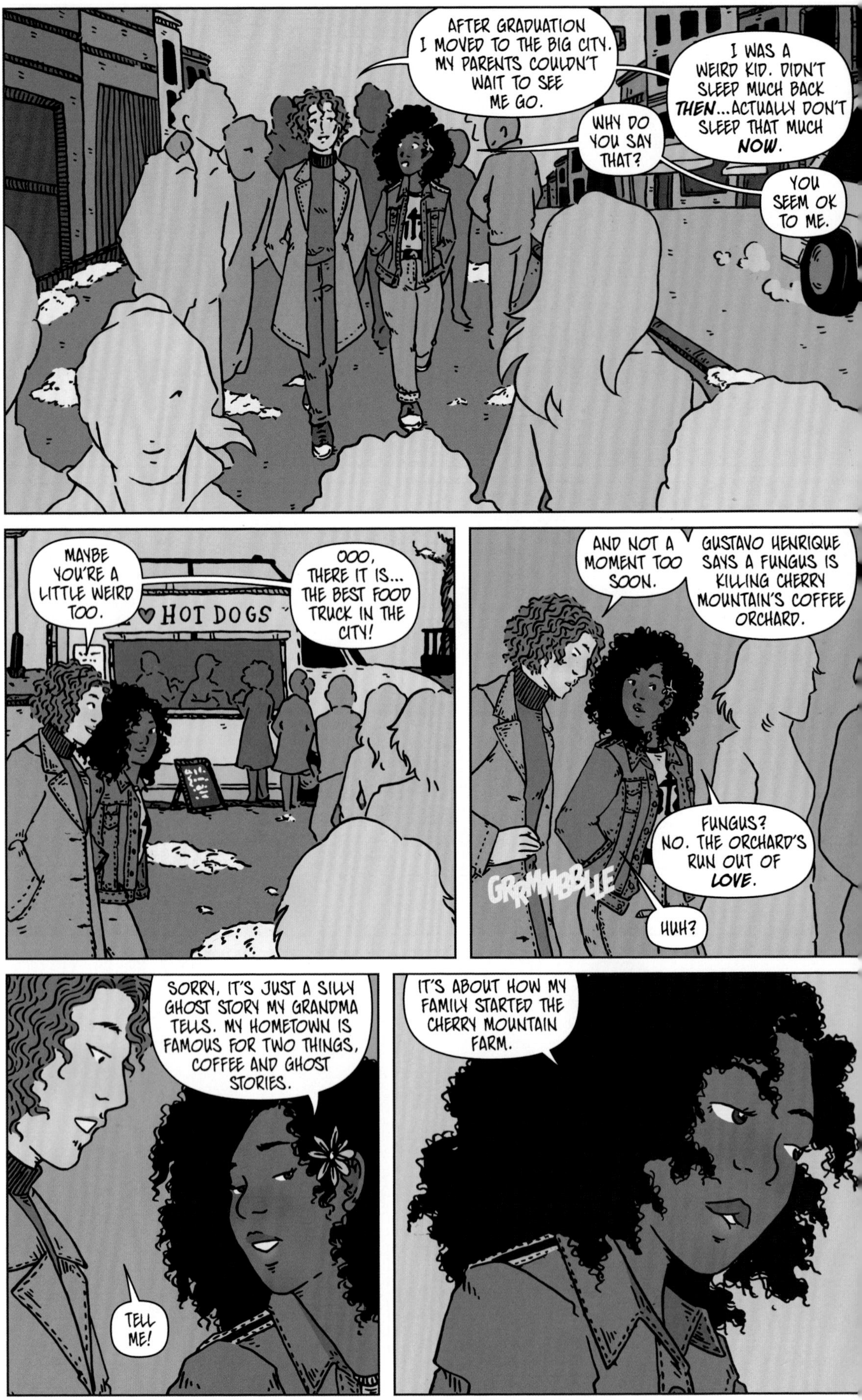
AFTER GRADUATION I MOVED TO THE BIG CITY. MY PARENTS COULDN'T WAIT TO SEE ME GO.
WHY DO YOU SAY THAT?
I WAS A WEIRD KID. DIDN'T SLEEP MUCH BACK **THEN**...ACTUALLY DON'T SLEEP THAT MUCH **NOW**.
YOU SEEM OK TO ME.
MAYBE YOU'RE A LITTLE WEIRD TOO.
OOO, THERE IT IS... THE BEST FOOD TRUCK IN THE CITY!
HOT DOGS
AND NOT A MOMENT TOO SOON.
GUSTAVO HENRIQUE SAYS A FUNGUS IS KILLING CHERRY MOUNTAIN'S COFFEE ORCHARD.
FUNGUS? NO. THE ORCHARD'S RUN OUT OF **LOVE**.
GRRMMBBLLE
HUH?
SORRY, IT'S JUST A SILLY GHOST STORY MY GRANDMA TELLS. MY HOMETOWN IS FAMOUS FOR TWO THINGS, COFFEE AND GHOST STORIES.
TELL ME!
IT'S ABOUT HOW MY FAMILY STARTED THE CHERRY MOUNTAIN FARM.

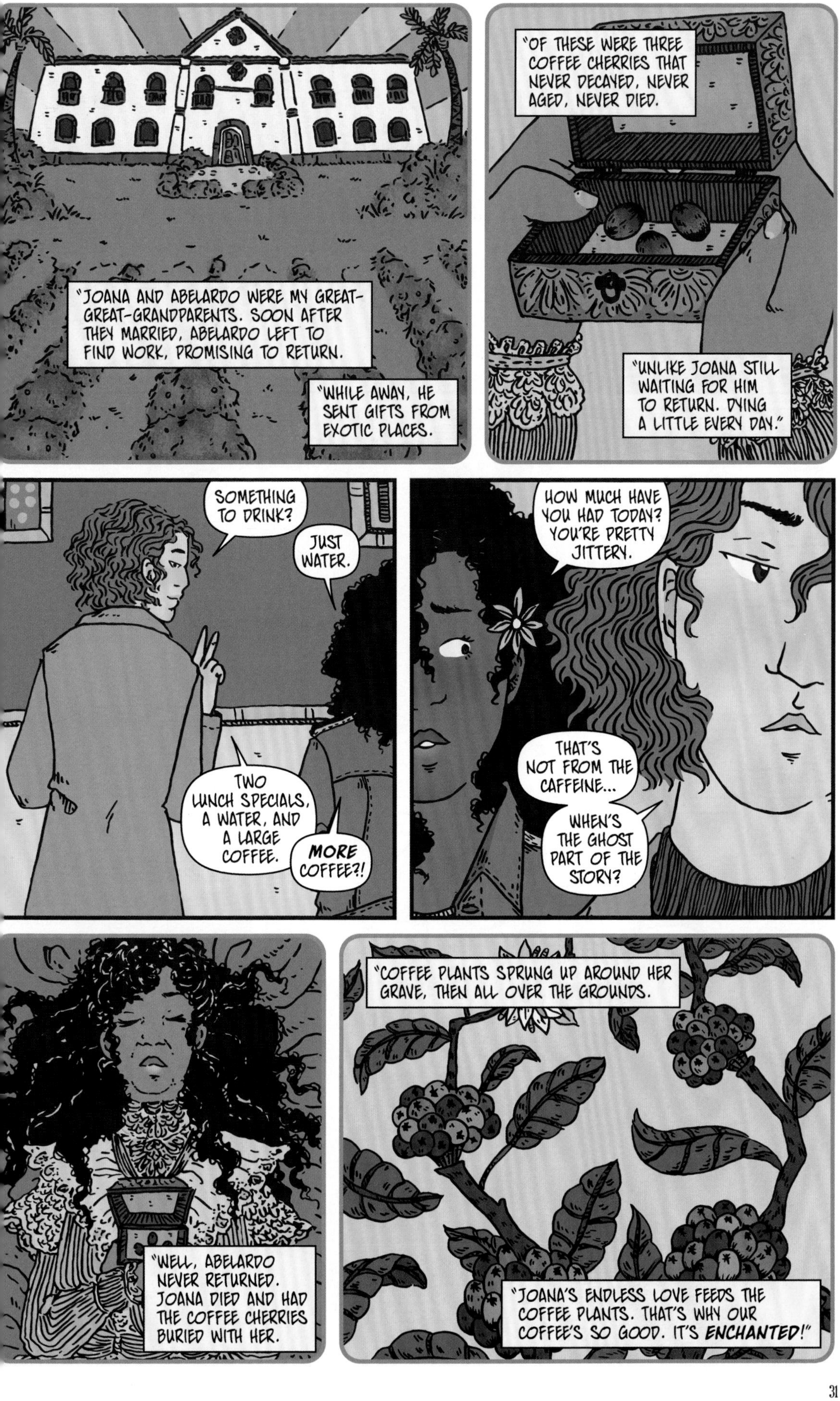
"JOANA AND ABELARDO WERE MY GREAT-GREAT-GRANDPARENTS. SOON AFTER THEY MARRIED, ABELARDO LEFT TO FIND WORK, PROMISING TO RETURN.
"WHILE AWAY, HE SENT GIFTS FROM EXOTIC PLACES.
"OF THESE WERE THREE COFFEE CHERRIES THAT NEVER DECAYED, NEVER AGED, NEVER DIED.
"UNLIKE JOANA STILL WAITING FOR HIM TO RETURN. DYING A LITTLE EVERY DAY."
SOMETHING TO DRINK?
JUST WATER.
TWO LUNCH SPECIALS, A WATER, AND A LARGE COFFEE.
MORE COFFEE?!
HOW MUCH HAVE YOU HAD TODAY? YOU'RE PRETTY JITTERY.
THAT'S NOT FROM THE CAFFEINE...
WHEN'S THE GHOST PART OF THE STORY?
"WELL, ABELARDO NEVER RETURNED. JOANA DIED AND HAD THE COFFEE CHERRIES BURIED WITH HER.
"COFFEE PLANTS SPRUNG UP AROUND HER GRAVE, THEN ALL OVER THE GROUNDS.
"JOANA'S ENDLESS LOVE FEEDS THE COFFEE PLANTS. THAT'S WHY OUR COFFEE'S SO GOOD. IT'S ***ENCHANTED!***"

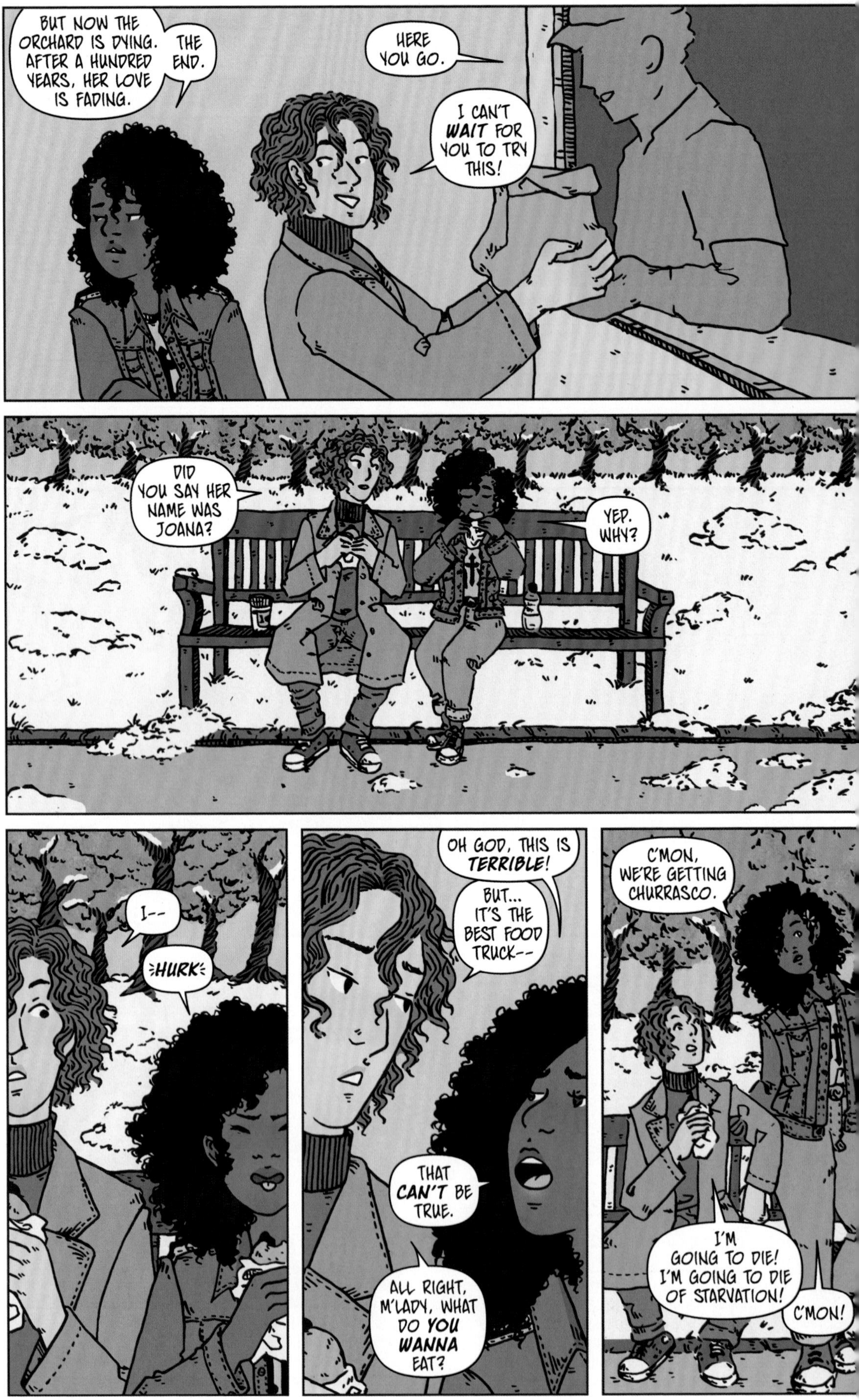
BUT NOW THE ORCHARD IS DYING. AFTER A HUNDRED YEARS, HER LOVE IS FADING.
THE END.
HERE YOU GO.
I CAN'T WAIT FOR YOU TO TRY THIS!
DID YOU SAY HER NAME WAS JOANA?
YEP. WHY?
I--
HURK
OH GOD, THIS IS TERRIBLE!
BUT... IT'S THE BEST FOOD TRUCK--
THAT CAN'T BE TRUE.
ALL RIGHT, M'LADY, WHAT DO YOU WANNA EAT?
C'MON, WE'RE GETTING CHURRASCO.
I'M GOING TO DIE! I'M GOING TO DIE OF STARVATION!
C'MON!

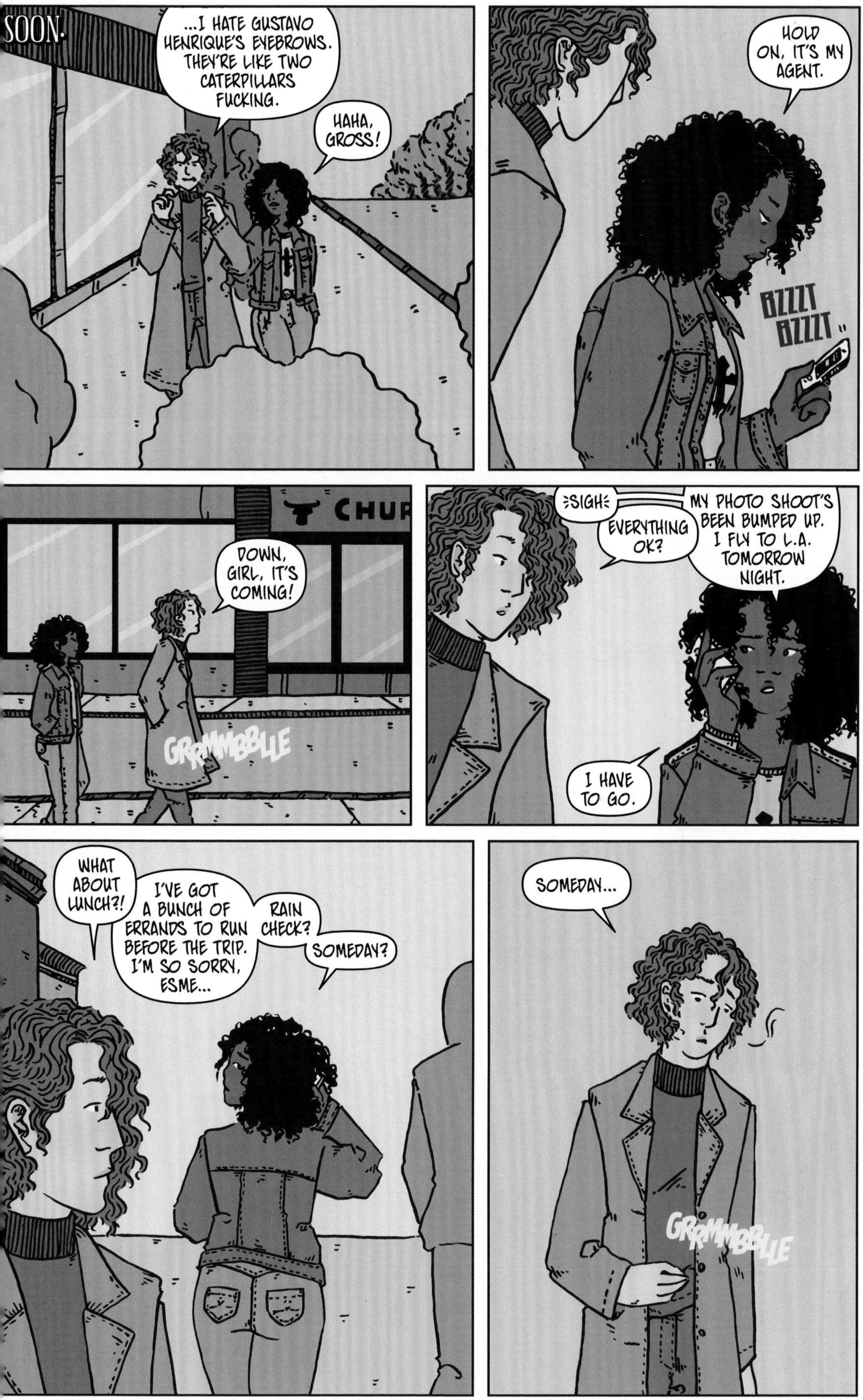
SOON.
...I HATE GUSTAVO HENRIQUE'S EYEBROWS. THEY'RE LIKE TWO CATERPILLARS FUCKING.
HAHA, GROSS!
HOLD ON, IT'S MY AGENT.
BZZZT BZZZT
CHUR
DOWN, GIRL, IT'S COMING!
GRRMMBBLLE
≈SIGH≈
EVERYTHING OK?
MY PHOTO SHOOT'S BEEN BUMPED UP. I FLY TO L.A. TOMORROW NIGHT.
I HAVE TO GO.
WHAT ABOUT LUNCH?!
I'VE GOT A BUNCH OF ERRANDS TO RUN BEFORE THE TRIP. I'M SO SORRY, ESME...
RAIN CHECK?
SOMEDAY?
SOMEDAY...
GRRMMBBLLE

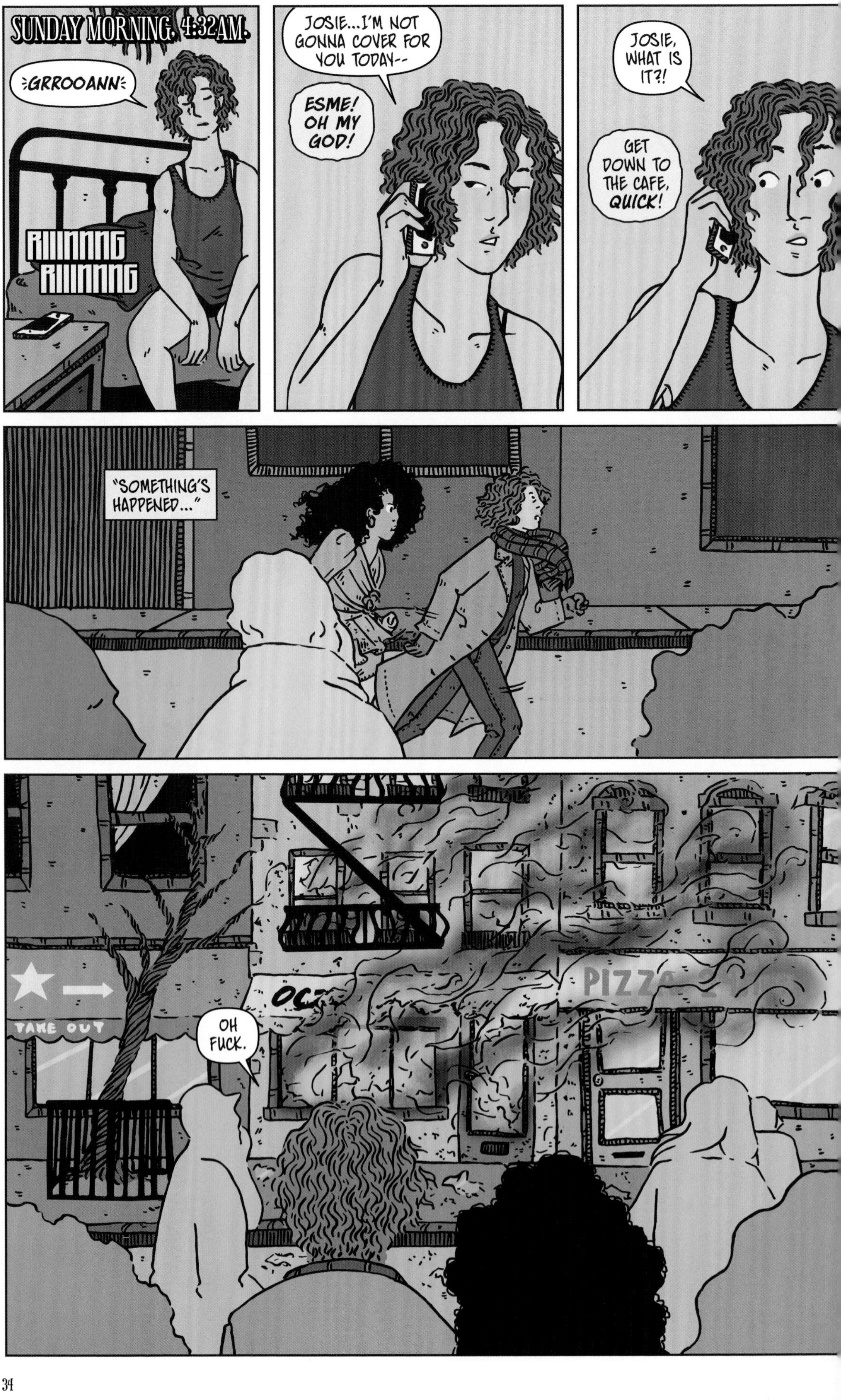
SUNDAY MORNING, 4:32AM.
GRROOANN
RIIINNNG RIIINNNG
JOSIE...I'M NOT GONNA COVER FOR YOU TODAY--
ESME! OH MY GOD!
JOSIE, WHAT IS IT?!
GET DOWN TO THE CAFE, QUICK!
"SOMETHING'S HAPPENED..."
TAKE OUT
OH FUCK.
PIZZA

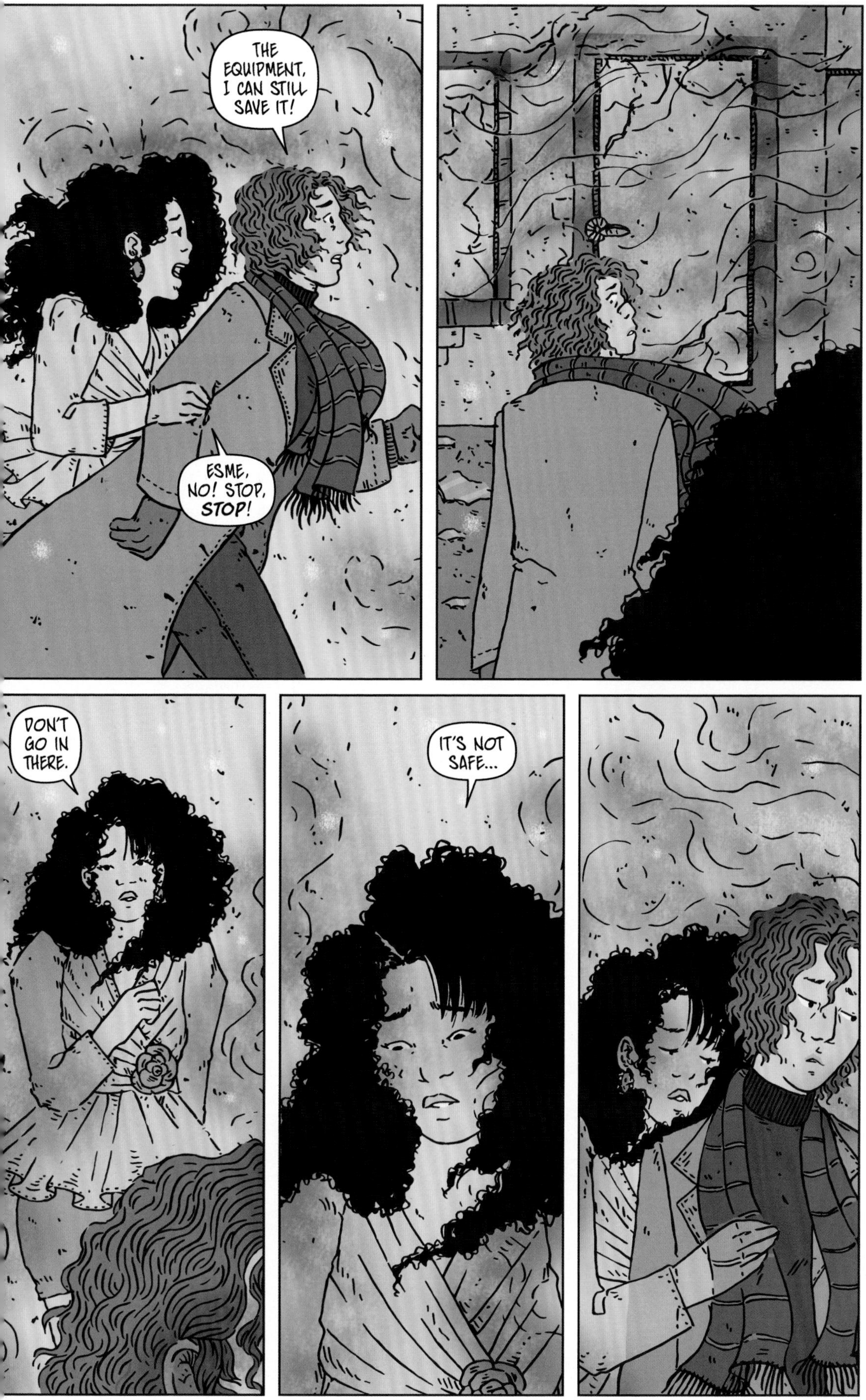
THE EQUIPMENT, I CAN STILL SAVE IT!
ESME, NO! STOP, **STOP!**
DON'T GO IN THERE.
IT'S NOT SAFE...

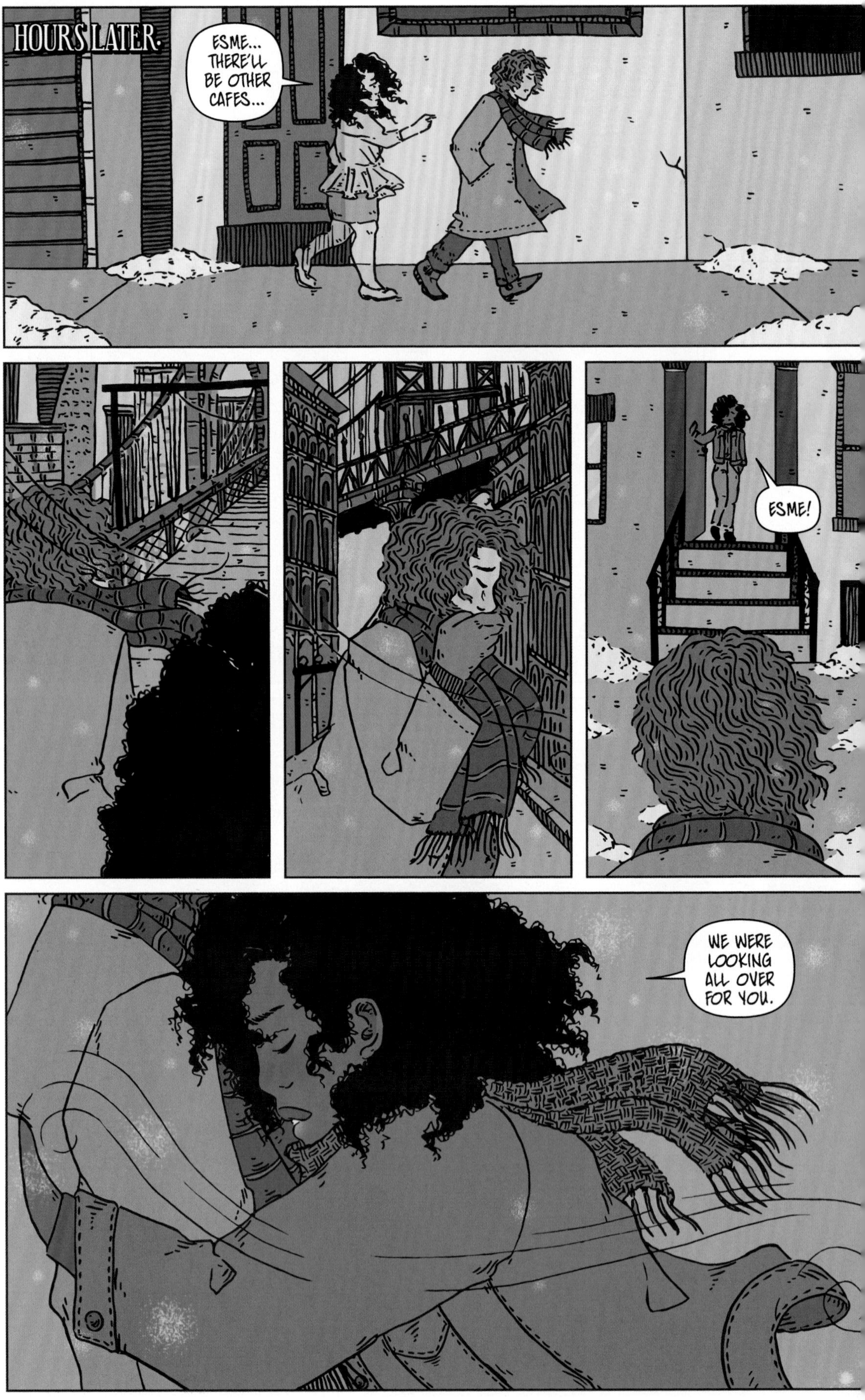
HOURS LATER.
ESME... THERE'LL BE OTHER CAFES...
ESME!
WE WERE LOOKING ALL OVER FOR YOU.

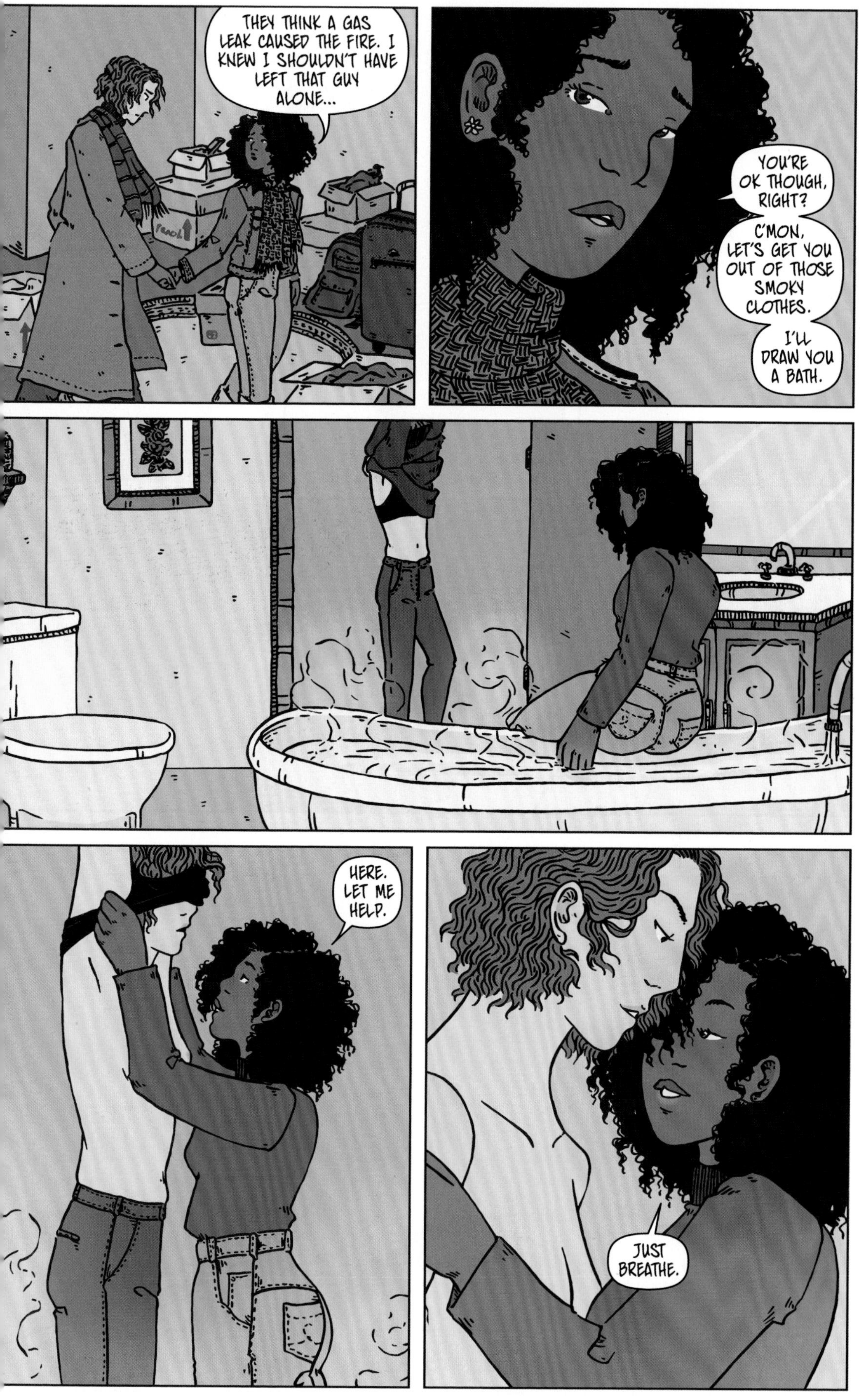
THEY THINK A GAS LEAK CAUSED THE FIRE. I KNEW I SHOULDN'T HAVE LEFT THAT GUY ALONE...
YOU'RE OK THOUGH, RIGHT?
C'MON, LET'S GET YOU OUT OF THOSE SMOKY CLOTHES.
I'LL DRAW YOU A BATH.
HERE. LET ME HELP.
JUST BREATHE.

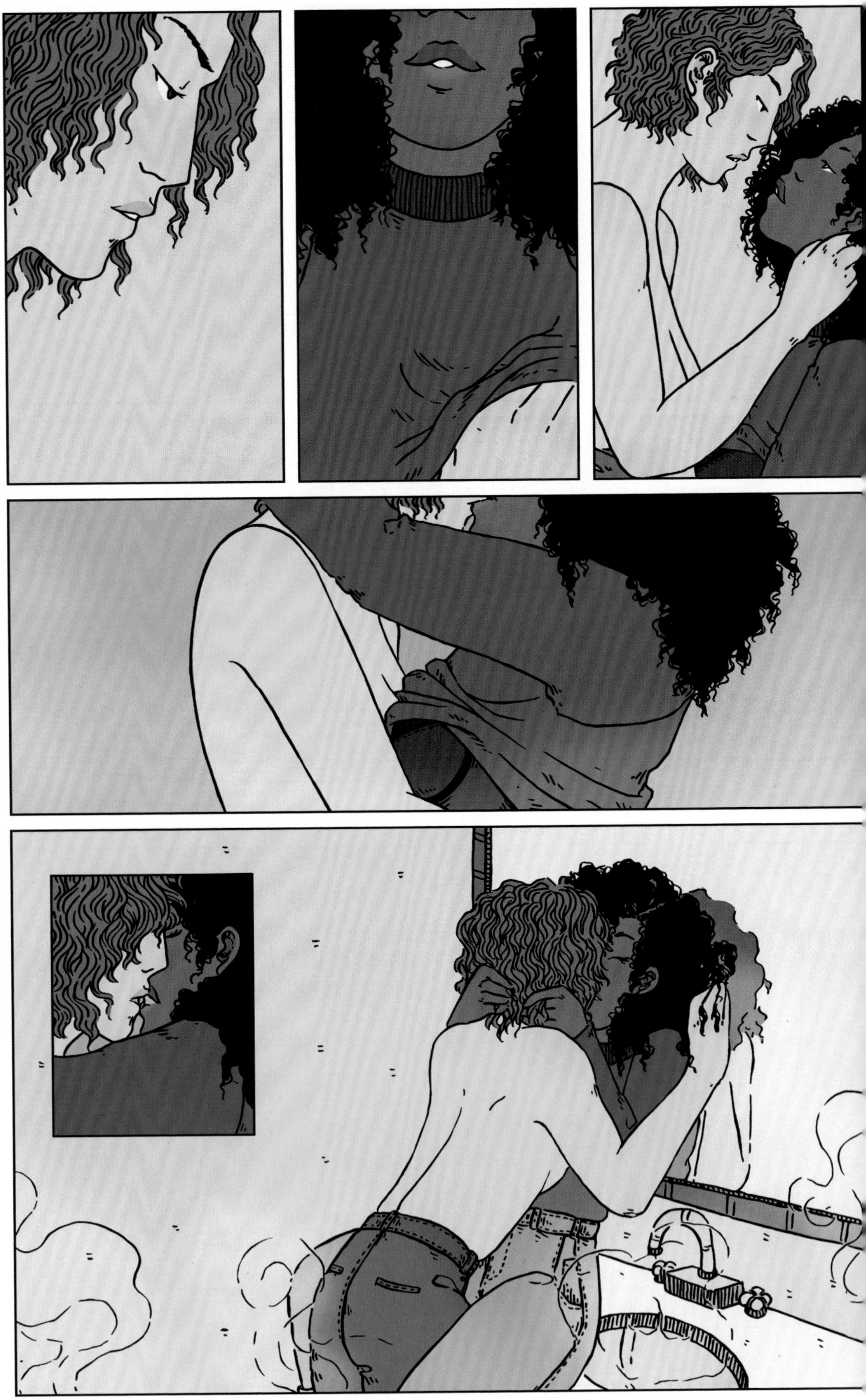

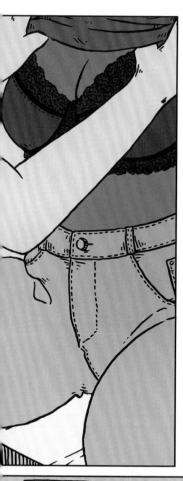

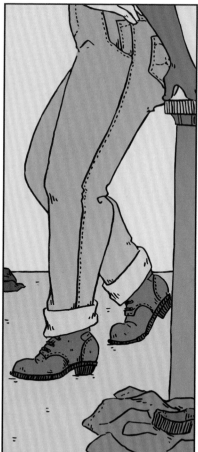

C'MON...

SORRY ABOUT THE MESS. I'M STILL PACKING...

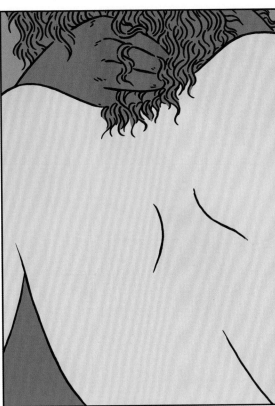
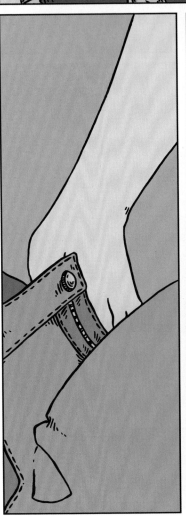

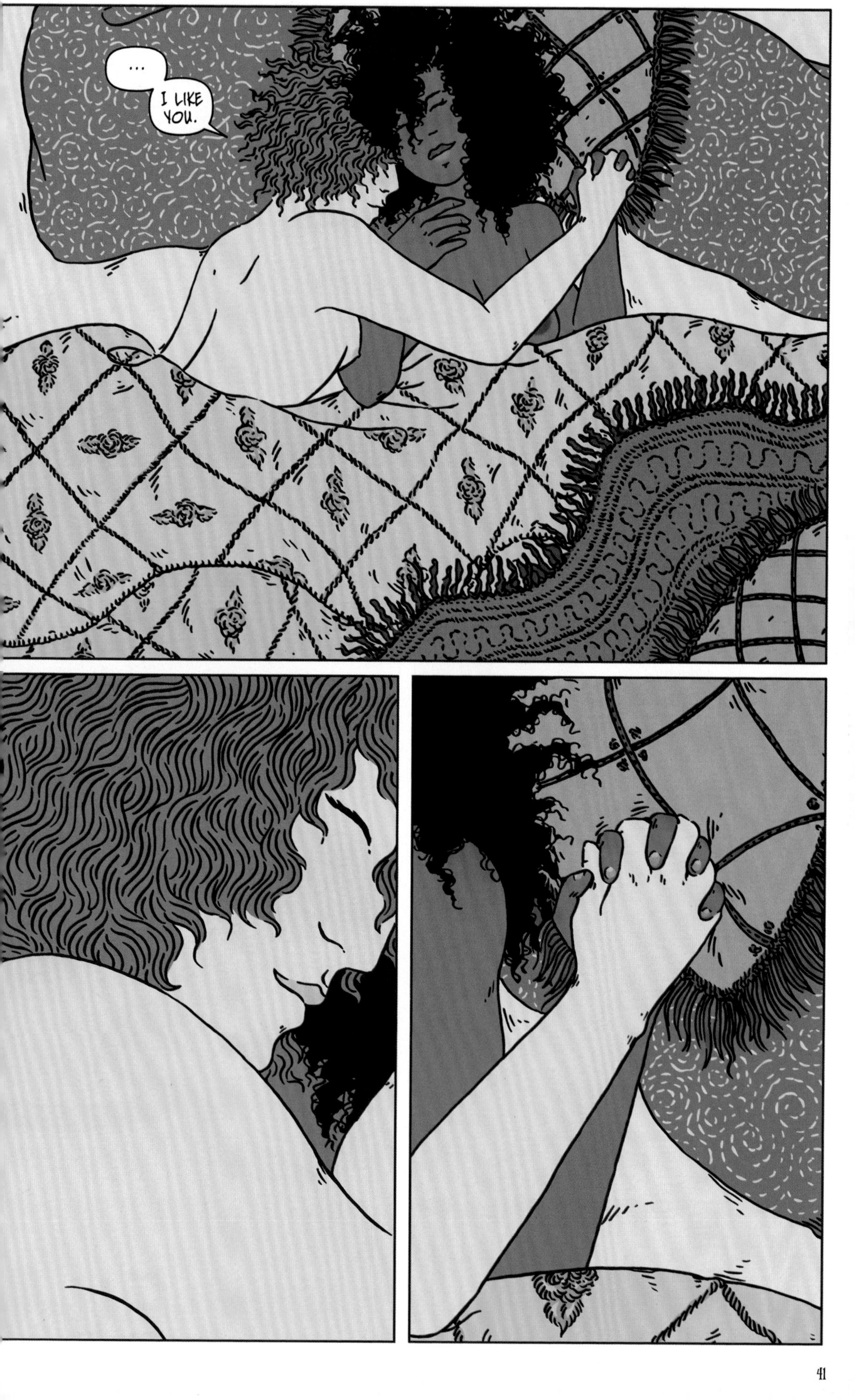
...
I LIKE YOU.

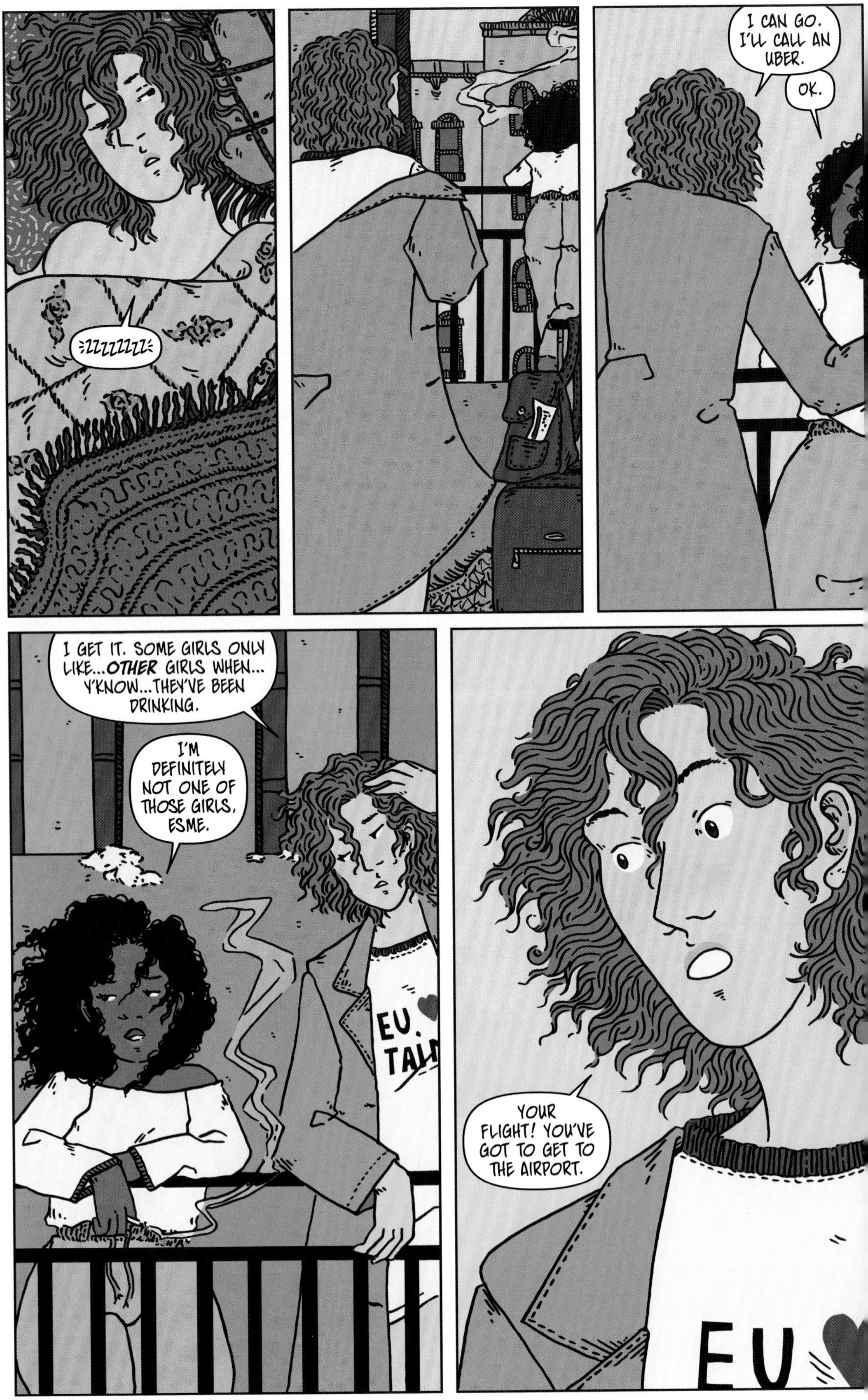
ZZZZZZZZ
I CAN GO. I'LL CALL AN UBER.
OK.
I GET IT. SOME GIRLS ONLY LIKE...OTHER GIRLS WHEN... Y'KNOW...THEY'VE BEEN DRINKING.
I'M DEFINITELY NOT ONE OF THOSE GIRLS, ESME.
EU.
TAI
YOUR FLIGHT! YOU'VE GOT TO GET TO THE AIRPORT.
EU

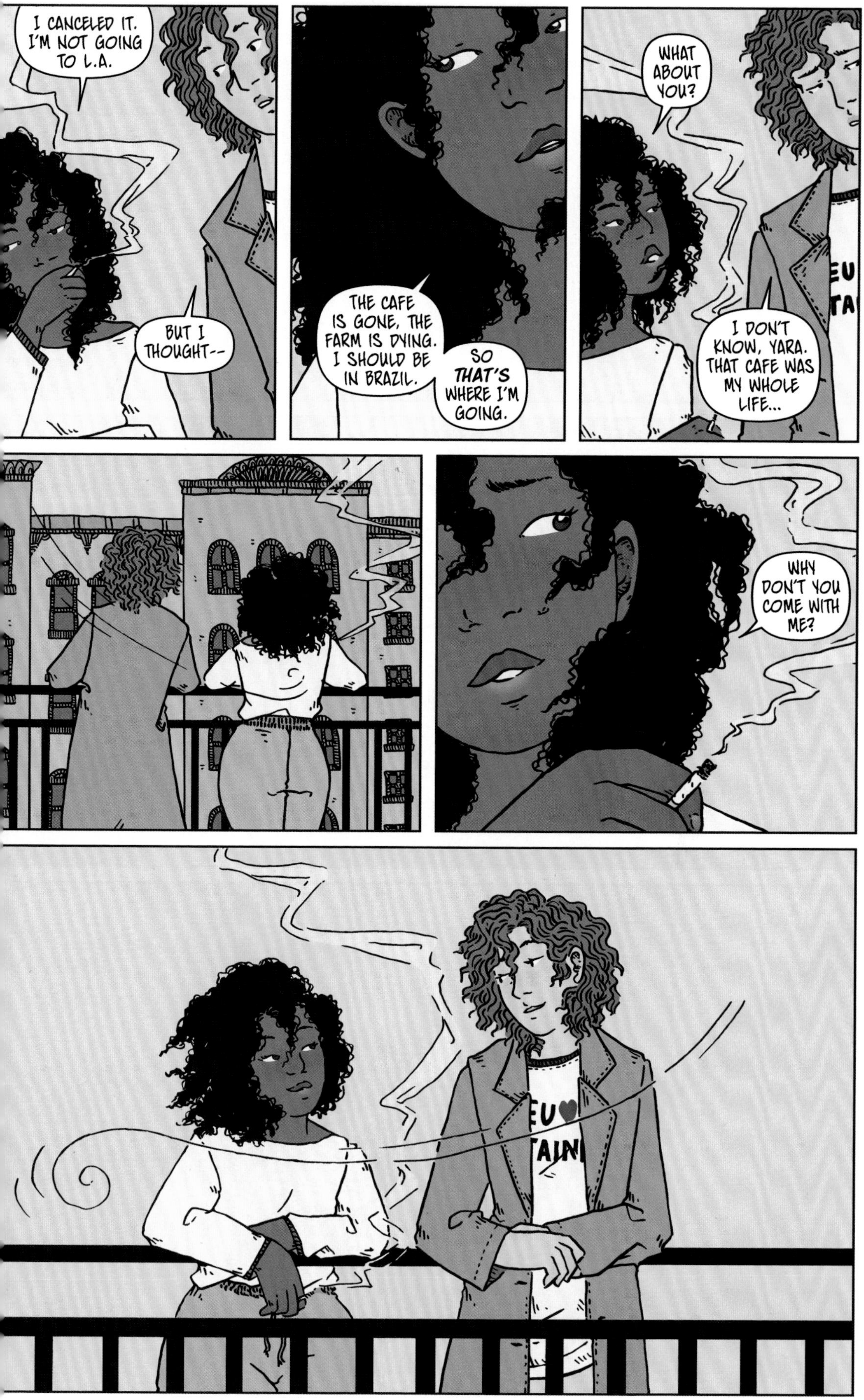
I CANCELED IT. I'M NOT GOING TO L.A.
BUT I THOUGHT--
THE CAFE IS GONE, THE FARM IS DYING. I SHOULD BE IN BRAZIL.
SO THAT'S WHERE I'M GOING.
WHAT ABOUT YOU?
I DON'T KNOW, YARA. THAT CAFE WAS MY WHOLE LIFE...
WHY DON'T YOU COME WITH ME?
EU ♥ TAIN

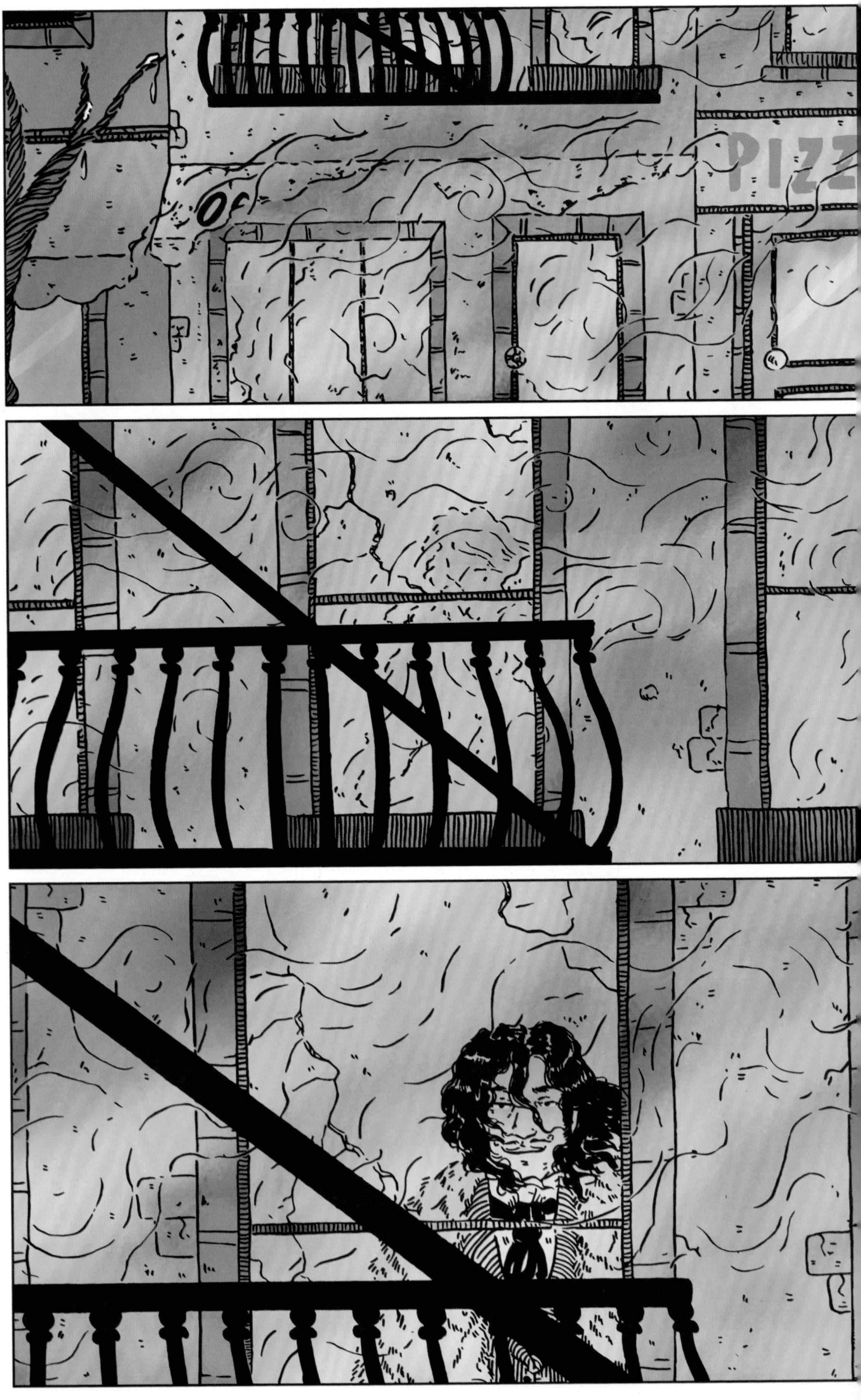

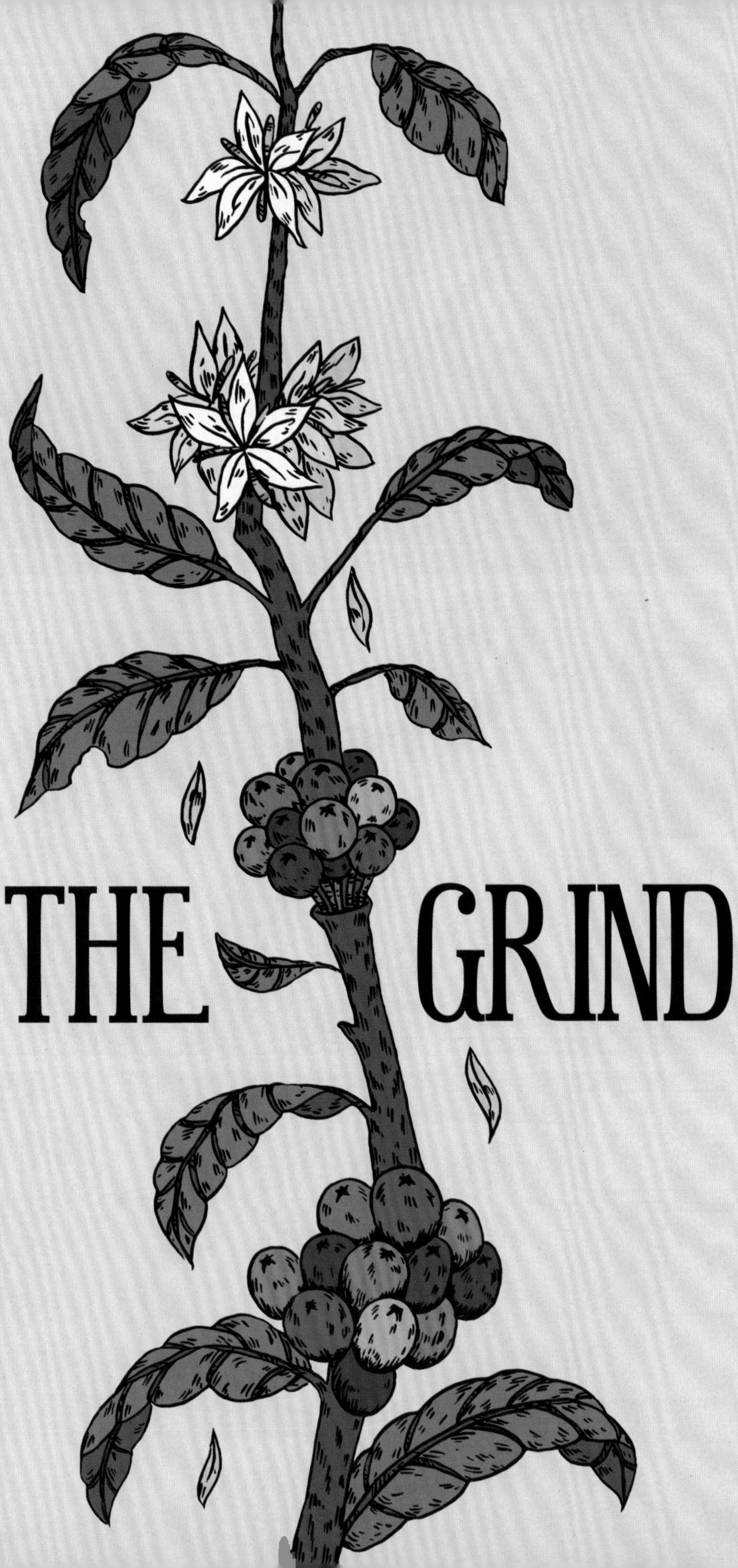

THE GRIND

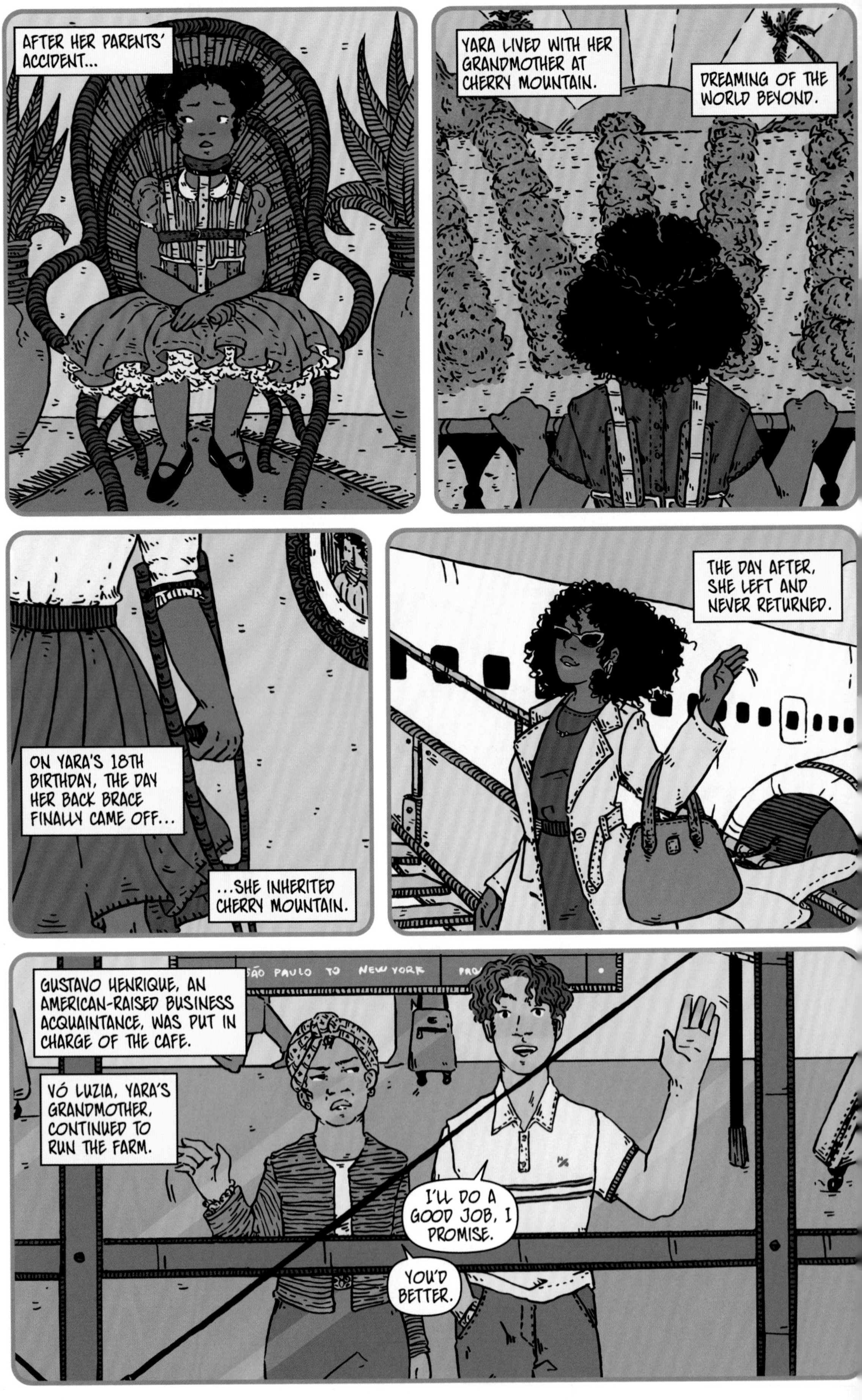
AFTER HER PARENTS' ACCIDENT...
YARA LIVED WITH HER GRANDMOTHER AT CHERRY MOUNTAIN.
DREAMING OF THE WORLD BEYOND.
ON YARA'S 18TH BIRTHDAY, THE DAY HER BACK BRACE FINALLY CAME OFF...
...SHE INHERITED CHERRY MOUNTAIN.
THE DAY AFTER, SHE LEFT AND NEVER RETURNED.
SÃO PAULO TO NEW YORK
GUSTAVO HENRIQUE, AN AMERICAN-RAISED BUSINESS ACQUAINTANCE, WAS PUT IN CHARGE OF THE CAFE.
VÓ LUZIA, YARA'S GRANDMOTHER, CONTINUED TO RUN THE FARM.
I'LL DO A GOOD JOB, I PROMISE.
YOU'D BETTER.

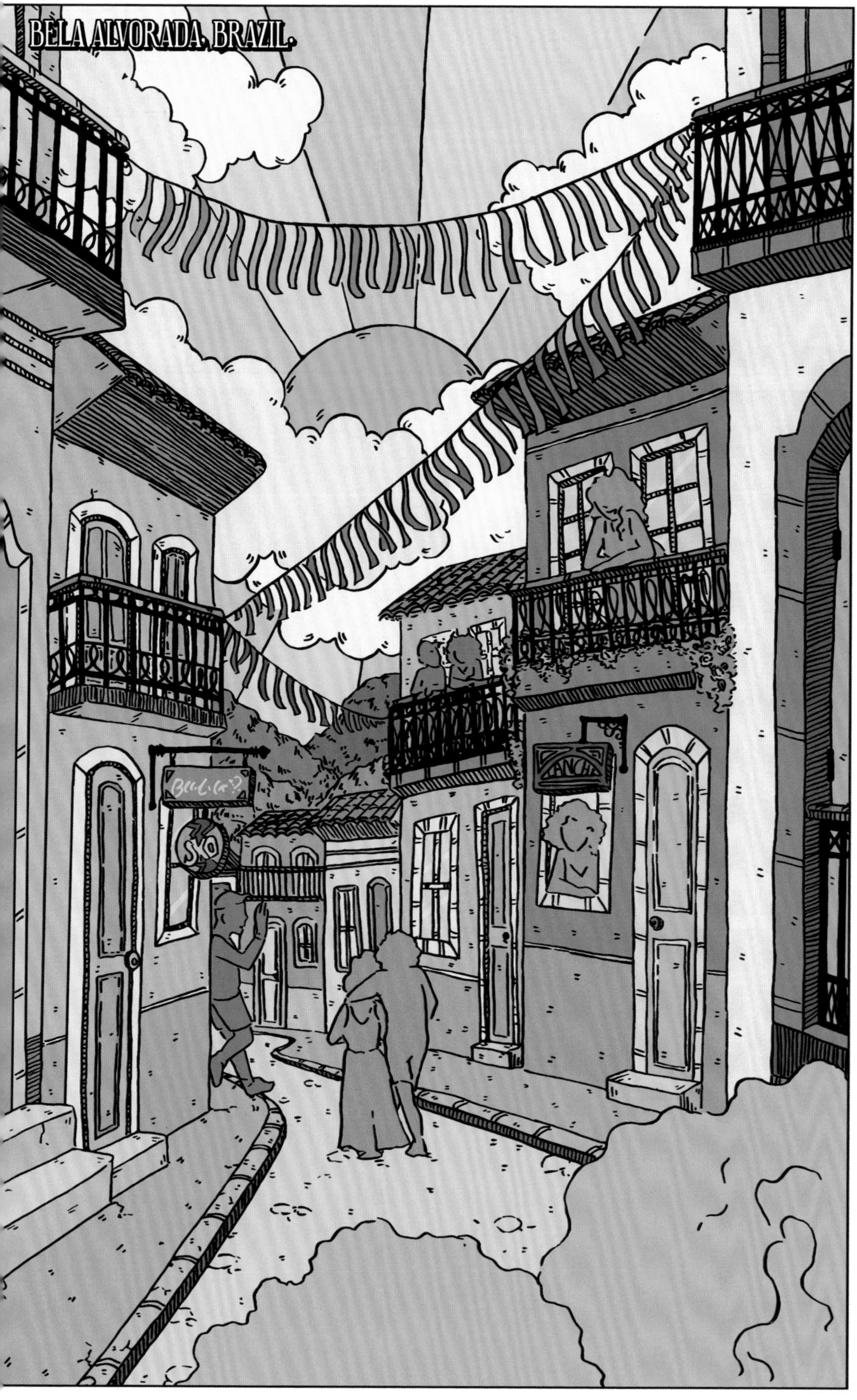
BELA ALVORADA, BRAZIL.

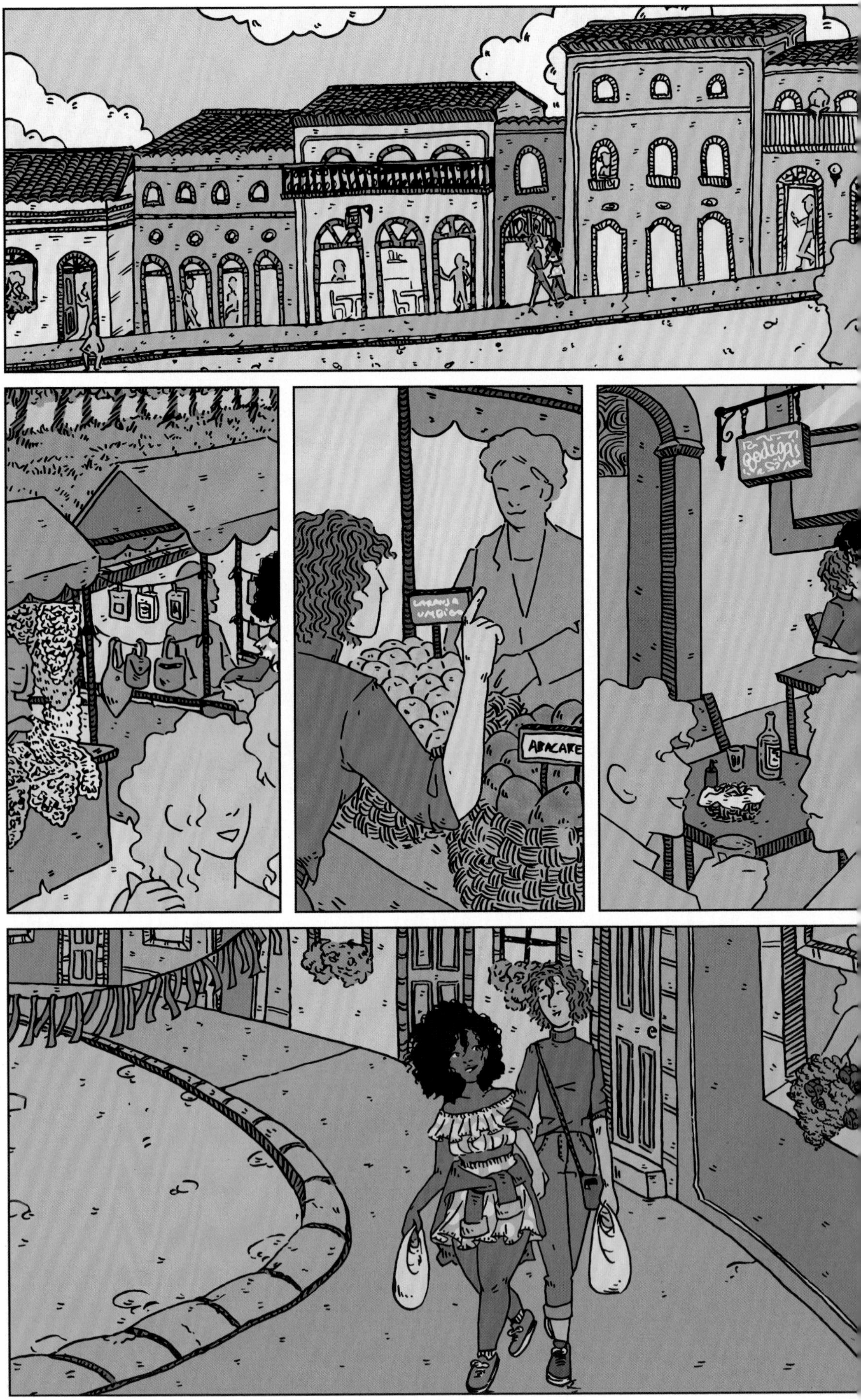
LARANJA
UMBIGO
ABACATE
Bodega's

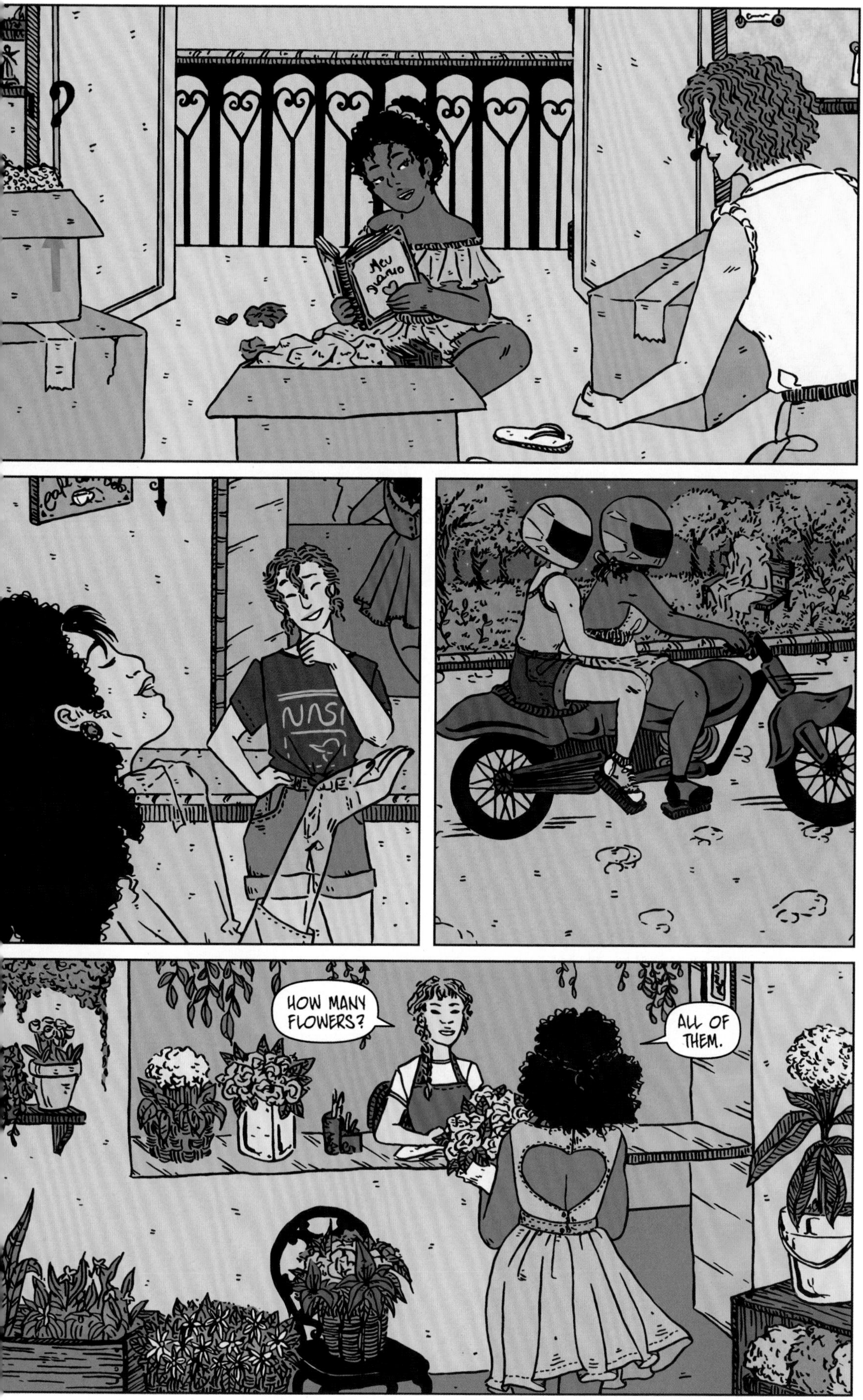

Meu diario
HOW MANY FLOWERS?
ALL OF THEM.

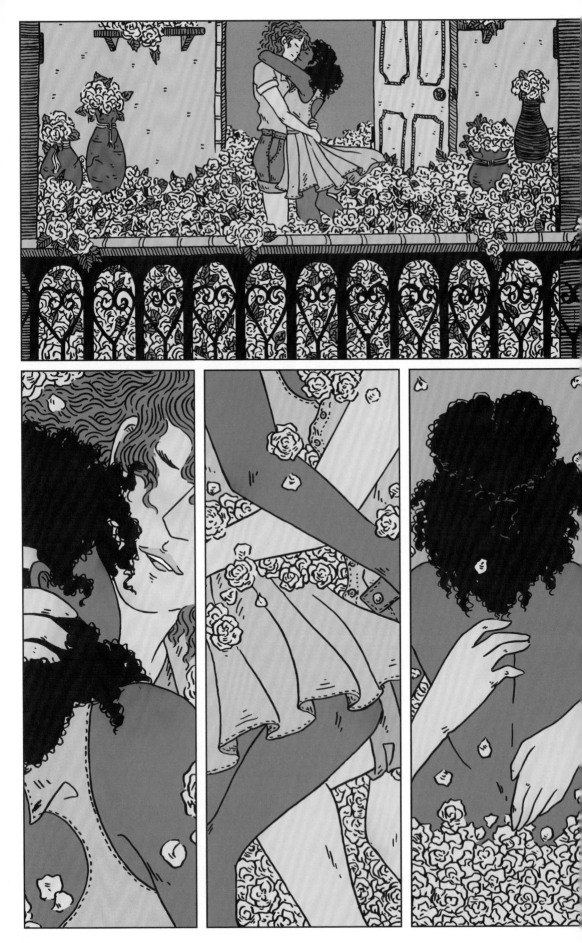

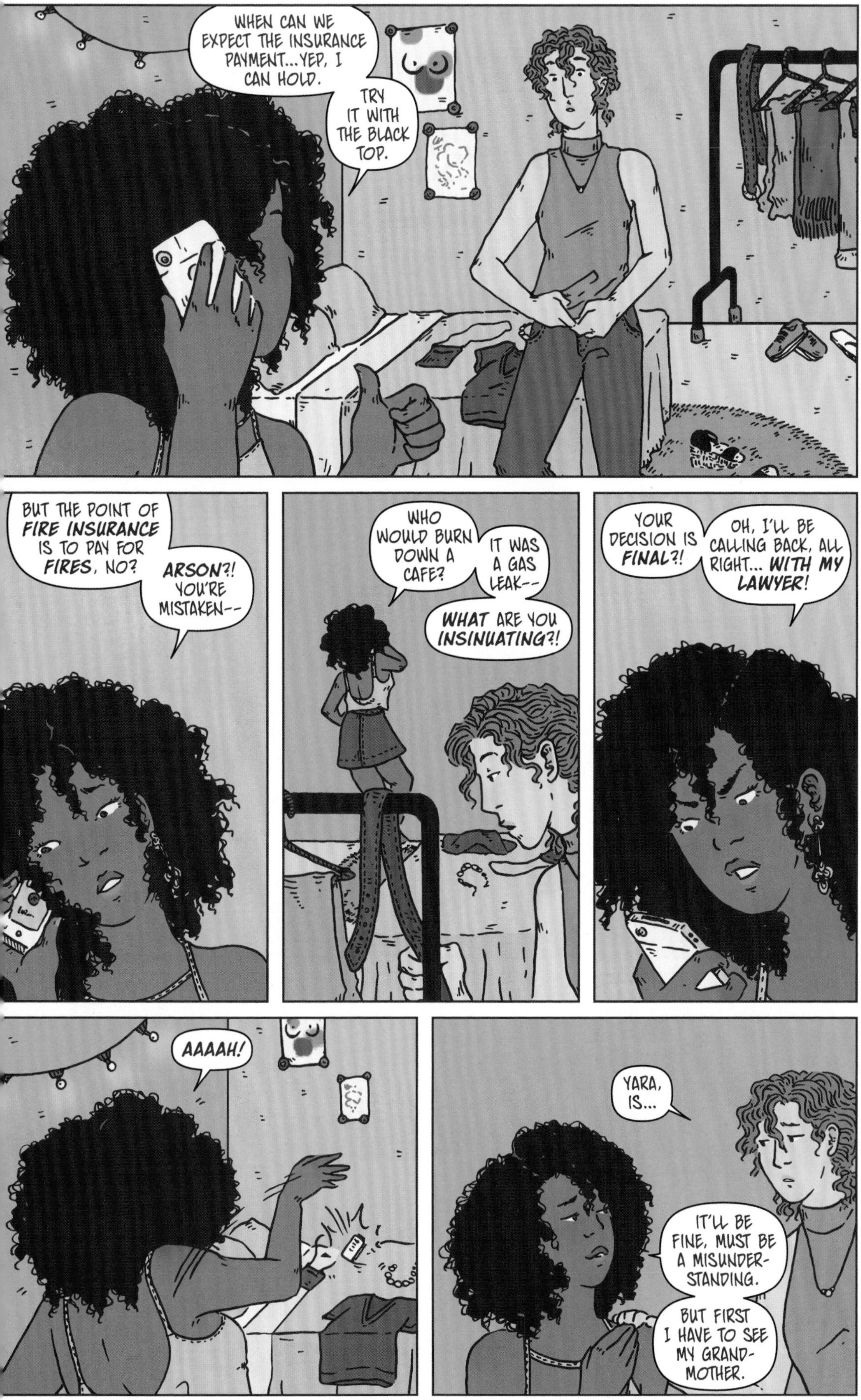
WHEN CAN WE EXPECT THE INSURANCE PAYMENT...YEP, I CAN HOLD.
TRY IT WITH THE BLACK TOP.
BUT THE POINT OF FIRE INSURANCE IS TO PAY FOR FIRES, NO?
ARSON?! YOU'RE MISTAKEN--
WHO WOULD BURN DOWN A CAFE?
IT WAS A GAS LEAK--
WHAT ARE YOU INSINUATING?!
YOUR DECISION IS FINAL?!
OH, I'LL BE CALLING BACK, ALL RIGHT... WITH MY LAWYER!
AAAAH!
YARA, IS...
IT'LL BE FINE, MUST BE A MISUNDERSTANDING.
BUT FIRST I HAVE TO SEE MY GRANDMOTHER.

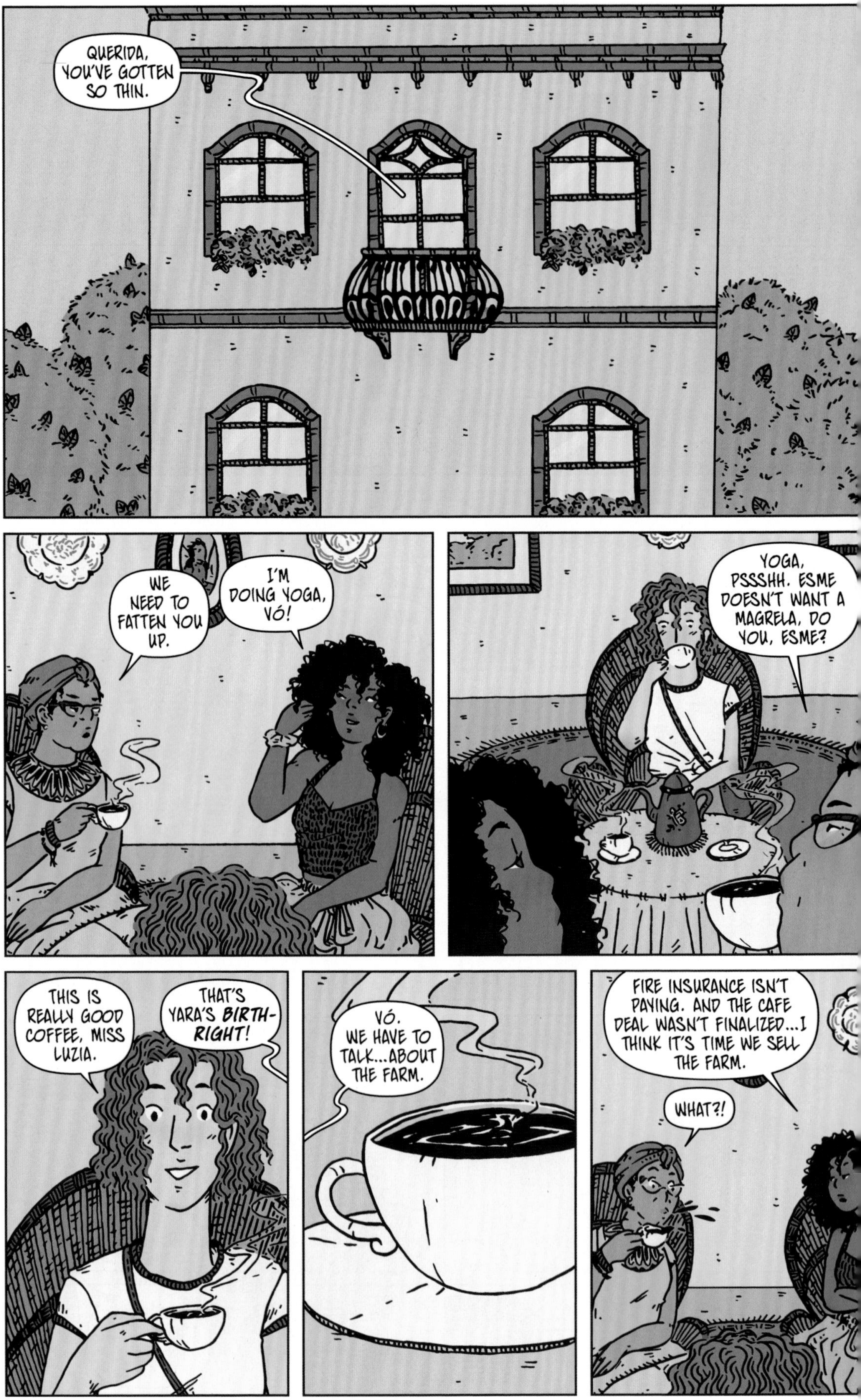
QUERIDA, YOU'VE GOTTEN SO THIN.
WE NEED TO FATTEN YOU UP.
I'M DOING YOGA, VÓ!
YOGA, PSSSHH. ESME DOESN'T WANT A MAGRELA, DO YOU, ESME?
THIS IS REALLY GOOD COFFEE, MISS LUZIA.
THAT'S YARA'S **BIRTH-RIGHT**!
VÓ. WE HAVE TO TALK...ABOUT THE FARM.
FIRE INSURANCE ISN'T PAYING. AND THE CAFE DEAL WASN'T FINALIZED...I THINK IT'S TIME WE SELL THE FARM.
WHAT?!

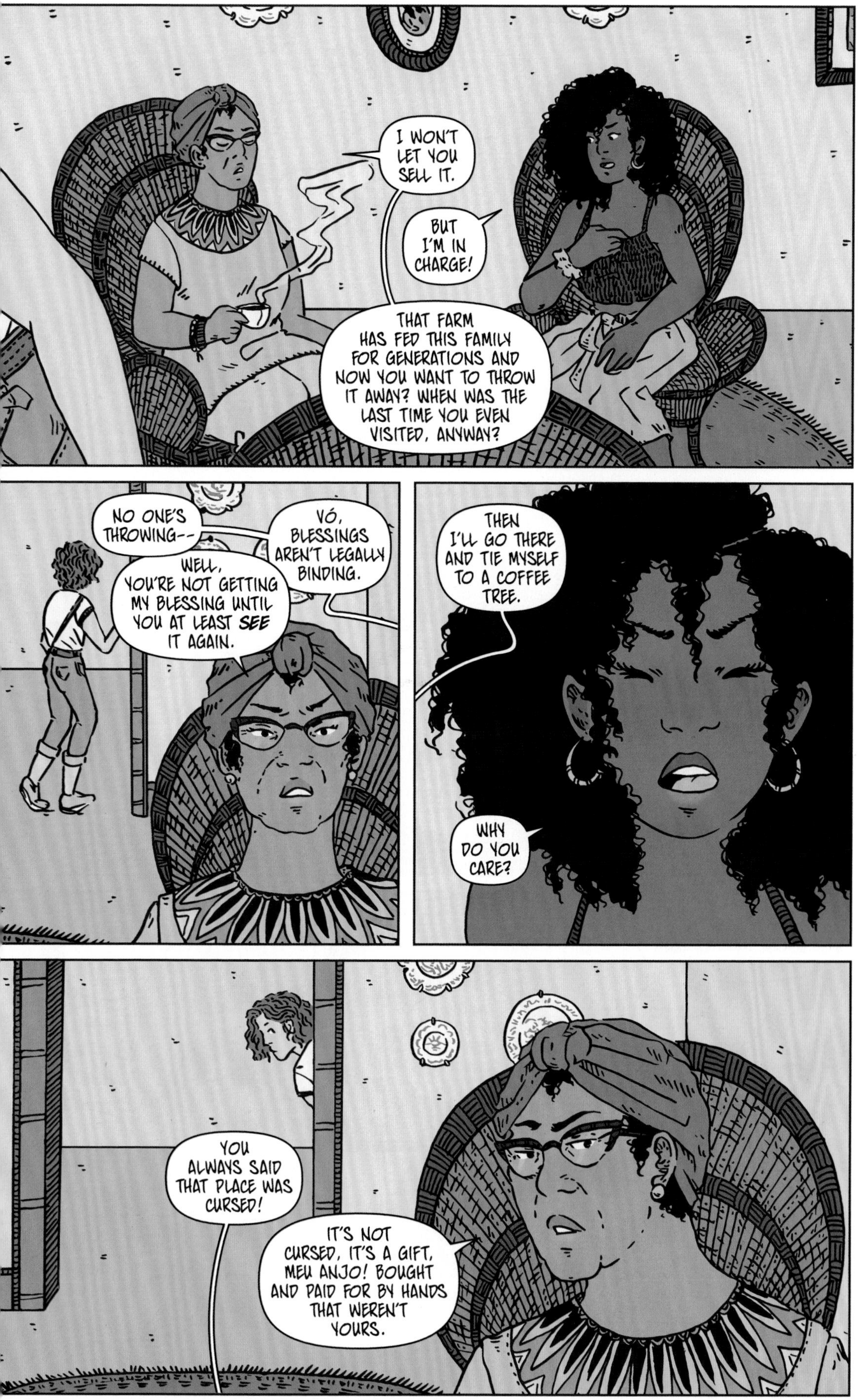
I WON'T LET YOU SELL IT.
BUT I'M IN CHARGE!
THAT FARM HAS FED THIS FAMILY FOR GENERATIONS AND NOW YOU WANT TO THROW IT AWAY? WHEN WAS THE LAST TIME YOU EVEN VISITED, ANYWAY?
NO ONE'S THROWING--
WELL, YOU'RE NOT GETTING MY BLESSING UNTIL YOU AT LEAST SEE IT AGAIN.
VÓ, BLESSINGS AREN'T LEGALLY BINDING.
THEN I'LL GO THERE AND TIE MYSELF TO A COFFEE TREE.
WHY DO YOU CARE?
YOU ALWAYS SAID THAT PLACE WAS CURSED!
IT'S NOT CURSED, IT'S A GIFT, MEU ANJO! BOUGHT AND PAID FOR BY HANDS THAT WEREN'T YOURS.

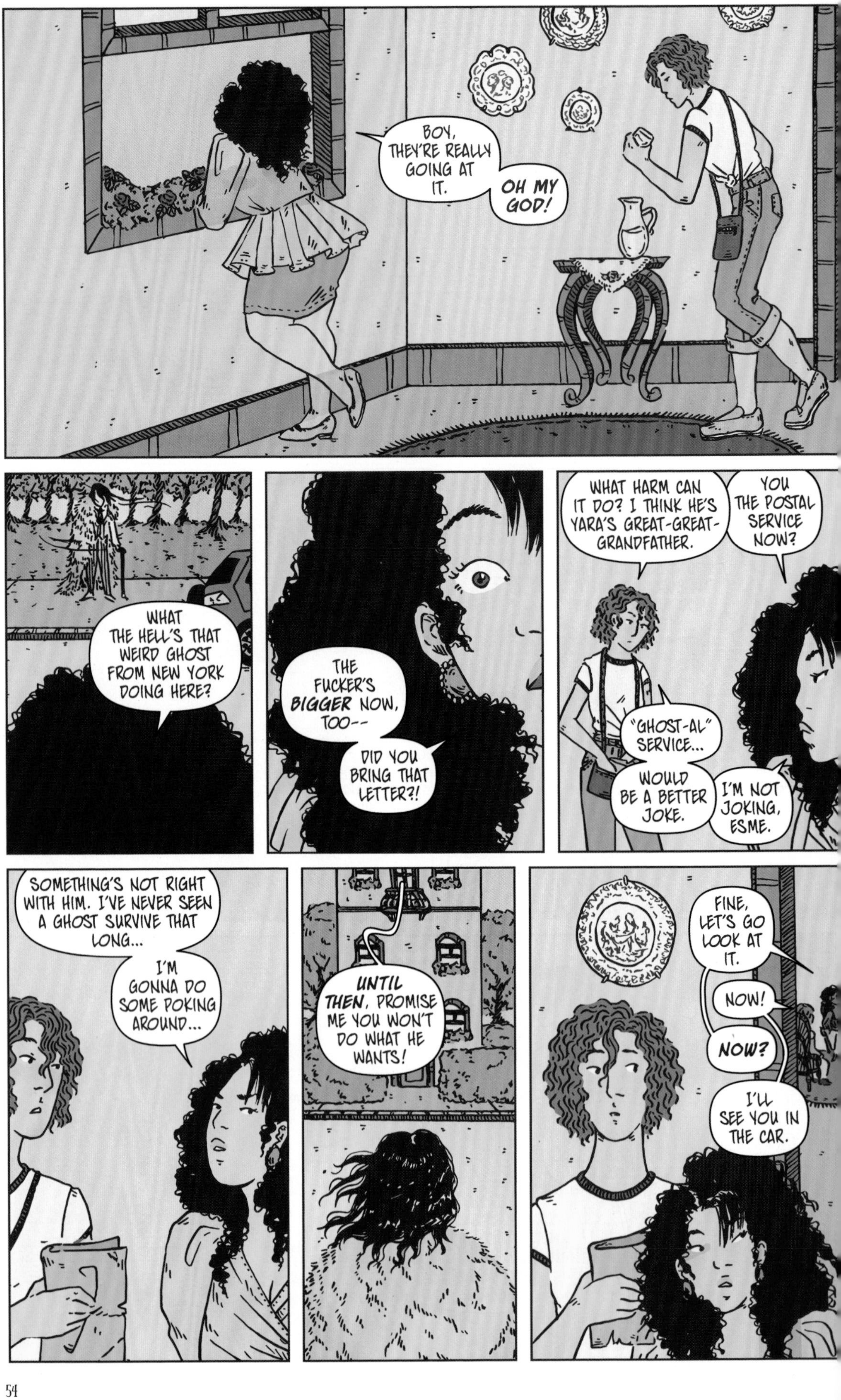
BOY, THEY'RE REALLY GOING AT IT.
OH MY GOD!
WHAT THE HELL'S THAT WEIRD GHOST FROM NEW YORK DOING HERE?
THE FUCKER'S BIGGER NOW, TOO--
DID YOU BRING THAT LETTER?!
WHAT HARM CAN IT DO? I THINK HE'S YARA'S GREAT-GREAT-GRANDFATHER.
YOU THE POSTAL SERVICE NOW?
"GHOST-AL" SERVICE...
WOULD BE A BETTER JOKE.
I'M NOT JOKING, ESME.
SOMETHING'S NOT RIGHT WITH HIM. I'VE NEVER SEEN A GHOST SURVIVE THAT LONG...
I'M GONNA DO SOME POKING AROUND...
UNTIL THEN, PROMISE ME YOU WON'T DO WHAT HE WANTS!
FINE, LET'S GO LOOK AT IT.
NOW!
NOW?
I'LL SEE YOU IN THE CAR.

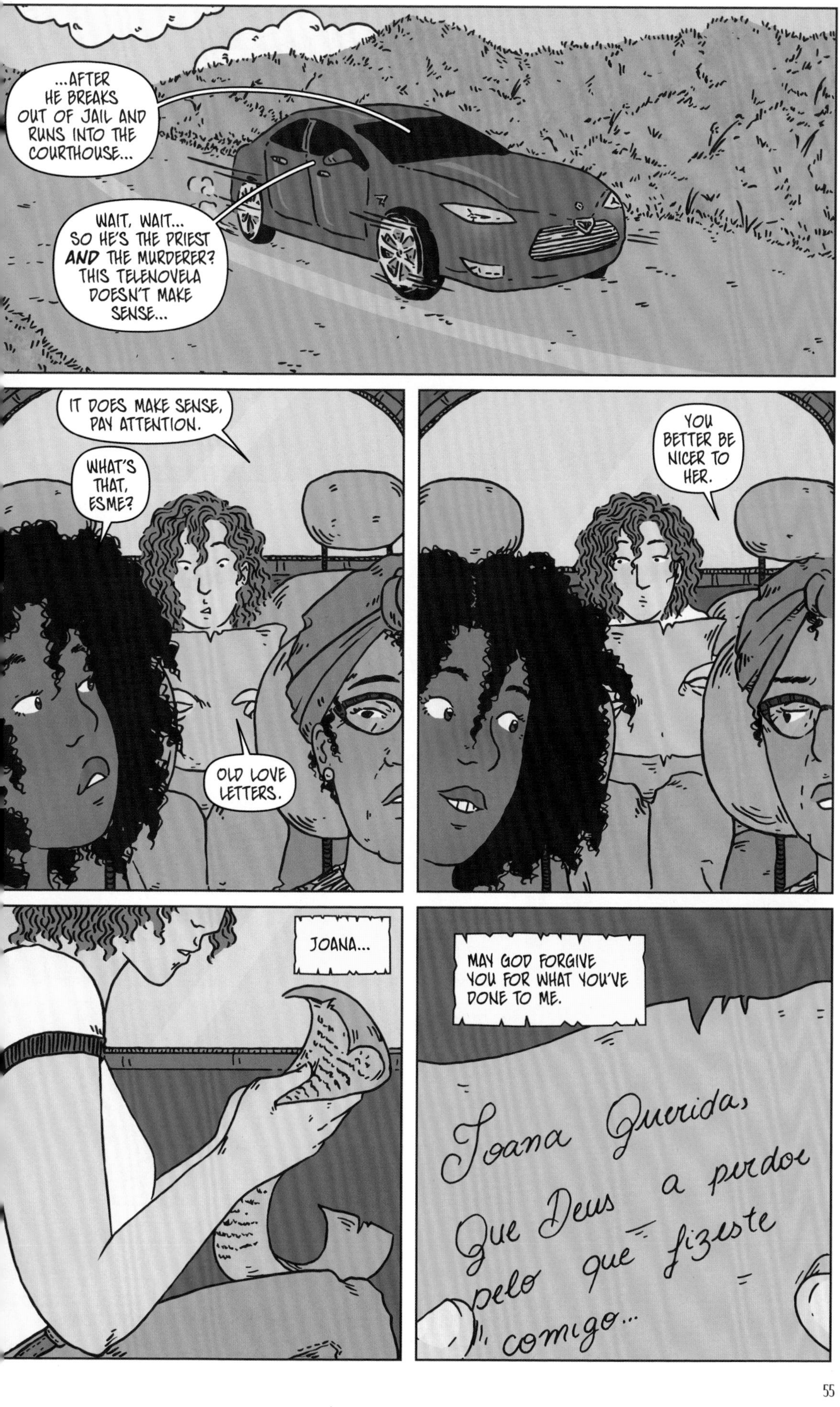
...AFTER HE BREAKS OUT OF JAIL AND RUNS INTO THE COURTHOUSE...
WAIT, WAIT... SO HE'S THE PRIEST **AND** THE MURDERER? THIS TELENOVELA DOESN'T MAKE SENSE...
IT DOES MAKE SENSE, PAY ATTENTION.
WHAT'S THAT, ESME?
OLD LOVE LETTERS.
YOU BETTER BE NICER TO HER.
JOANA...
MAY GOD FORGIVE YOU FOR WHAT YOU'VE DONE TO ME.
Joana Querida,
Que Deus a perdoe pelo que fizeste comigo...

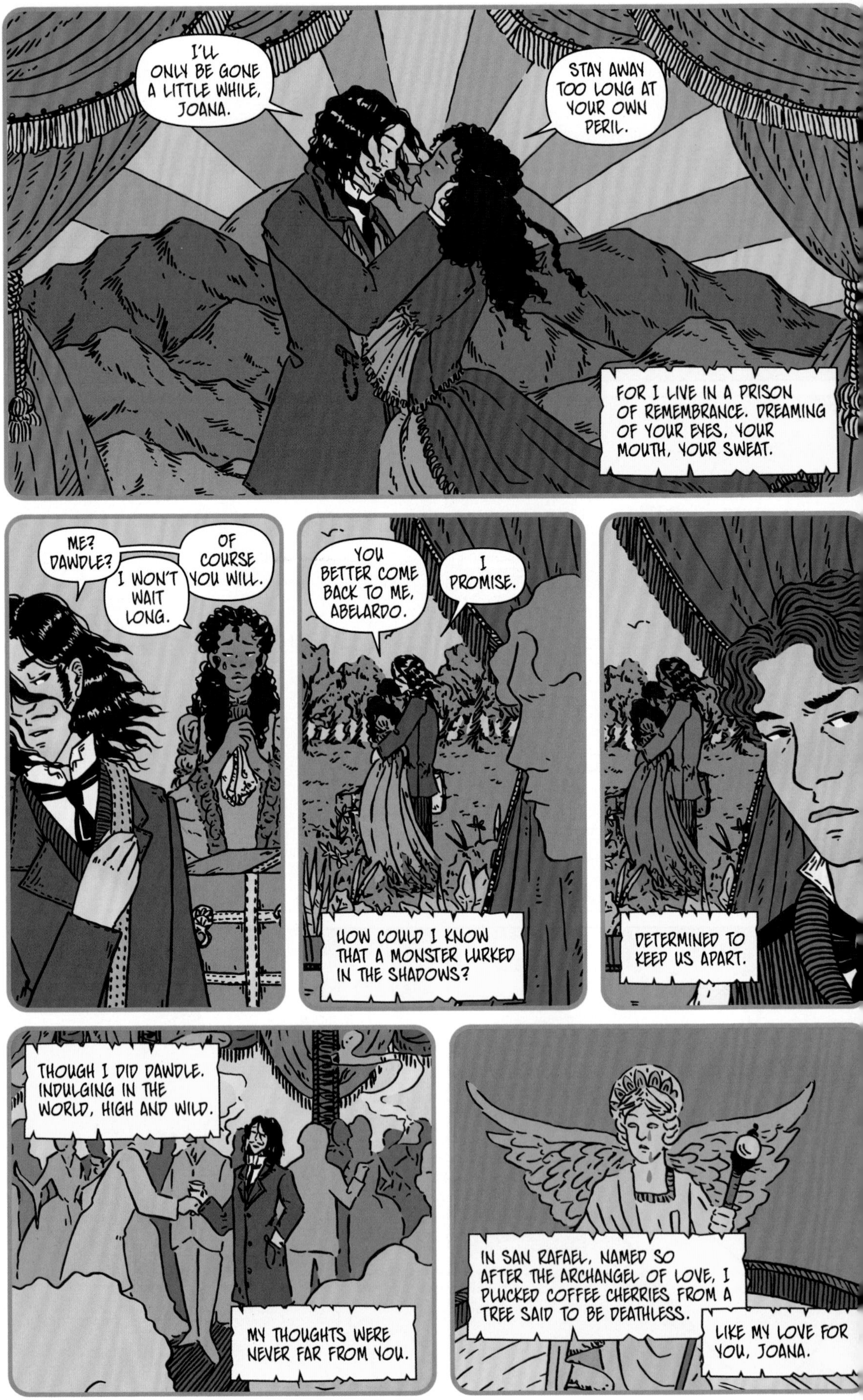
I'LL ONLY BE GONE A LITTLE WHILE, JOANA.
STAY AWAY TOO LONG AT YOUR OWN PERIL.
FOR I LIVE IN A PRISON OF REMEMBRANCE. DREAMING OF YOUR EYES, YOUR MOUTH, YOUR SWEAT.
ME? DAWDLE?
I WON'T WAIT LONG.
OF COURSE YOU WILL.
YOU BETTER COME BACK TO ME, ABELARDO.
I PROMISE.
HOW COULD I KNOW THAT A MONSTER LURKED IN THE SHADOWS?
DETERMINED TO KEEP US APART.
THOUGH I DID DAWDLE. INDULGING IN THE WORLD, HIGH AND WILD.
MY THOUGHTS WERE NEVER FAR FROM YOU.
IN SAN RAFAEL, NAMED SO AFTER THE ARCHANGEL OF LOVE, I PLUCKED COFFEE CHERRIES FROM A TREE SAID TO BE DEATHLESS.
LIKE MY LOVE FOR YOU, JOANA.

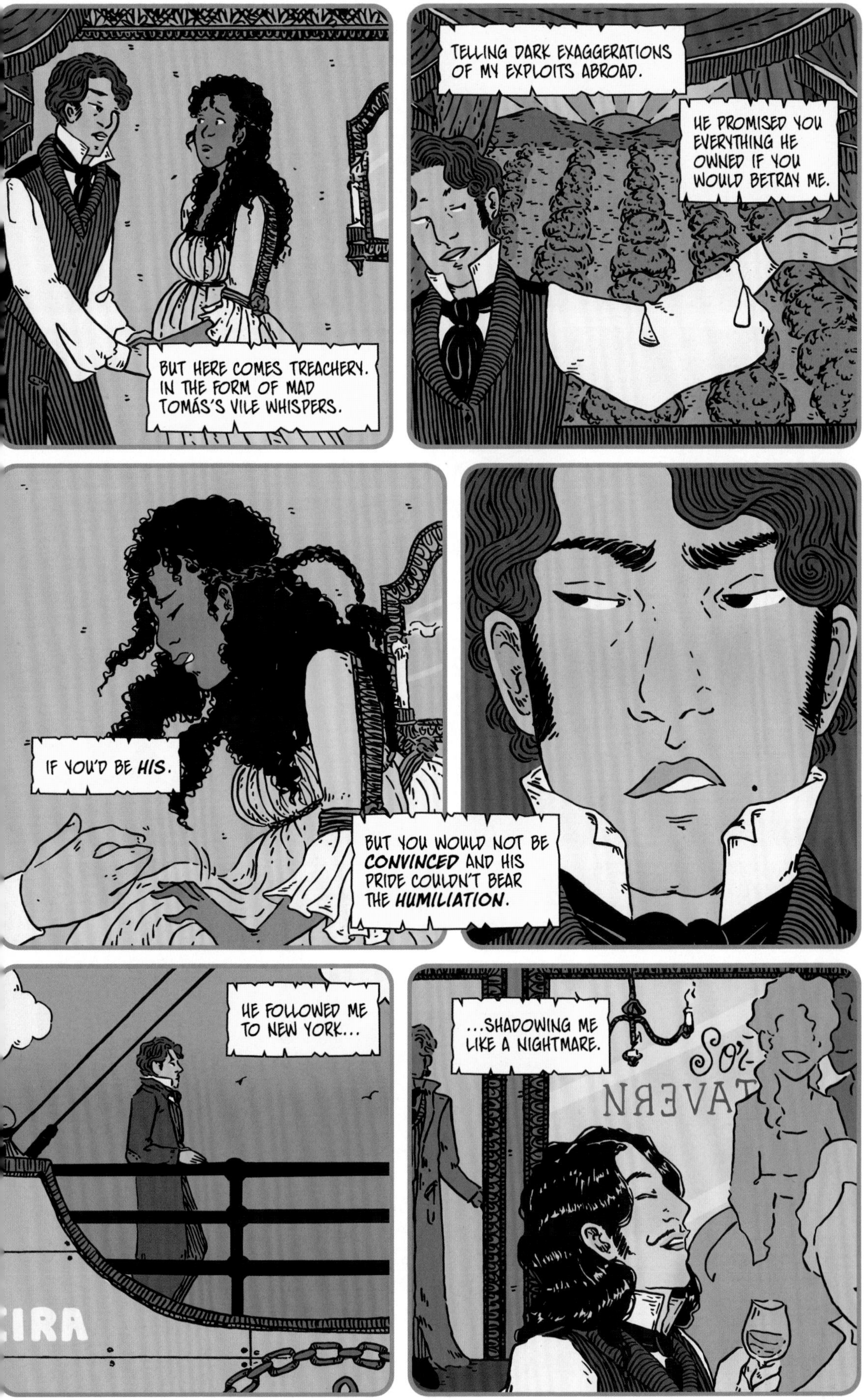
BUT HERE COMES TREACHERY. IN THE FORM OF MAD TOMÁS'S VILE WHISPERS.
TELLING DARK EXAGGERATIONS OF MY EXPLOITS ABROAD.
HE PROMISED YOU EVERYTHING HE OWNED IF YOU WOULD BETRAY ME.
IF YOU'D BE **HIS**.
BUT YOU WOULD NOT BE **CONVINCED** AND HIS PRIDE COULDN'T BEAR THE **HUMILIATION**.
HE FOLLOWED ME TO NEW YORK...
...SHADOWING ME LIKE A NIGHTMARE.

LECHER!

THIS AWOKE MY FURY.

HIS HANDS, WEAK. HIS AIM, FALSE.

MY FISTS, POWDER KEGS. MY HEART, TRUE.

CRACK

MY LOVE BURNED TOO BRIGHTLY, CONSUMING EVERYTHING IT TOUCHED.

TRUE TO HIS WORD, MAD TOMÁS WILLED HIS LANDS TO YOU. CERTAIN THAT HE WOULD BEST ME.

DELUSIONAL TO THE VERY END.

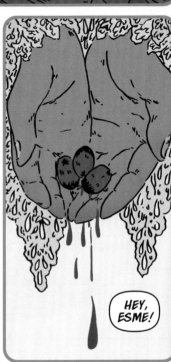

HEY, ESME!

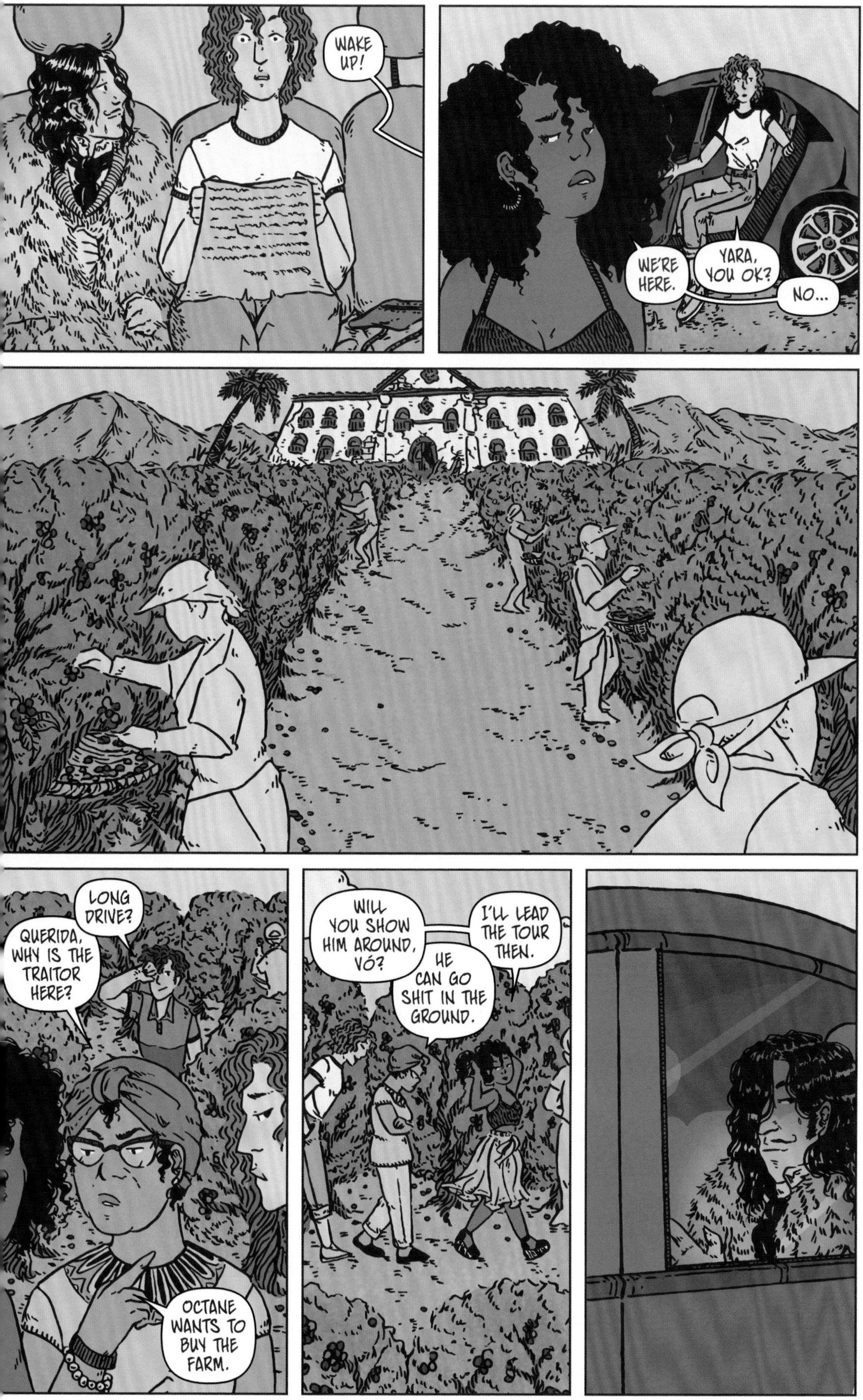
WAKE UP!
WE'RE HERE.
YARA, YOU OK?
NO...
QUERIDA, WHY IS THE TRAITOR HERE?
LONG DRIVE?
OCTANE WANTS TO BUY THE FARM.
WILL YOU SHOW HIM AROUND, VÓ?
HE CAN GO SHIT IN THE GROUND.
I'LL LEAD THE TOUR THEN.

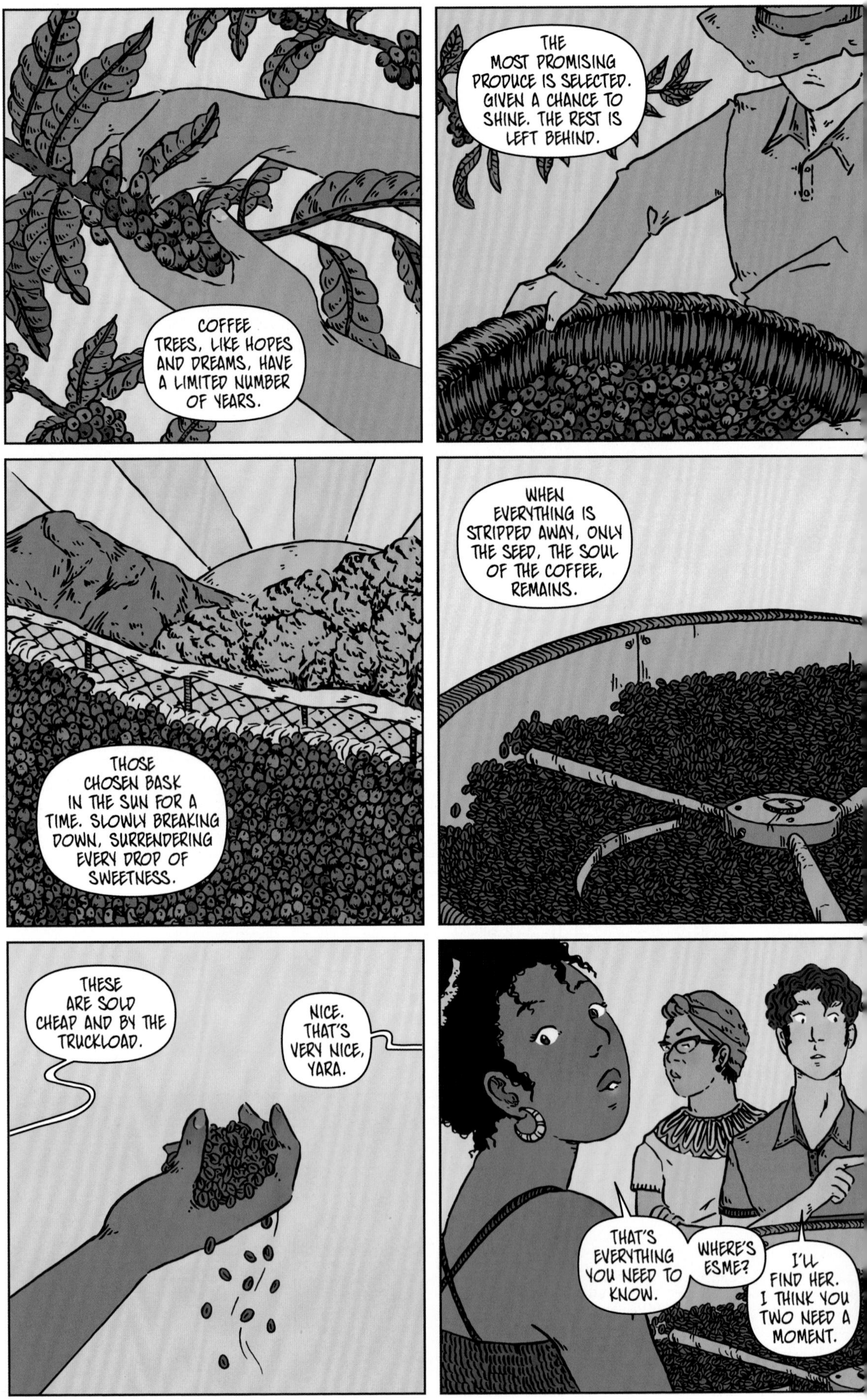
COFFEE TREES, LIKE HOPES AND DREAMS, HAVE A LIMITED NUMBER OF YEARS.
THE MOST PROMISING PRODUCE IS SELECTED. GIVEN A CHANCE TO SHINE. THE REST IS LEFT BEHIND.
THOSE CHOSEN BASK IN THE SUN FOR A TIME. SLOWLY BREAKING DOWN, SURRENDERING EVERY DROP OF SWEETNESS.
WHEN EVERYTHING IS STRIPPED AWAY, ONLY THE SEED, THE SOUL OF THE COFFEE, REMAINS.
THESE ARE SOLD CHEAP AND BY THE TRUCKLOAD.
NICE. THAT'S VERY NICE, YARA.
THAT'S EVERYTHING YOU NEED TO KNOW.
WHERE'S ESME?
I'LL FIND HER. I THINK YOU TWO NEED A MOMENT.

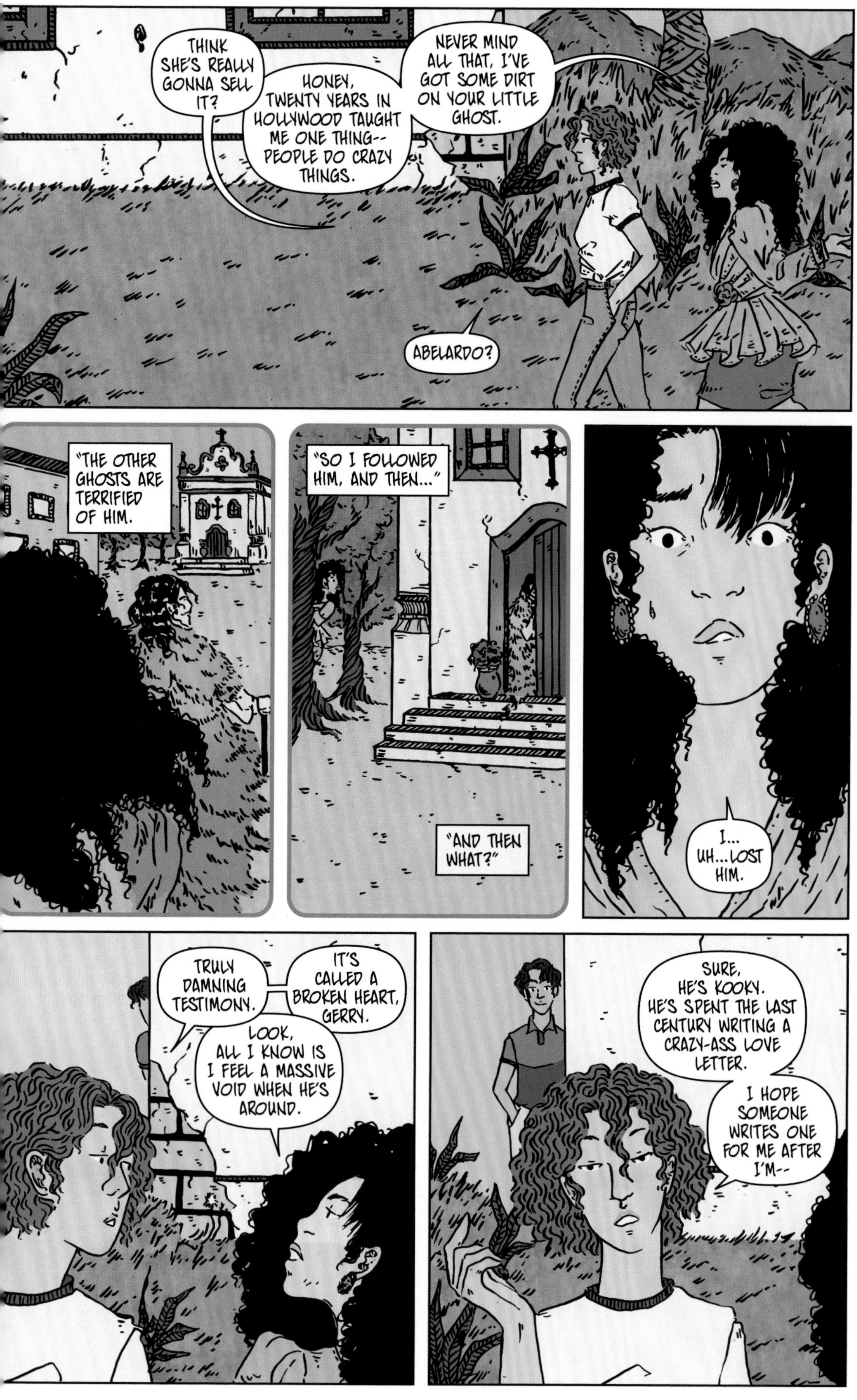
THINK SHE'S REALLY GONNA SELL IT?
HONEY, TWENTY YEARS IN HOLLYWOOD TAUGHT ME ONE THING-- PEOPLE DO CRAZY THINGS.
NEVER MIND ALL THAT, I'VE GOT SOME DIRT ON YOUR LITTLE GHOST.
ABELARDO?
"THE OTHER GHOSTS ARE TERRIFIED OF HIM.
"SO I FOLLOWED HIM, AND THEN..."
"AND THEN WHAT?"
I... UH...LOST HIM.
TRULY DAMNING TESTIMONY.
IT'S CALLED A BROKEN HEART, GERRY.
LOOK, ALL I KNOW IS I FEEL A MASSIVE VOID WHEN HE'S AROUND.
SURE, HE'S KOOKY. HE'S SPENT THE LAST CENTURY WRITING A CRAZY-ASS LOVE LETTER.
I HOPE SOMEONE WRITES ONE FOR ME AFTER I'M--

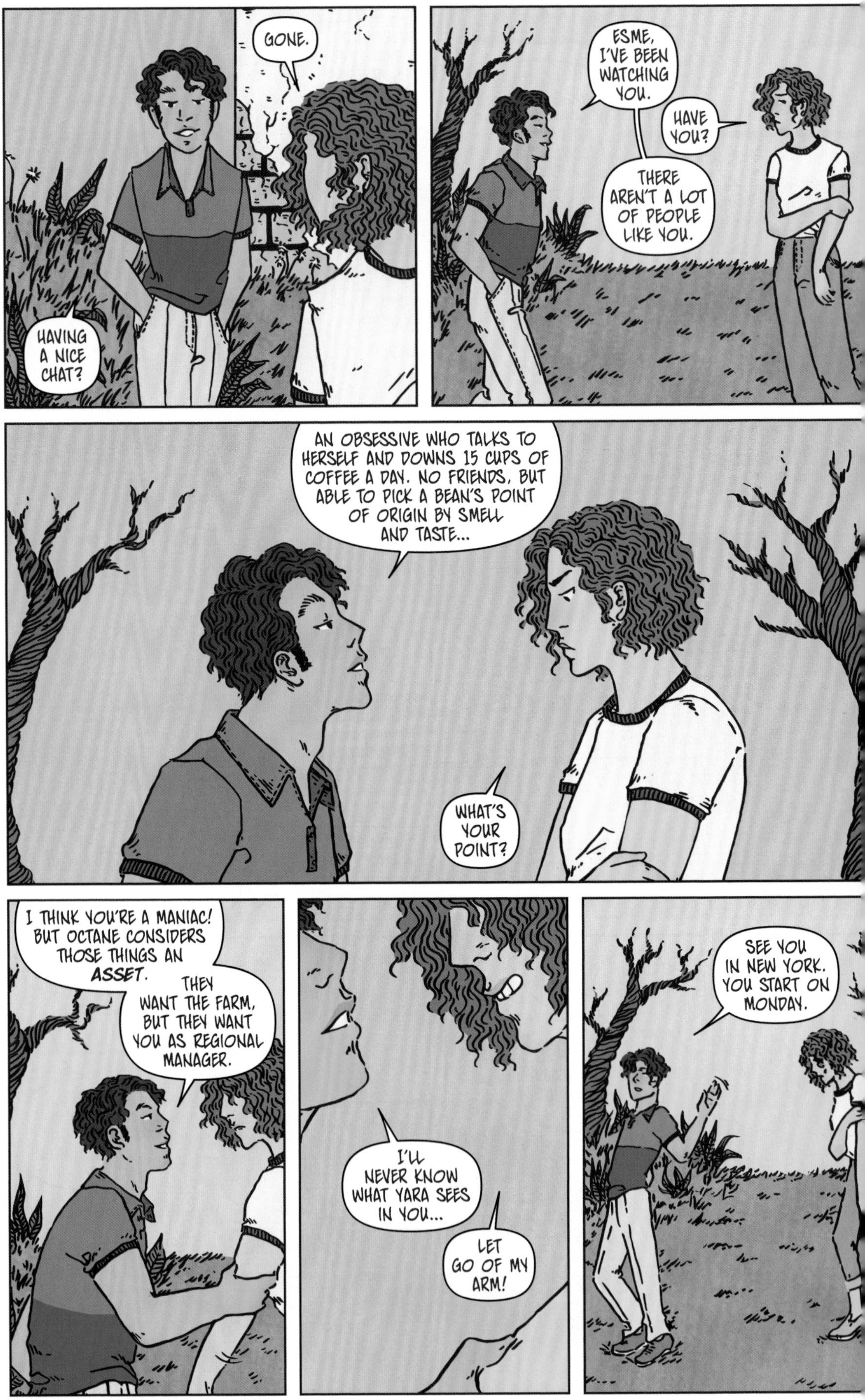
GONE.
HAVING A NICE CHAT?
ESME, I'VE BEEN WATCHING YOU.
HAVE YOU?
THERE AREN'T A LOT OF PEOPLE LIKE YOU.
AN OBSESSIVE WHO TALKS TO HERSELF AND DOWNS 15 CUPS OF COFFEE A DAY. NO FRIENDS, BUT ABLE TO PICK A BEAN'S POINT OF ORIGIN BY SMELL AND TASTE...
WHAT'S YOUR POINT?
I THINK YOU'RE A MANIAC! BUT OCTANE CONSIDERS THOSE THINGS AN **ASSET**.
THEY WANT THE FARM, BUT THEY WANT YOU AS REGIONAL MANAGER.
I'LL NEVER KNOW WHAT YARA SEES IN YOU...
LET GO OF MY ARM!
SEE YOU IN NEW YORK. YOU START ON MONDAY.

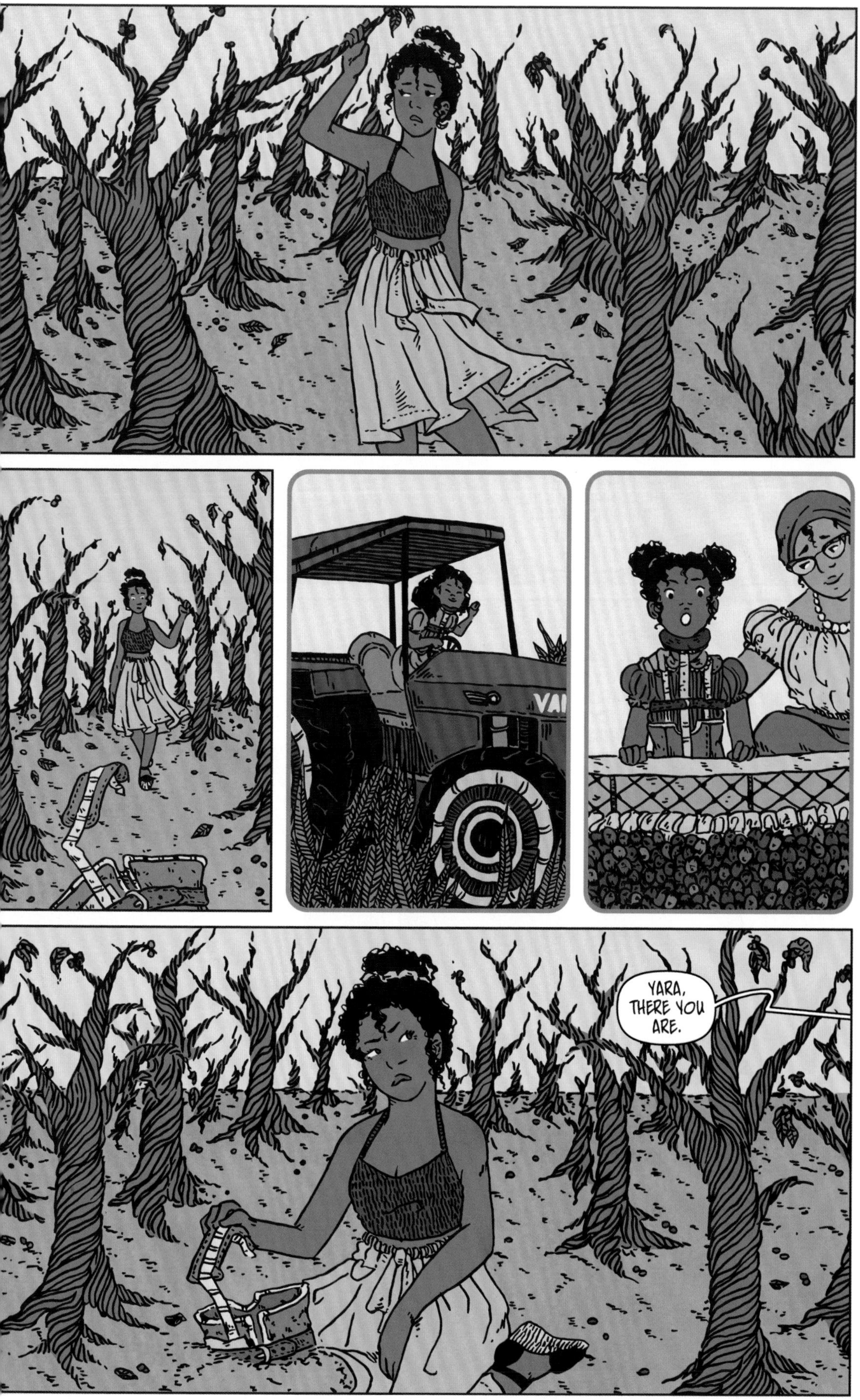
VAI
YARA, THERE YOU ARE.

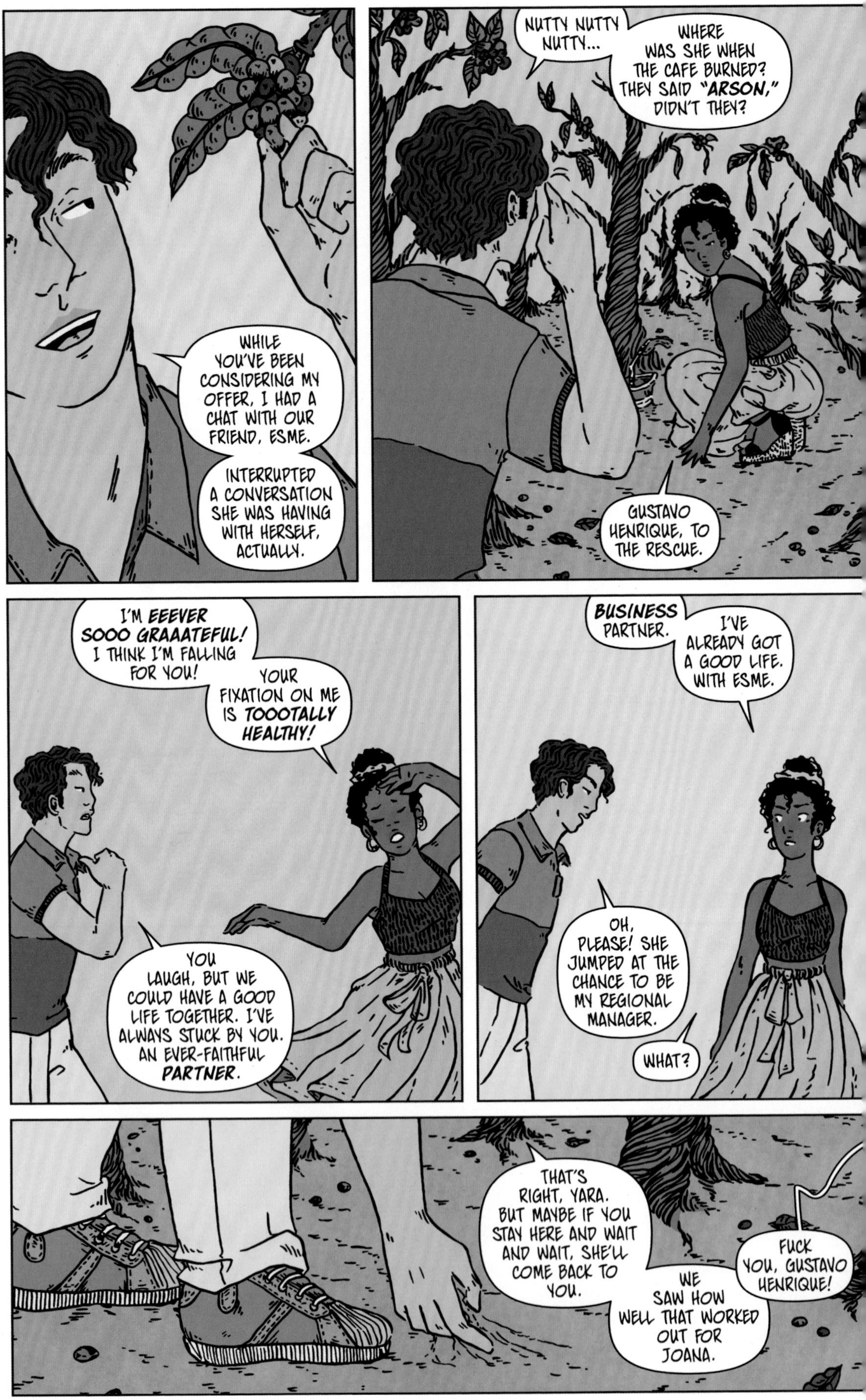
WHILE YOU'VE BEEN CONSIDERING MY OFFER, I HAD A CHAT WITH OUR FRIEND, ESME.
INTERRUPTED A CONVERSATION SHE WAS HAVING WITH HERSELF, ACTUALLY.
NUTTY NUTTY NUTTY...
WHERE WAS SHE WHEN THE CAFE BURNED? THEY SAID "ARSON," DIDN'T THEY?
GUSTAVO HENRIQUE, TO THE RESCUE.
I'M EEEVER SOOO GRAAATEFUL! I THINK I'M FALLING FOR YOU!
YOUR FIXATION ON ME IS TOOOTALLY HEALTHY!
YOU LAUGH, BUT WE COULD HAVE A GOOD LIFE TOGETHER. I'VE ALWAYS STUCK BY YOU. AN EVER-FAITHFUL PARTNER.
BUSINESS PARTNER.
I'VE ALREADY GOT A GOOD LIFE. WITH ESME.
OH, PLEASE! SHE JUMPED AT THE CHANCE TO BE MY REGIONAL MANAGER.
WHAT?
THAT'S RIGHT, YARA. BUT MAYBE IF YOU STAY HERE AND WAIT AND WAIT, SHE'LL COME BACK TO YOU.
WE SAW HOW WELL THAT WORKED OUT FOR JOANA.
FUCK YOU, GUSTAVO HENRIQUE!

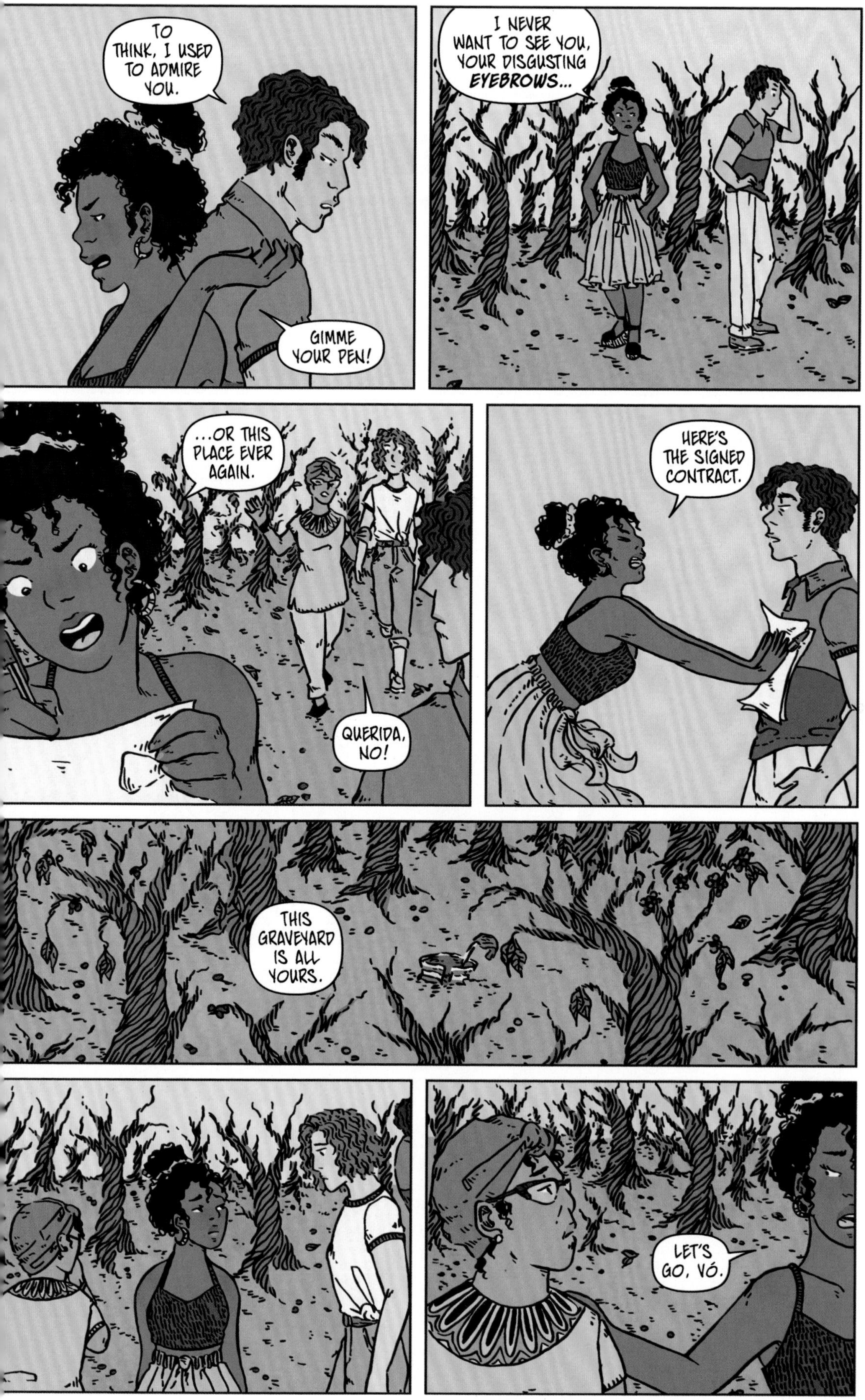
TO THINK, I USED TO ADMIRE YOU.
GIMME YOUR PEN!
I NEVER WANT TO SEE YOU, YOUR DISGUSTING EYEBROWS...
...OR THIS PLACE EVER AGAIN.
QUERIDA, NO!
HERE'S THE SIGNED CONTRACT.
THIS GRAVEYARD IS ALL YOURS.
LET'S GO, VÓ.

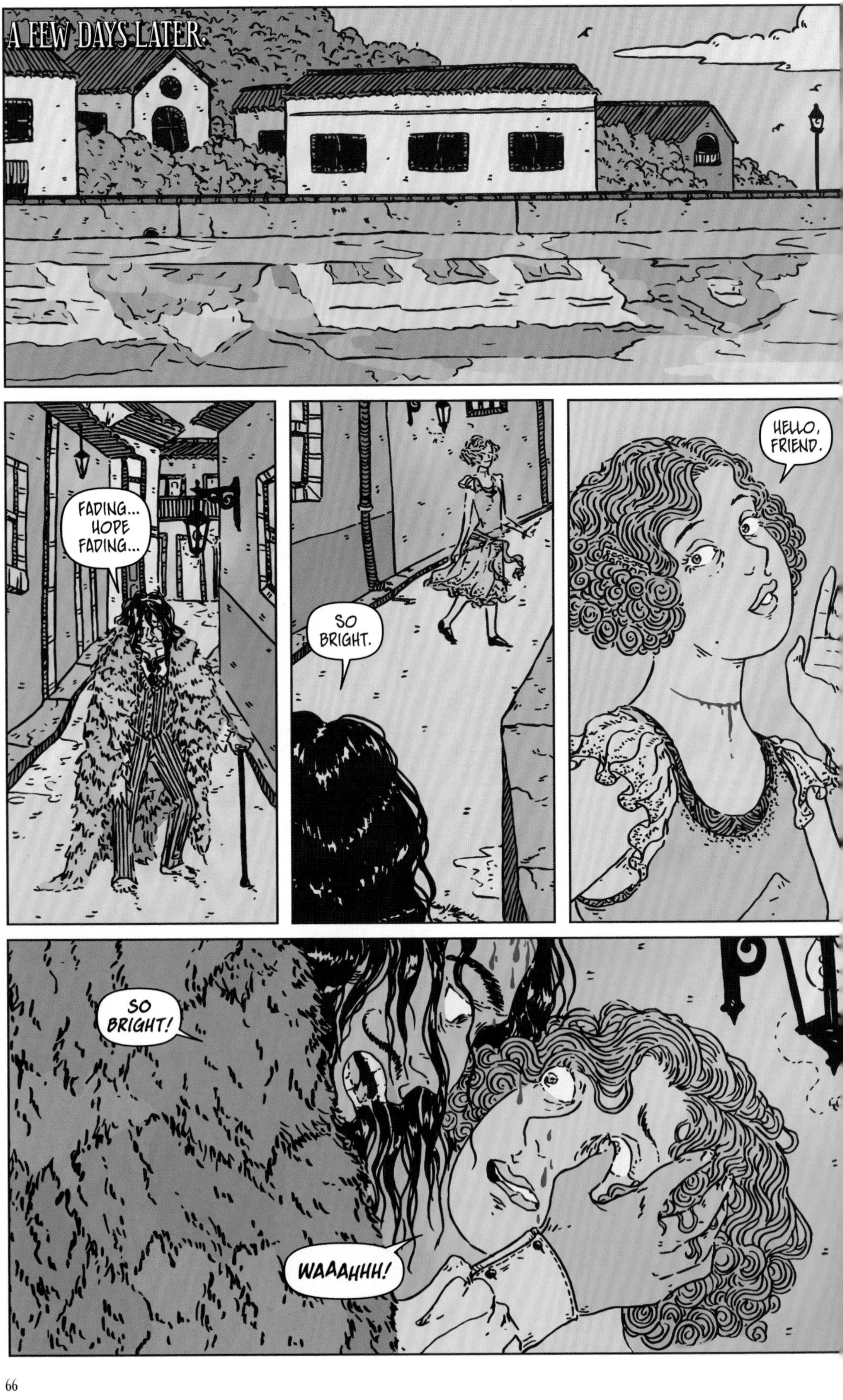
A FEW DAYS LATER.
FADING... HOPE FADING...
SO BRIGHT.
HELLO, FRIEND.
SO BRIGHT!
WAAAHHH!

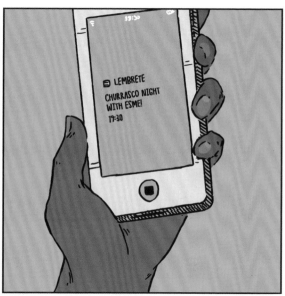

LEMBRETE
CHURRASCO NIGHT
WITH ESME!
19:30

Churras Gull

KEEP 'EM
COMING.

HOURS LATER.

IT'S
CLOSING
TIME...
SORRY.

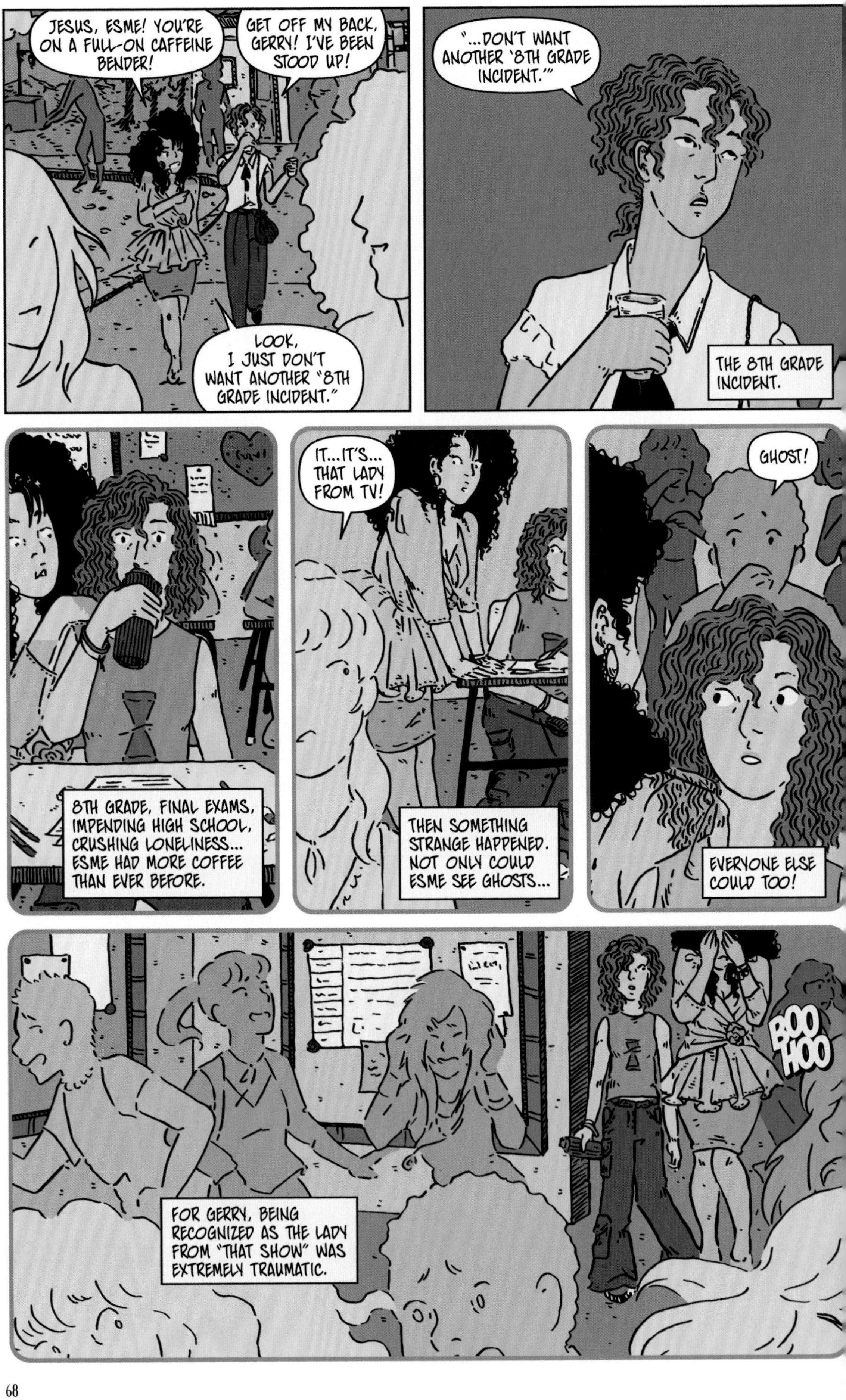

JESUS, ESME! YOU'RE ON A FULL-ON CAFFEINE BENDER!
GET OFF MY BACK, GERRY! I'VE BEEN STOOD UP!
LOOK, I JUST DON'T WANT ANOTHER "8TH GRADE INCIDENT."
"...DON'T WANT ANOTHER '8TH GRADE INCIDENT.'"
THE 8TH GRADE INCIDENT.
8TH GRADE, FINAL EXAMS, IMPENDING HIGH SCHOOL, CRUSHING LONELINESS... ESME HAD MORE COFFEE THAN EVER BEFORE.
IT...IT'S... THAT LADY FROM TV!
THEN SOMETHING STRANGE HAPPENED. NOT ONLY COULD ESME SEE GHOSTS...
GHOST!
EVERYONE ELSE COULD TOO!
BOO HOO
FOR GERRY, BEING RECOGNIZED AS THE LADY FROM "THAT SHOW" WAS EXTREMELY TRAUMATIC.

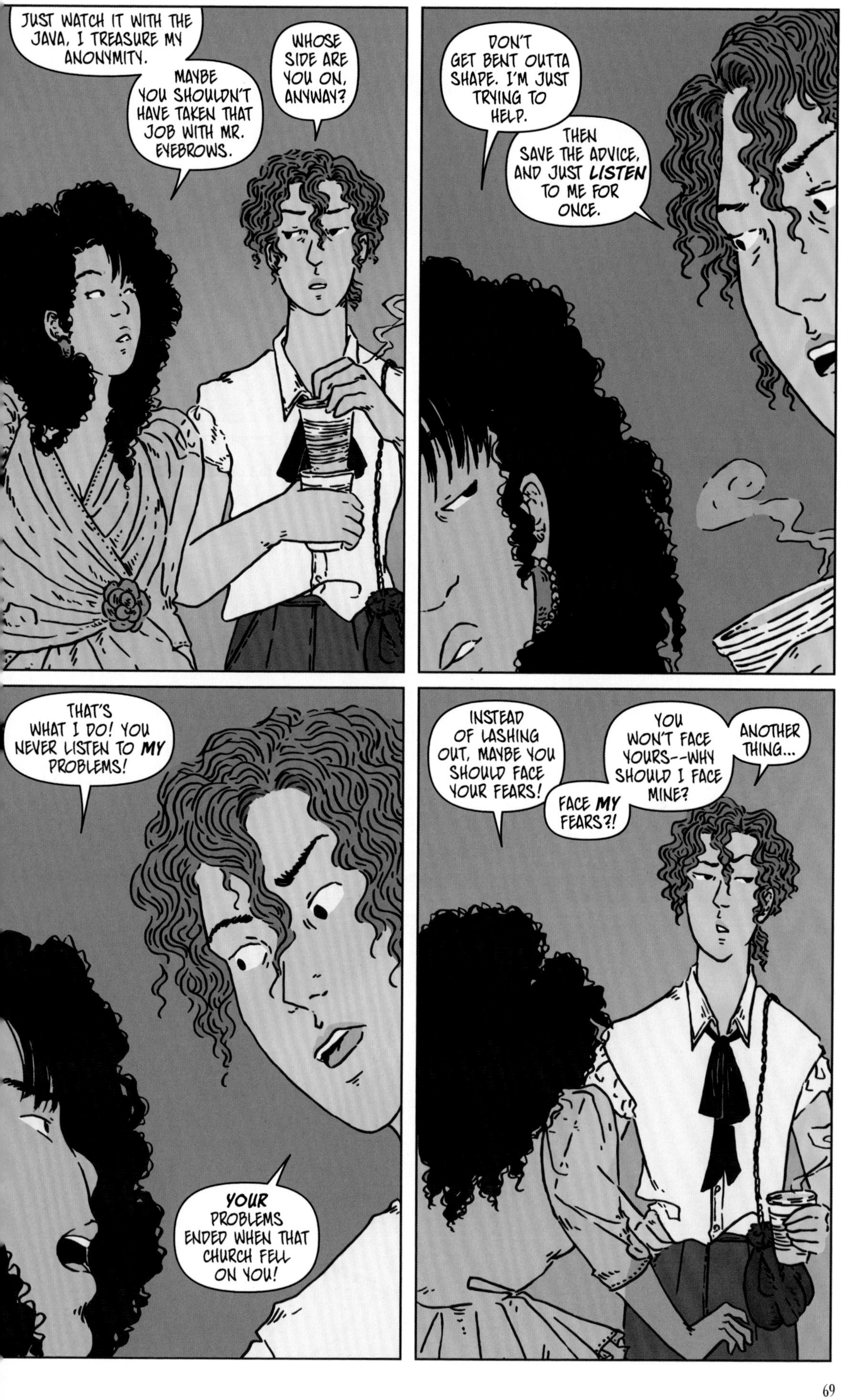
JUST WATCH IT WITH THE JAVA, I TREASURE MY ANONYMITY.
MAYBE YOU SHOULDN'T HAVE TAKEN THAT JOB WITH MR. EYEBROWS.
WHOSE SIDE ARE YOU ON, ANYWAY?
DON'T GET BENT OUTTA SHAPE. I'M JUST TRYING TO HELP.
THEN SAVE THE ADVICE, AND JUST **LISTEN** TO ME FOR ONCE.
THAT'S WHAT I DO! YOU NEVER LISTEN TO **MY** PROBLEMS!
YOUR PROBLEMS ENDED WHEN THAT CHURCH FELL ON YOU!
INSTEAD OF LASHING OUT, MAYBE YOU SHOULD FACE YOUR FEARS!
FACE **MY** FEARS?!
YOU WON'T FACE YOURS--WHY SHOULD I FACE MINE?
ANOTHER THING...

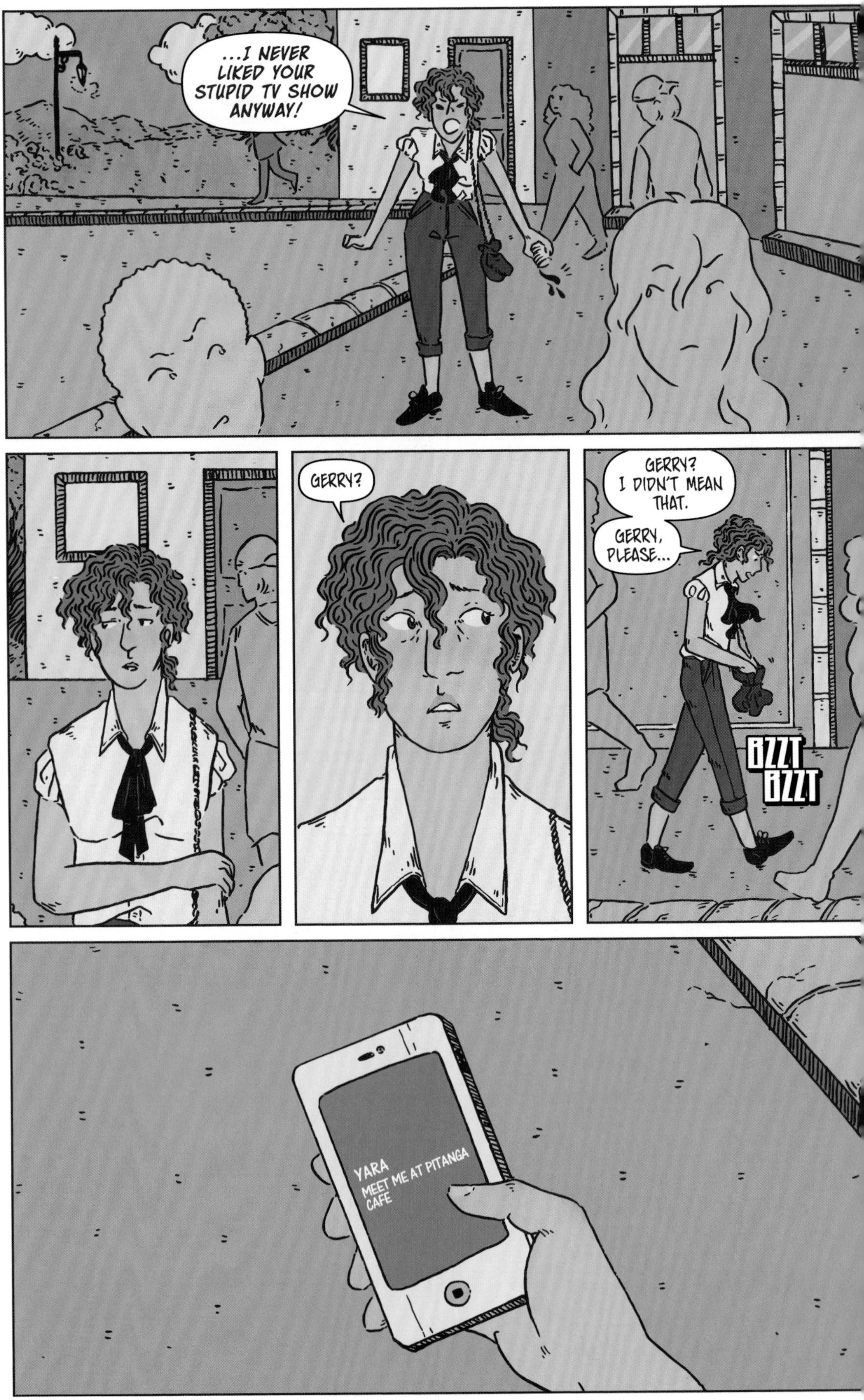
...I NEVER LIKED YOUR STUPID TV SHOW ANYWAY!
GERRY?
GERRY? I DIDN'T MEAN THAT.
GERRY, PLEASE...
BZZT BZZT
YARA
MEET ME AT PITANGA CAFE

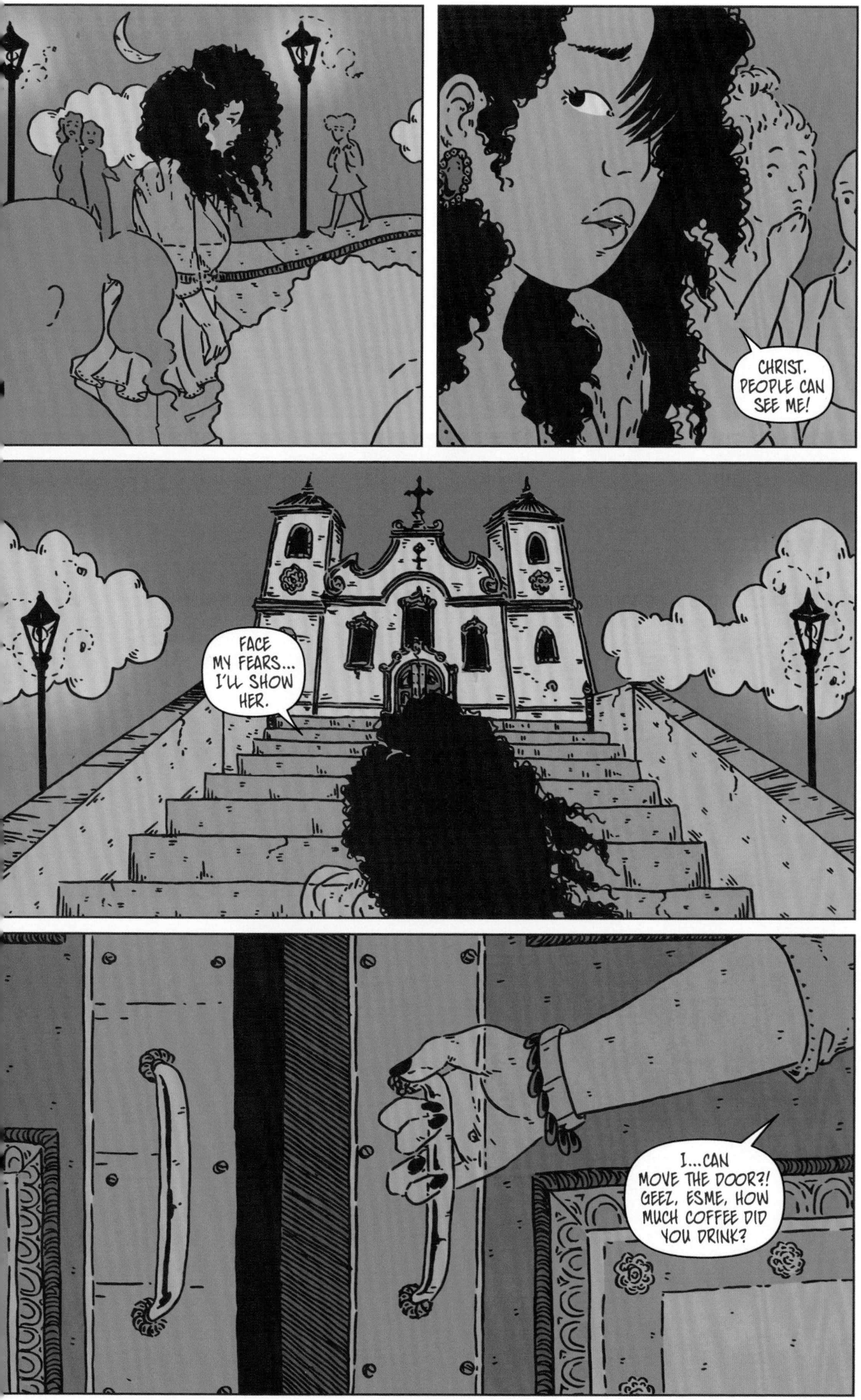
CHRIST. PEOPLE CAN SEE ME!
FACE MY FEARS... I'LL SHOW HER.
I...CAN MOVE THE DOOR?! GEEZ, ESME, HOW MUCH COFFEE DID YOU DRINK?

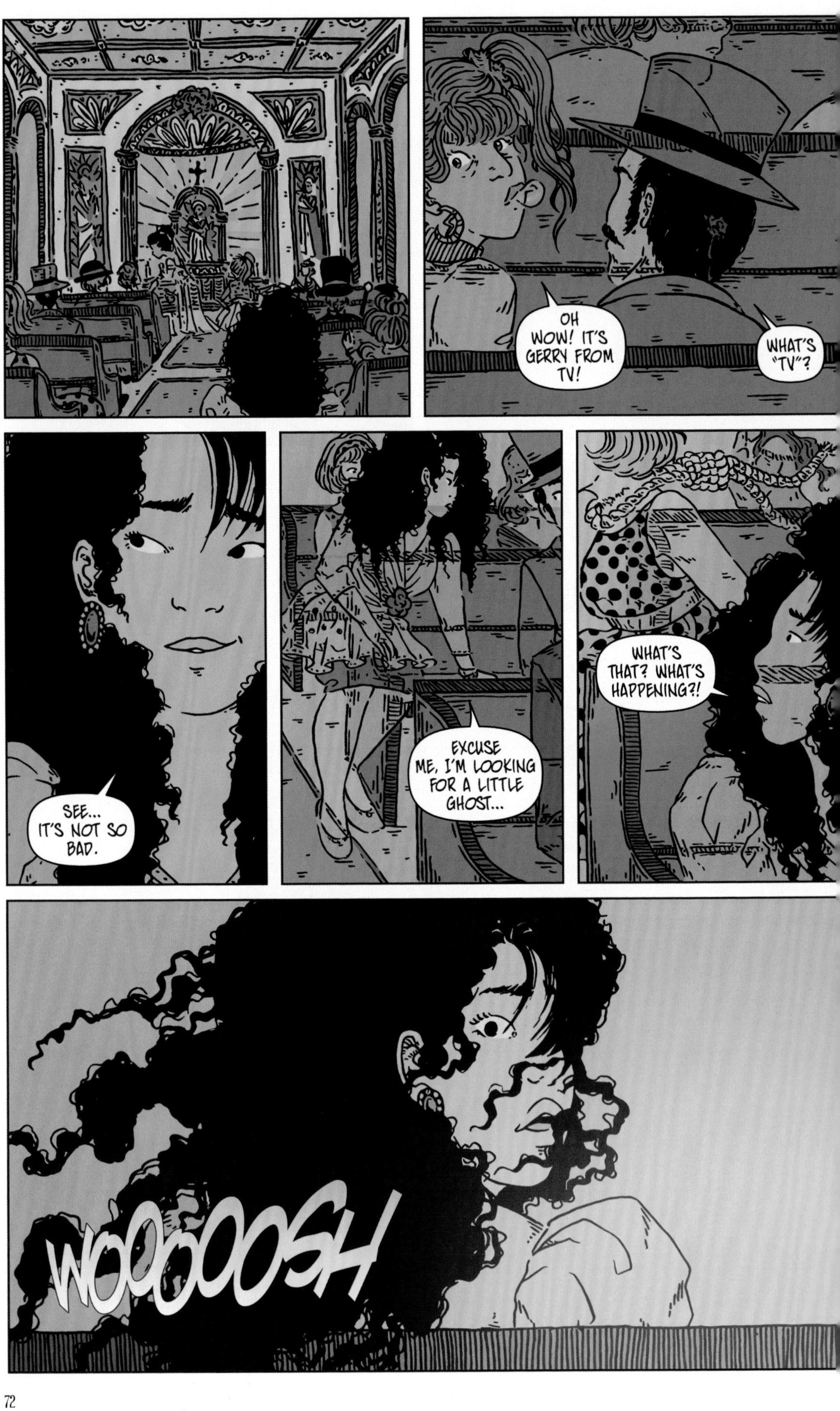
OH WOW! IT'S GERRY FROM TV!
WHAT'S "TV"?
SEE... IT'S NOT SO BAD.
EXCUSE ME, I'M LOOKING FOR A LITTLE GHOST...
WHAT'S THAT? WHAT'S HAPPENING?!
WOOOOOSH

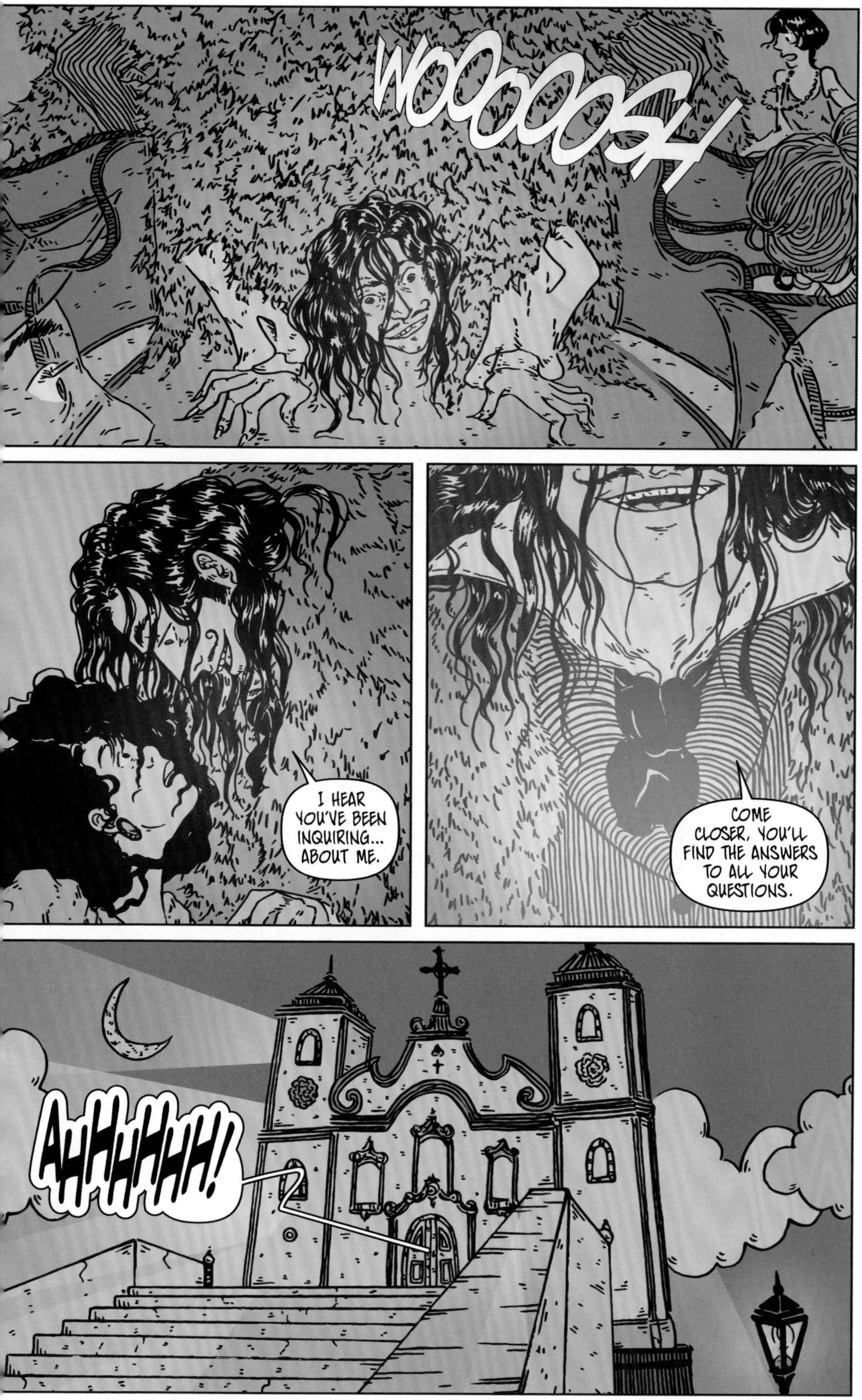
WOOOOOSH
I HEAR YOU'VE BEEN INQUIRING... ABOUT ME.
COME CLOSER, YOU'LL FIND THE ANSWERS TO ALL YOUR QUESTIONS.
AHHHHHH!

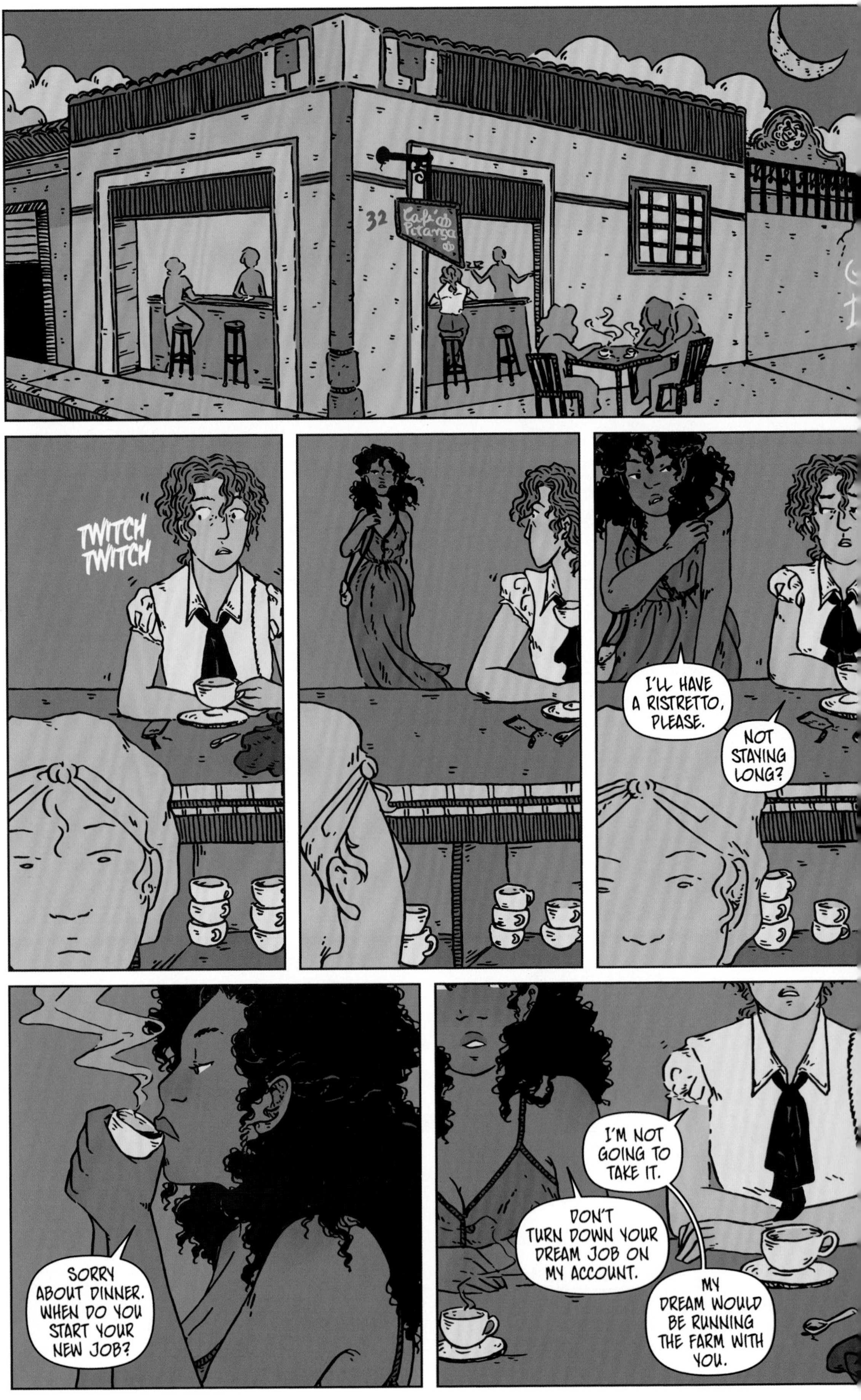
32
Café
Pitanga
TWITCH
TWITCH
I'LL HAVE A RISTRETTO, PLEASE.
NOT STAYING LONG?
SORRY ABOUT DINNER. WHEN DO YOU START YOUR NEW JOB?
I'M NOT GOING TO TAKE IT.
DON'T TURN DOWN YOUR DREAM JOB ON MY ACCOUNT.
MY DREAM WOULD BE RUNNING THE FARM WITH YOU.

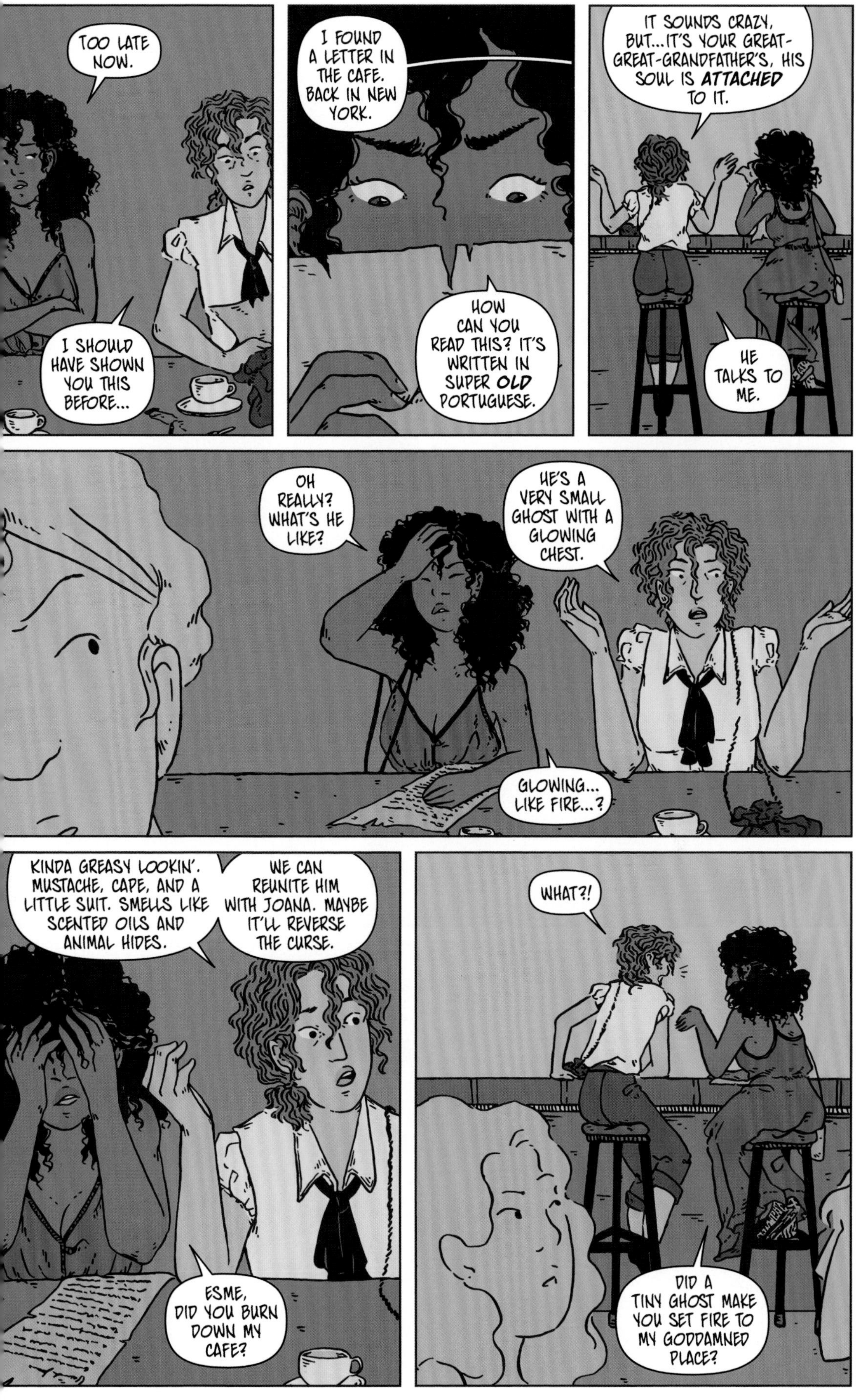
TOO LATE NOW.
I SHOULD HAVE SHOWN YOU THIS BEFORE...
I FOUND A LETTER IN THE CAFE. BACK IN NEW YORK.
HOW CAN YOU READ THIS? IT'S WRITTEN IN SUPER OLD PORTUGUESE.
IT SOUNDS CRAZY, BUT...IT'S YOUR GREAT-GREAT-GRANDFATHER'S, HIS SOUL IS ATTACHED TO IT.
HE TALKS TO ME.
OH REALLY? WHAT'S HE LIKE?
HE'S A VERY SMALL GHOST WITH A GLOWING CHEST.
GLOWING... LIKE FIRE...?
KINDA GREASY LOOKIN'. MUSTACHE, CAPE, AND A LITTLE SUIT. SMELLS LIKE SCENTED OILS AND ANIMAL HIDES.
WE CAN REUNITE HIM WITH JOANA. MAYBE IT'LL REVERSE THE CURSE.
ESME, DID YOU BURN DOWN MY CAFE?
WHAT?!
DID A TINY GHOST MAKE YOU SET FIRE TO MY GODDAMNED PLACE?

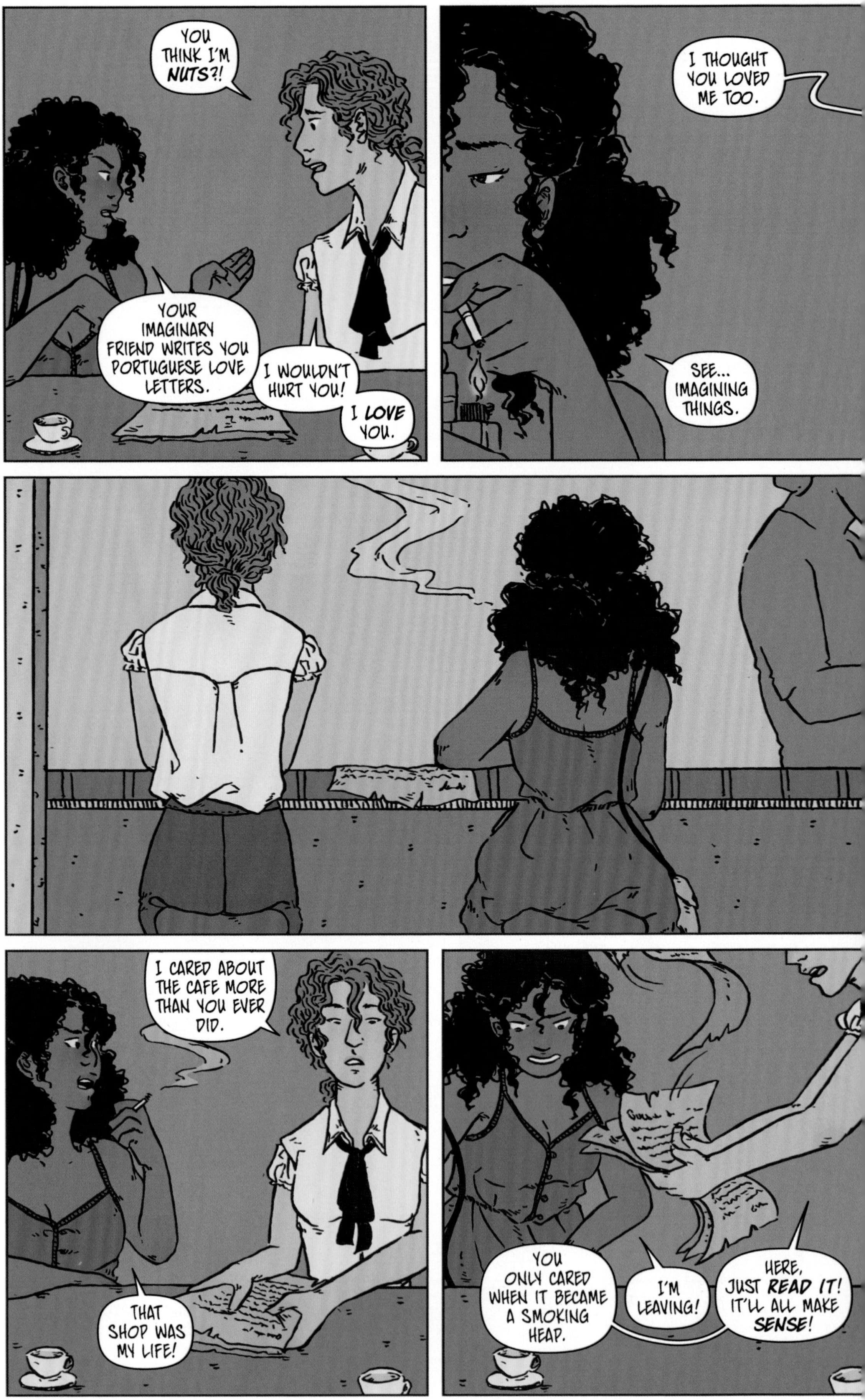

YOU THINK I'M NUTS?!
YOUR IMAGINARY FRIEND WRITES YOU PORTUGUESE LOVE LETTERS.
I WOULDN'T HURT YOU!
I LOVE YOU.
I THOUGHT YOU LOVED ME TOO.
SEE... IMAGINING THINGS.
I CARED ABOUT THE CAFE MORE THAN YOU EVER DID.
THAT SHOP WAS MY LIFE!
YOU ONLY CARED WHEN IT BECAME A SMOKING HEAP.
I'M LEAVING!
HERE, JUST READ IT! IT'LL ALL MAKE SENSE!

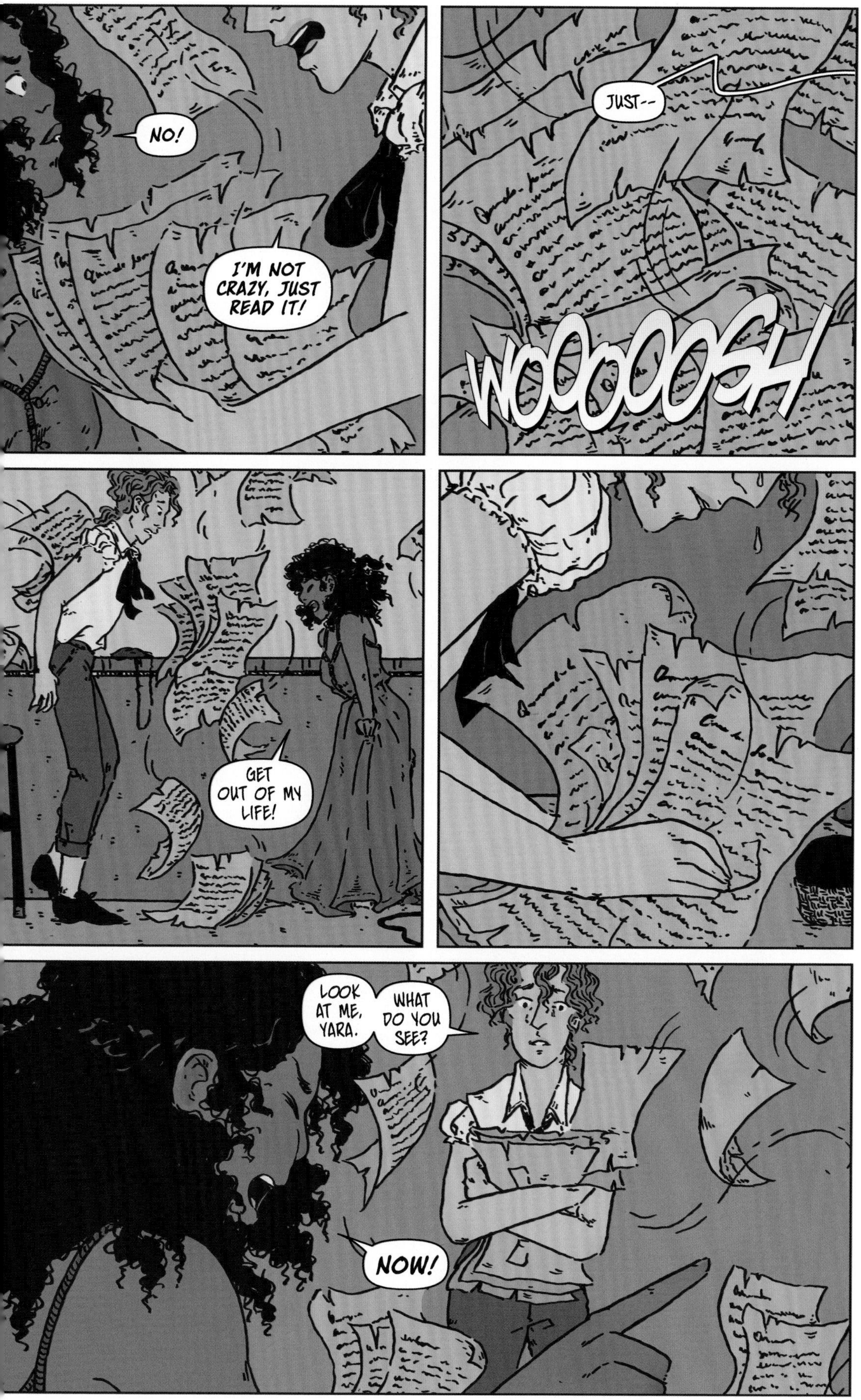
NO!
I'M NOT CRAZY, JUST READ IT!
JUST--
WOOOOOSH
GET OUT OF MY LIFE!
LOOK AT ME, YARA.
WHAT DO YOU SEE?
NOW!

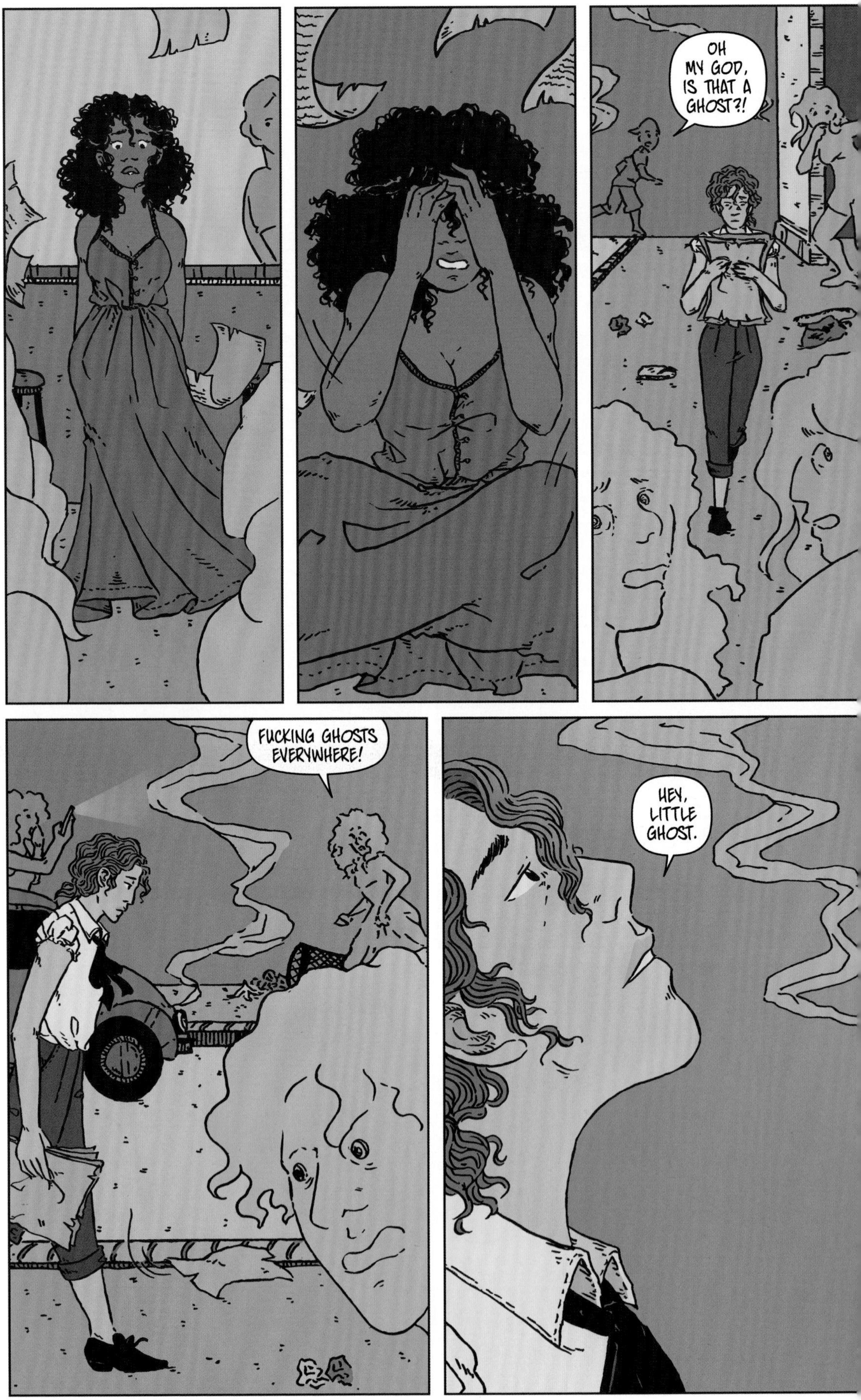
OH MY GOD, IS THAT A GHOST?!
FUCKING GHOSTS EVERYWHERE!
HEY, LITTLE GHOST.

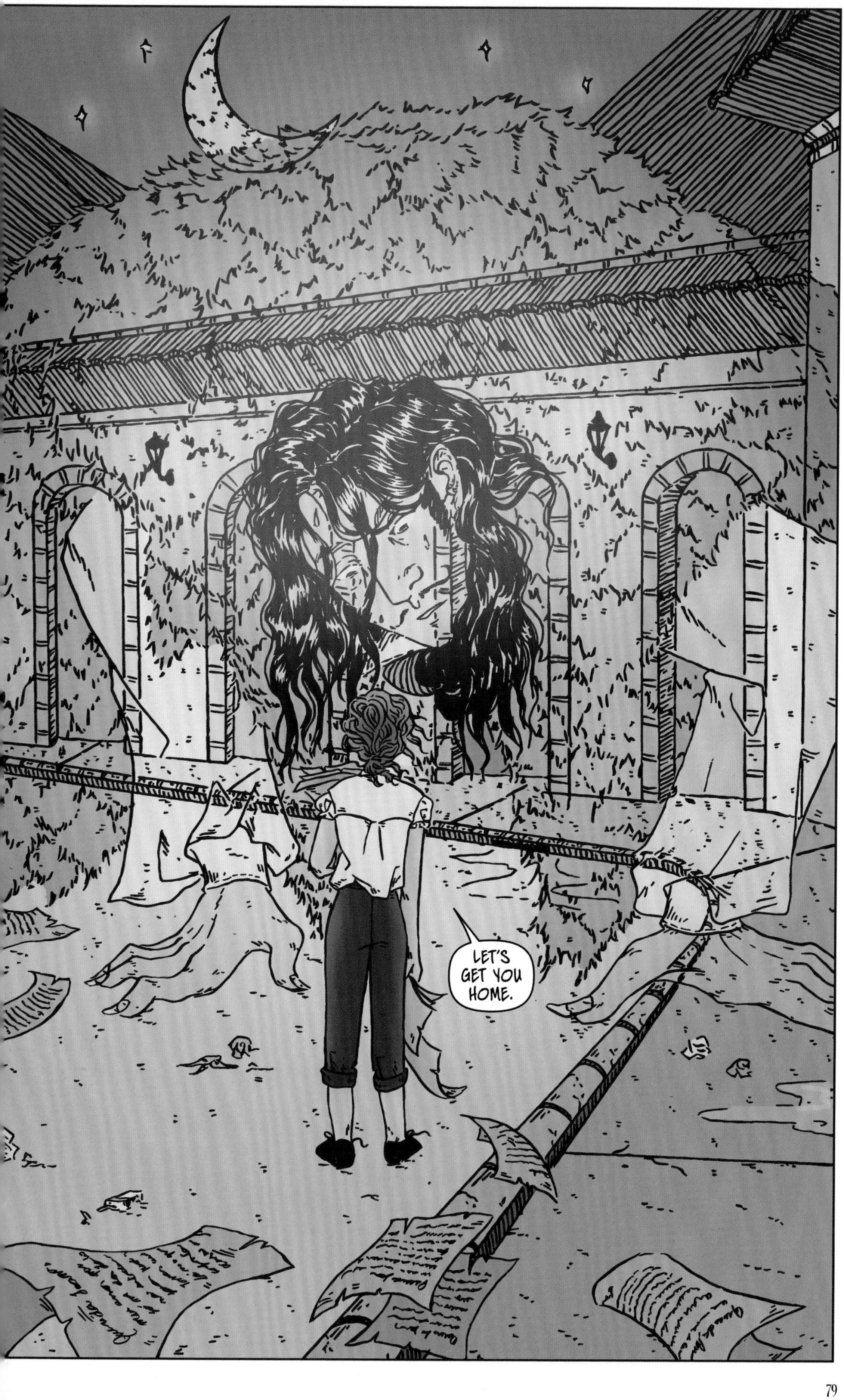
LET'S GET YOU HOME.

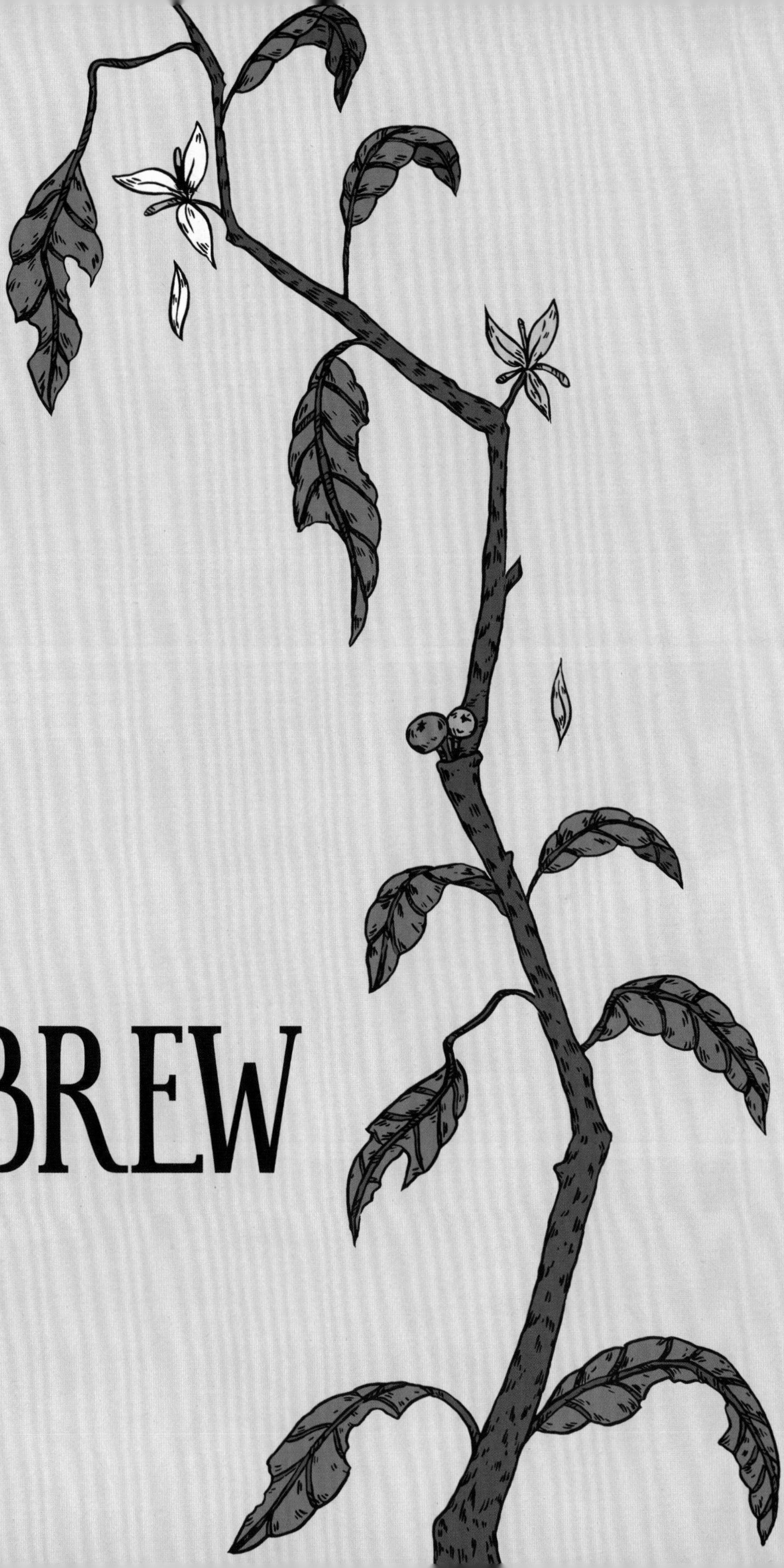

BREW

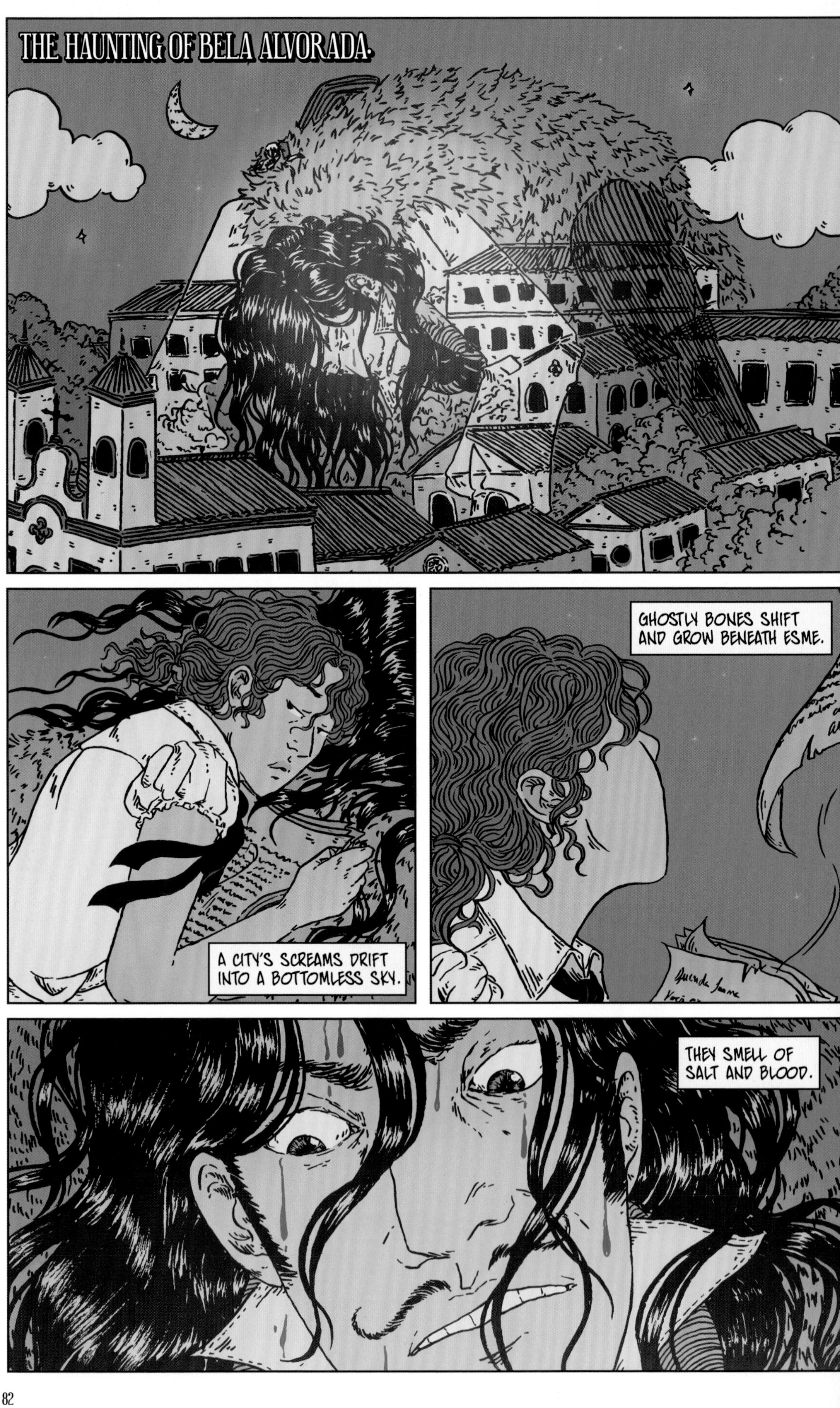
THE HAUNTING OF BELA ALVORADA.
A CITY'S SCREAMS DRIFT INTO A BOTTOMLESS SKY.
GHOSTLY BONES SHIFT AND GROW BENEATH ESME.
THEY SMELL OF SALT AND BLOOD.

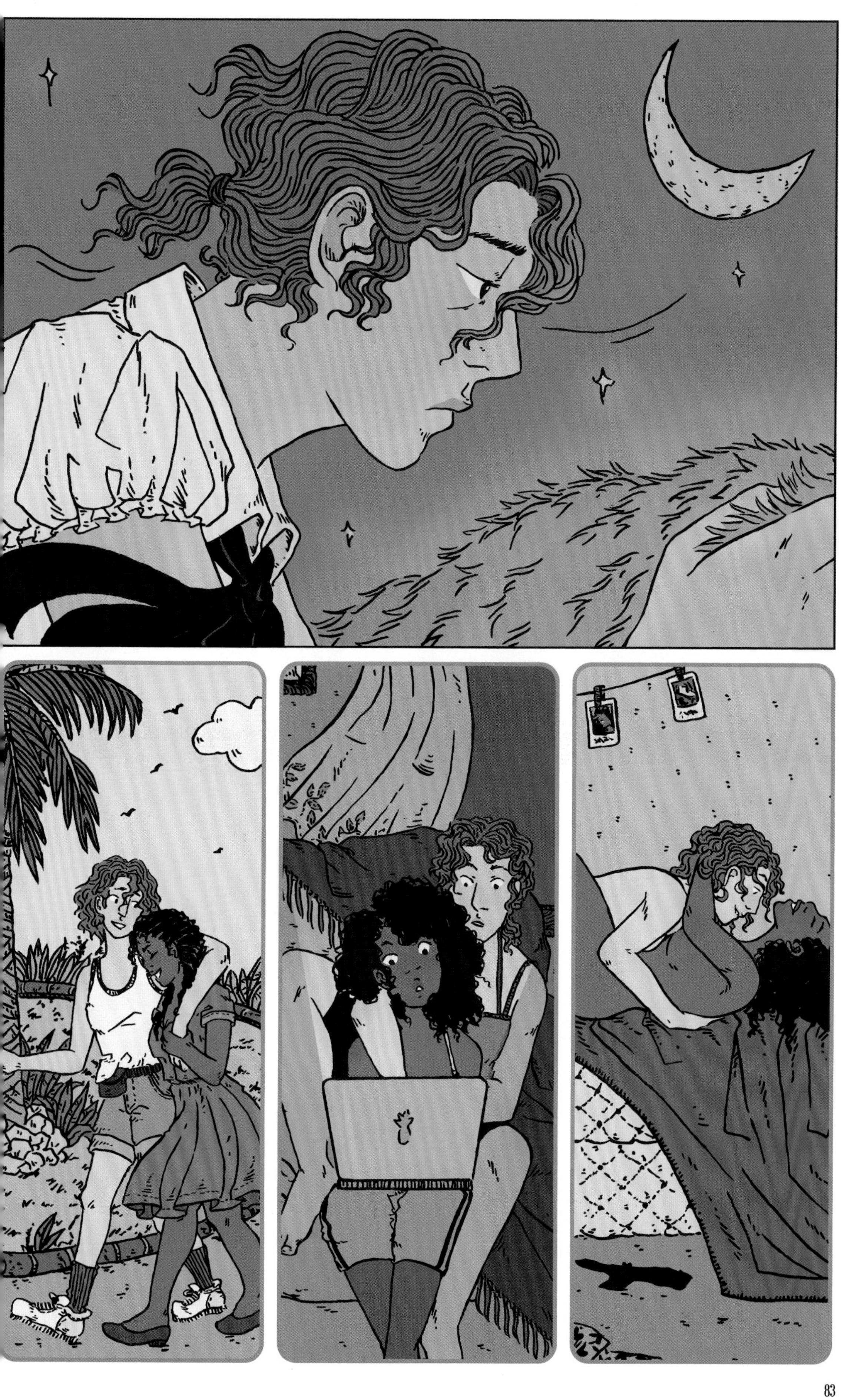

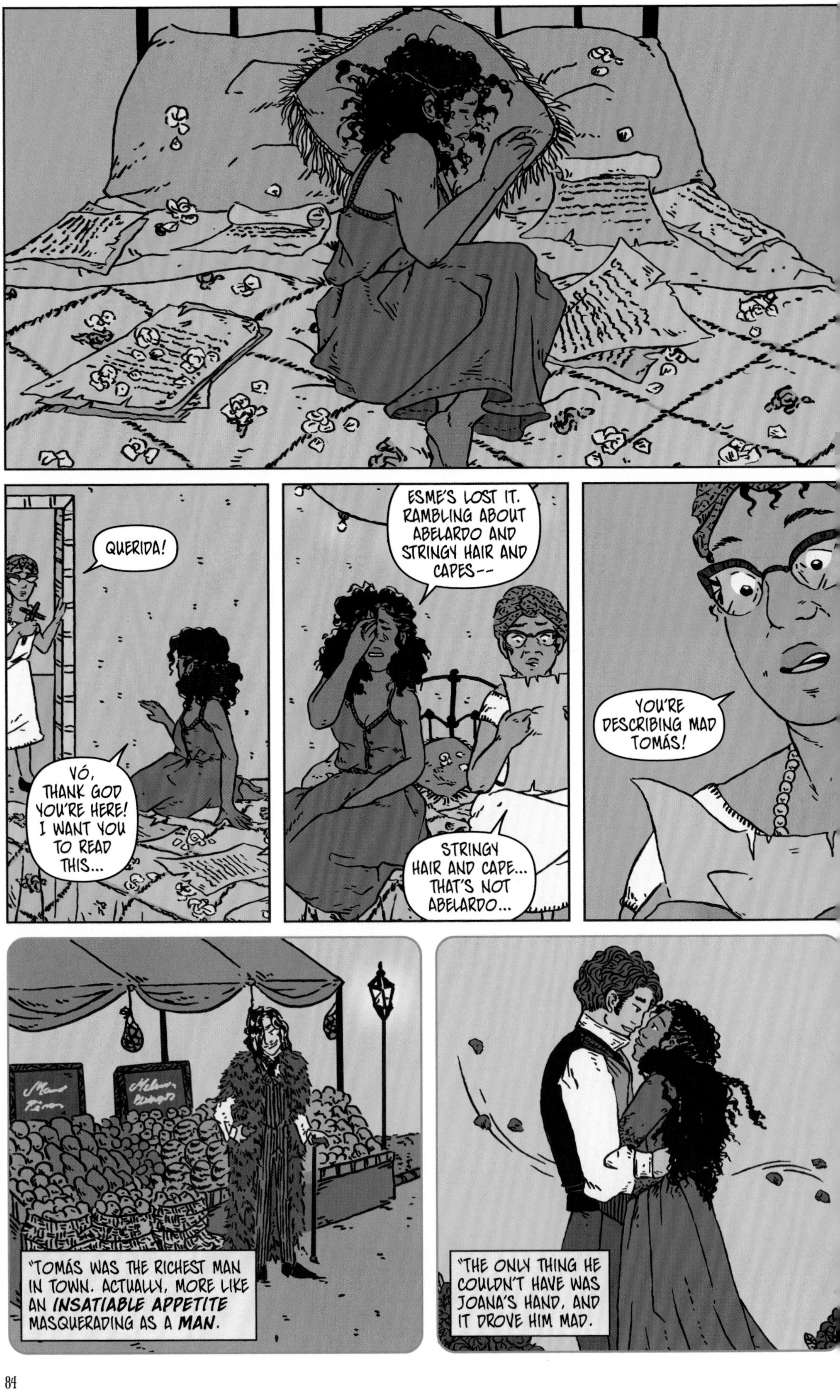

QUERIDA!
VÓ, THANK GOD YOU'RE HERE! I WANT YOU TO READ THIS...
ESME'S LOST IT. RAMBLING ABOUT ABELARDO AND STRINGY HAIR AND CAPES--
STRINGY HAIR AND CAPE... THAT'S NOT ABELARDO...
YOU'RE DESCRIBING MAD TOMÁS!
"TOMÁS WAS THE RICHEST MAN IN TOWN. ACTUALLY, MORE LIKE AN *INSATIABLE APPETITE* MASQUERADING AS A *MAN*.
"THE ONLY THING HE COULDN'T HAVE WAS JOANA'S HAND, AND IT DROVE HIM MAD.

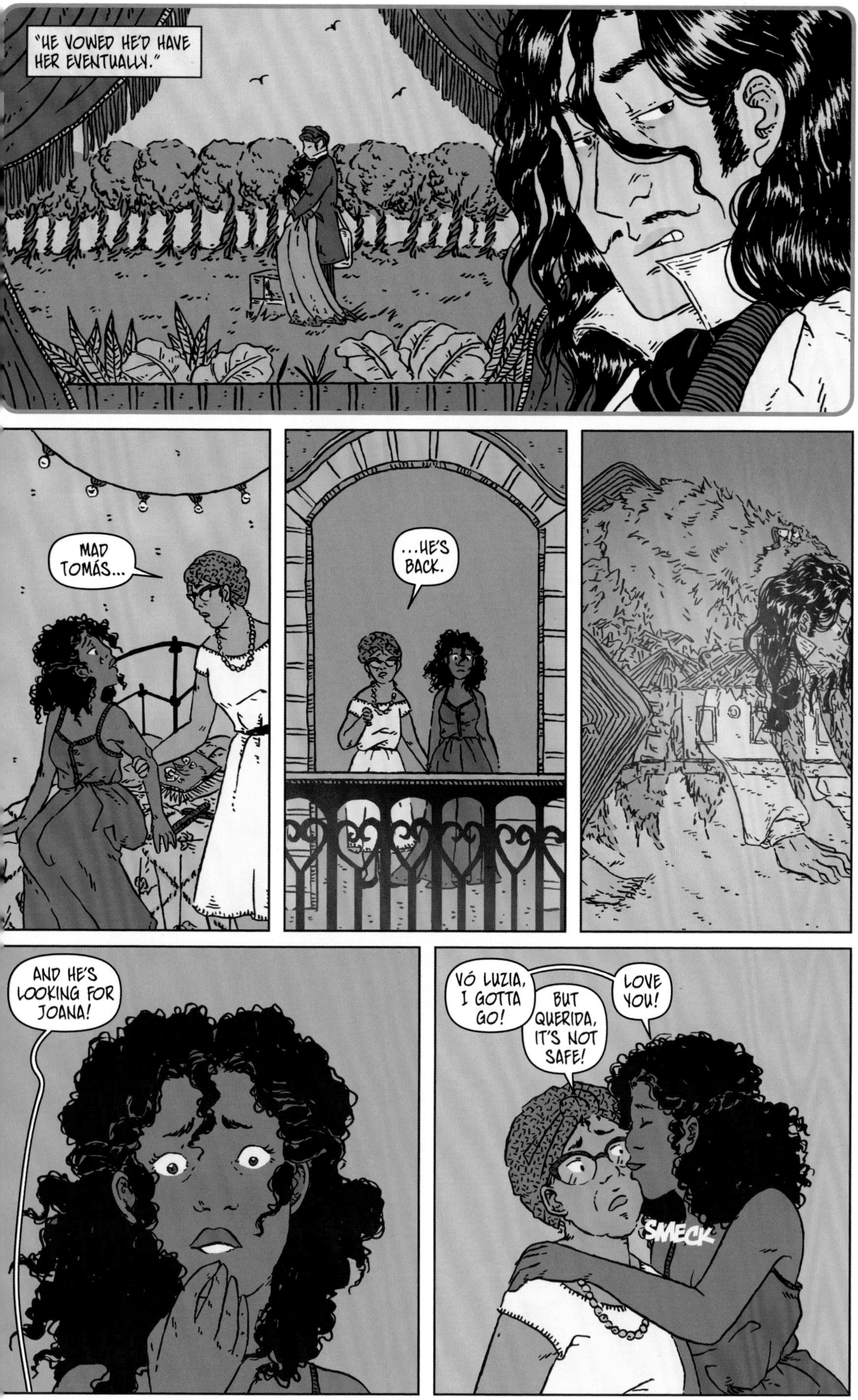
"HE VOWED HE'D HAVE HER EVENTUALLY."
MAD TOMÁS...
...HE'S BACK.
AND HE'S LOOKING FOR JOANA!
VÓ LUZIA, I GOTTA GO!
BUT QUERIDA, IT'S NOT SAFE!
LOVE YOU!
SMECK

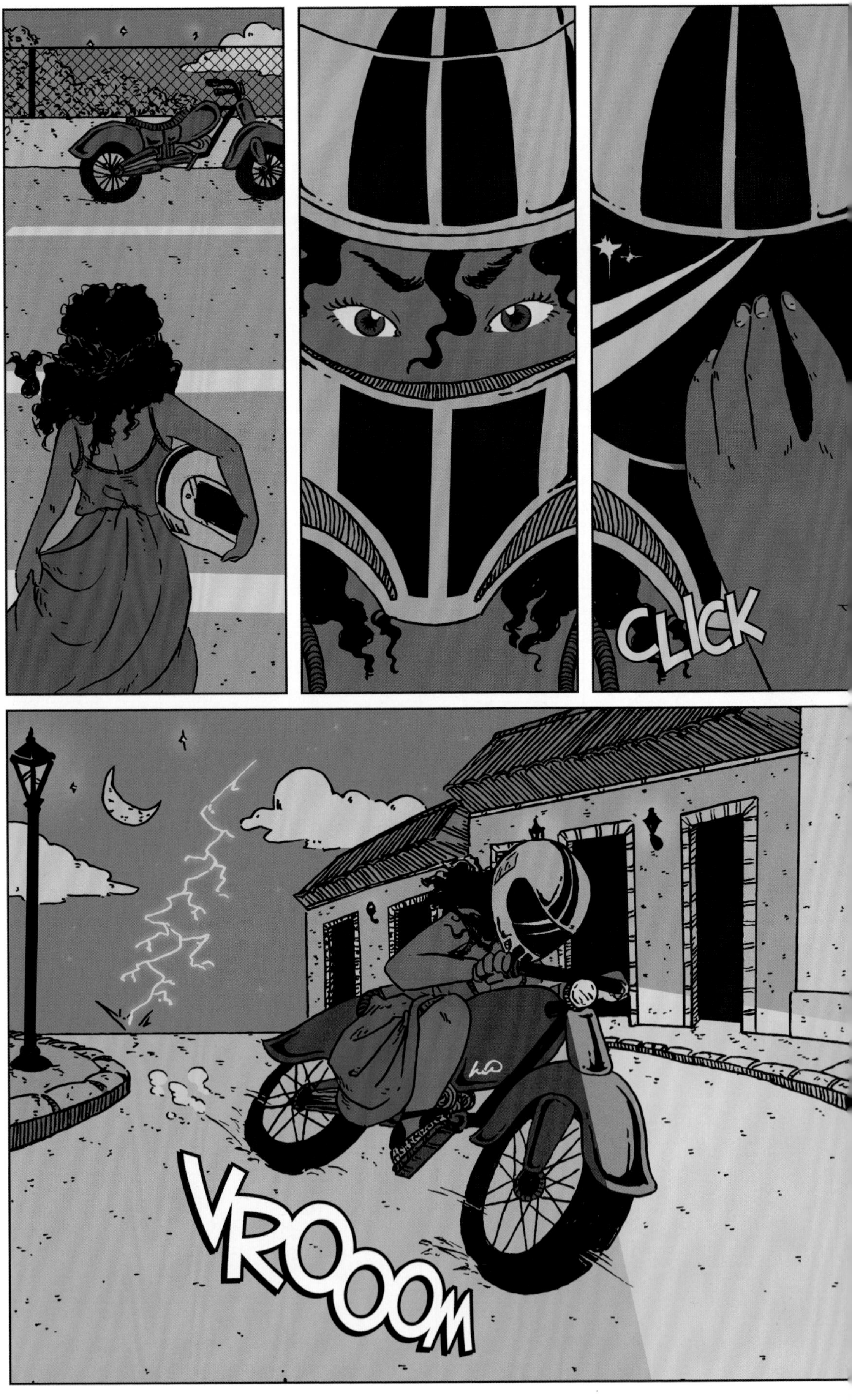
CLICK
VROOOM

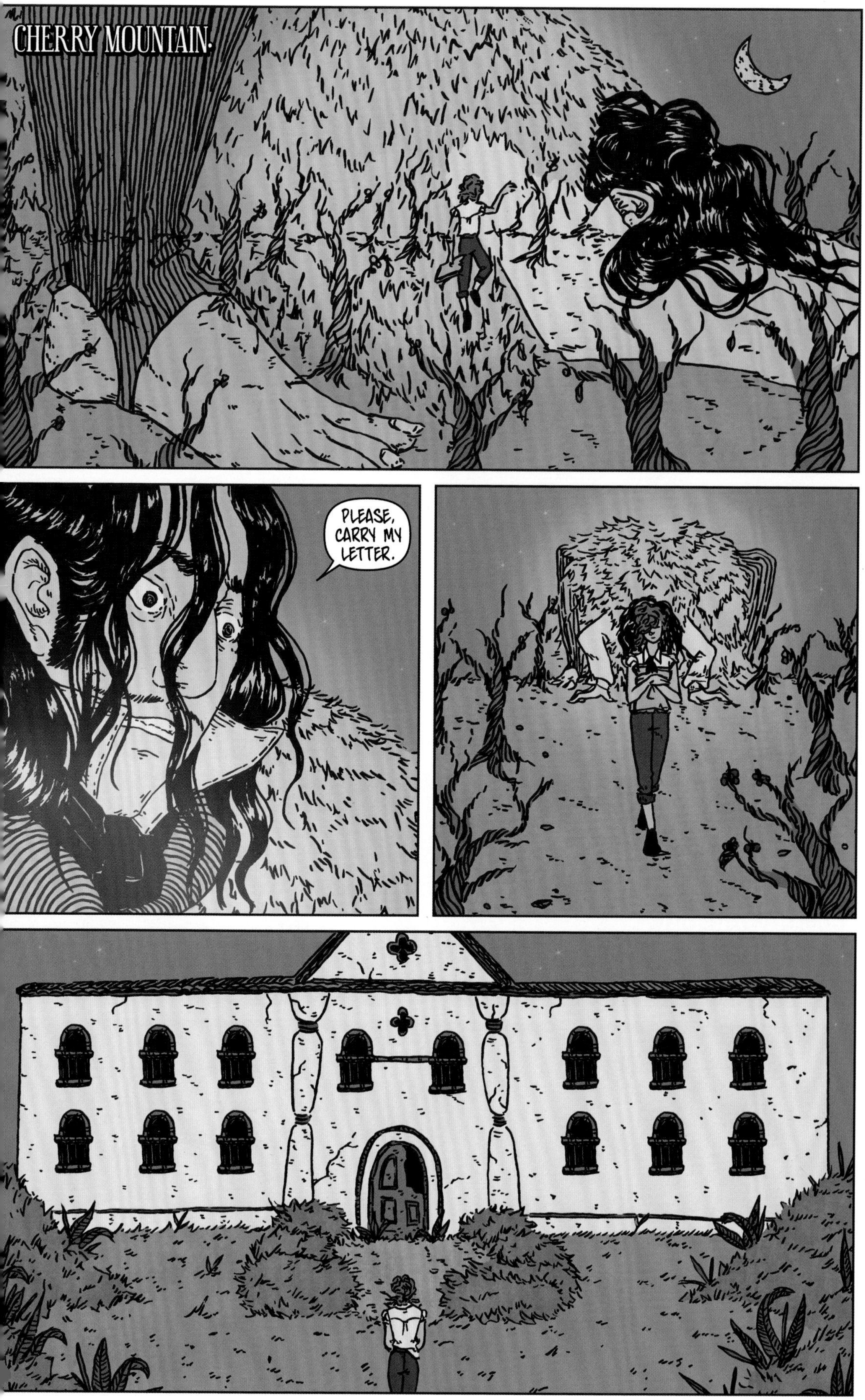
CHERRY MOUNTAIN.
PLEASE, CARRY MY LETTER.

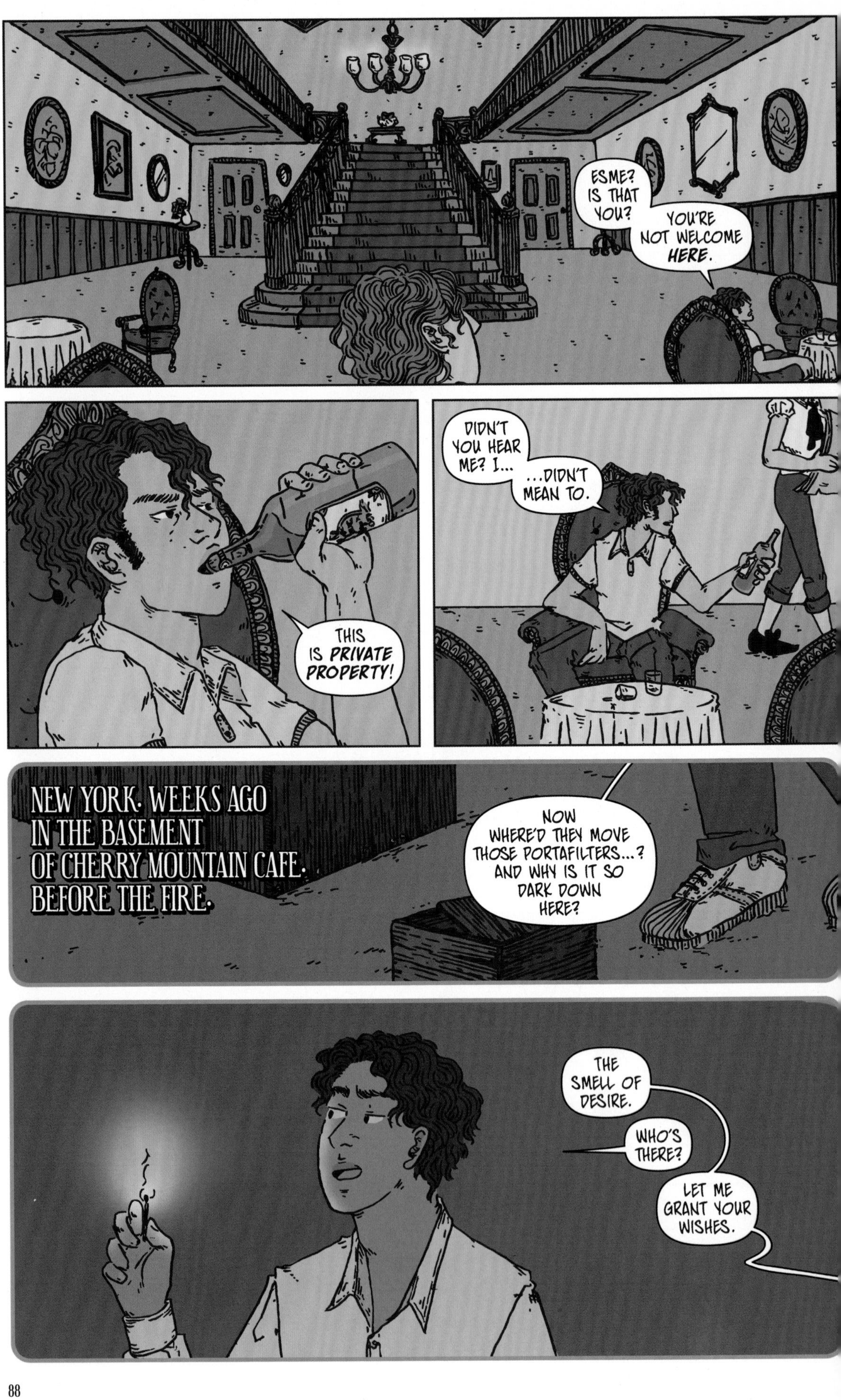
ESME? IS THAT YOU?
YOU'RE NOT WELCOME HERE.
THIS IS PRIVATE PROPERTY!
DIDN'T YOU HEAR ME? I...
...DIDN'T MEAN TO.
NEW YORK. WEEKS AGO IN THE BASEMENT OF CHERRY MOUNTAIN CAFE. BEFORE THE FIRE.
NOW WHERE'D THEY MOVE THOSE PORTAFILTERS...? AND WHY IS IT SO DARK DOWN HERE?
THE SMELL OF DESIRE.
WHO'S THERE?
LET ME GRANT YOUR WISHES.

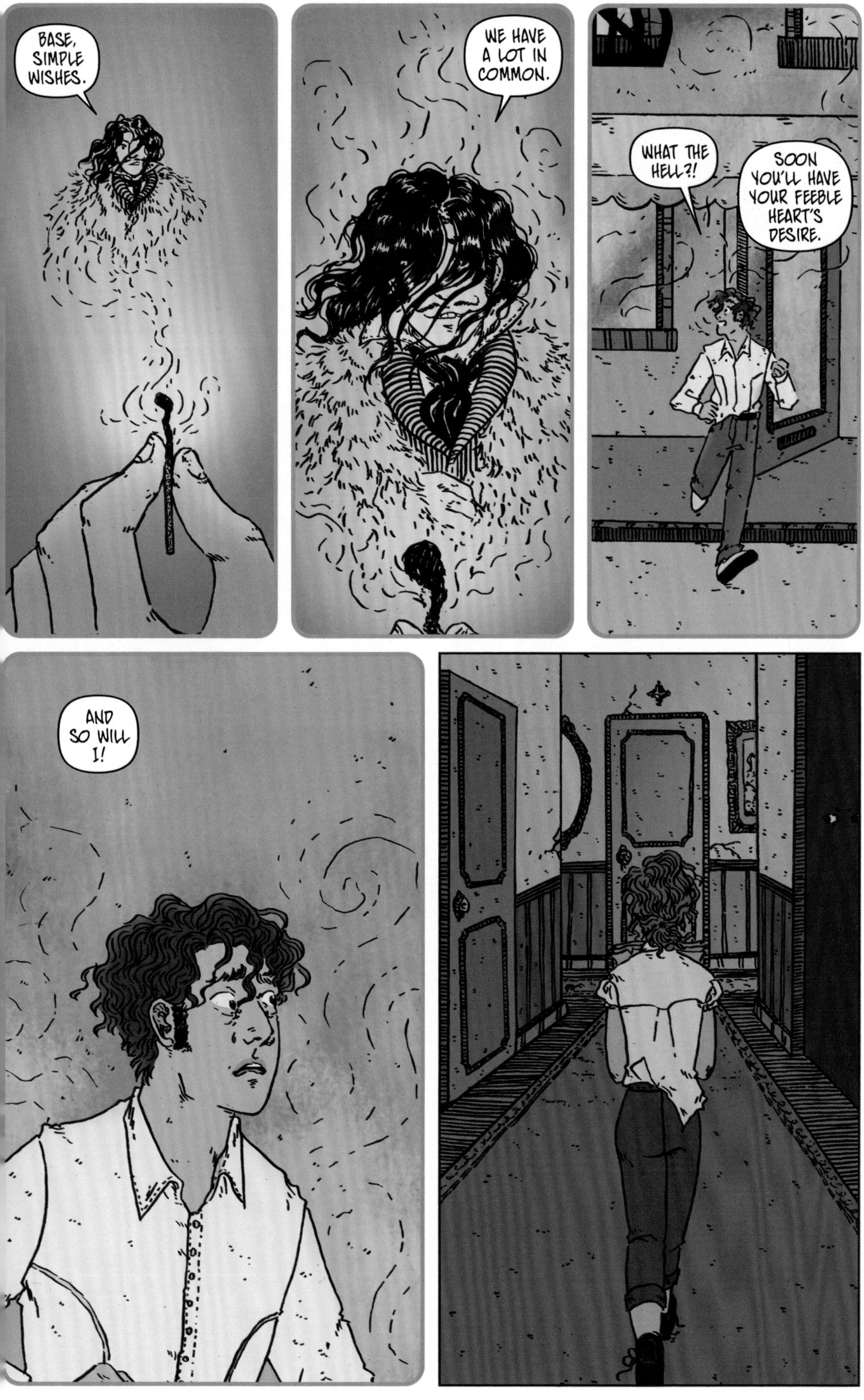
BASE, SIMPLE WISHES.
WE HAVE A LOT IN COMMON.
WHAT THE HELL?!
SOON YOU'LL HAVE YOUR FEEBLE HEART'S DESIRE.
AND SO WILL I!

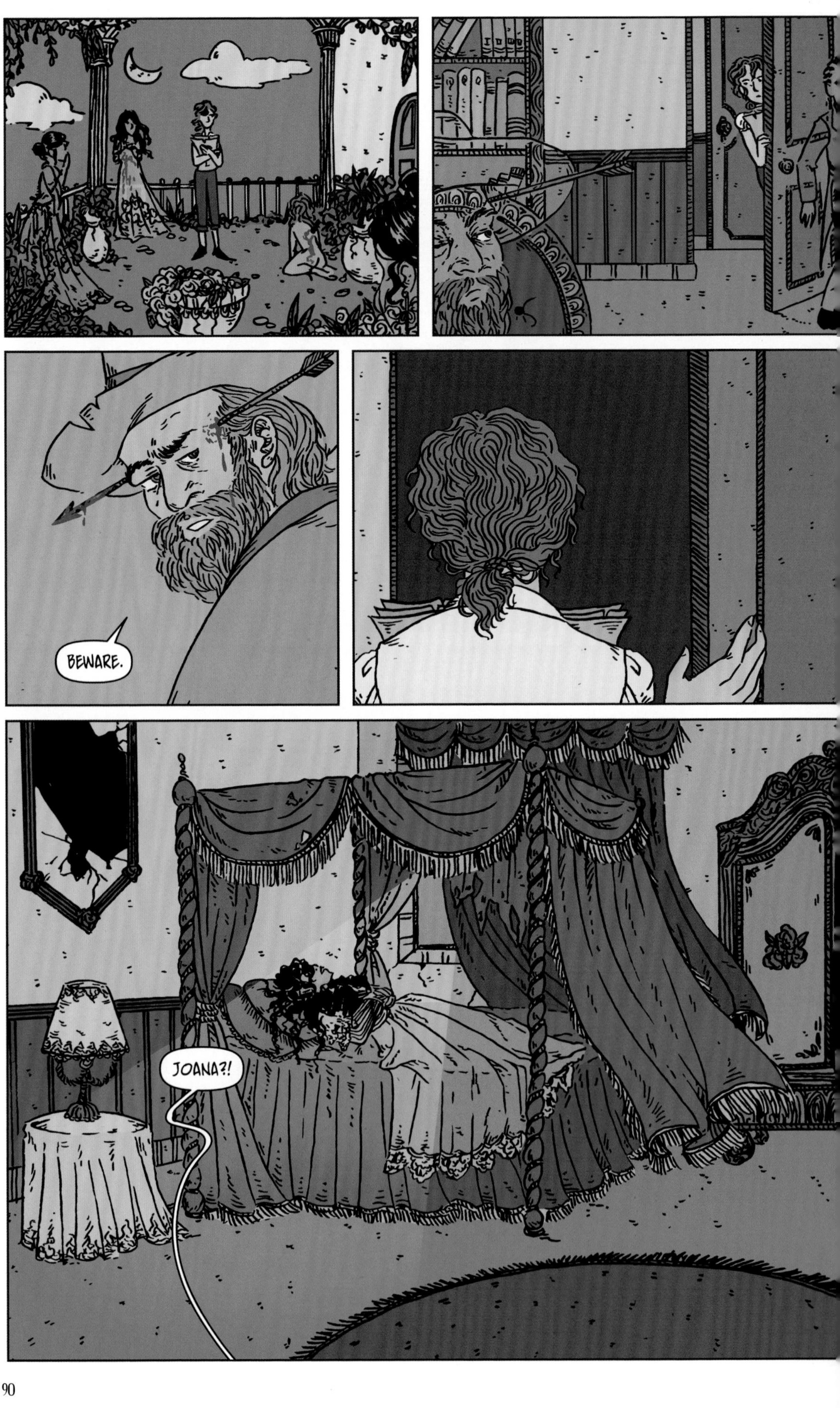
BEWARE.
JOANA?!

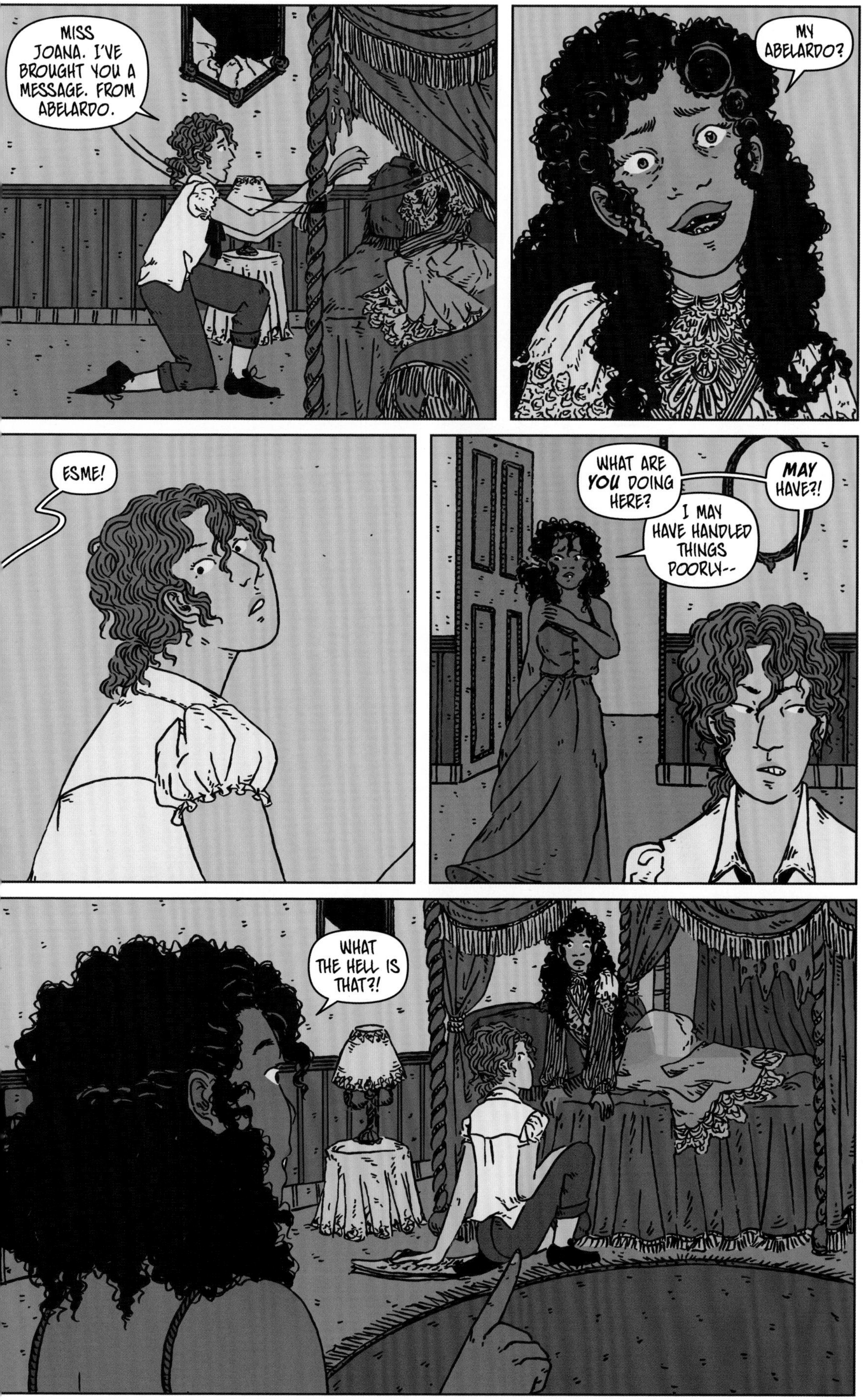
MISS JOANA. I'VE BROUGHT YOU A MESSAGE. FROM ABELARDO.
MY ABELARDO?
ESME!
WHAT ARE YOU DOING HERE?
I MAY HAVE HANDLED THINGS POORLY--
MAY HAVE?!
WHAT THE HELL IS THAT?!

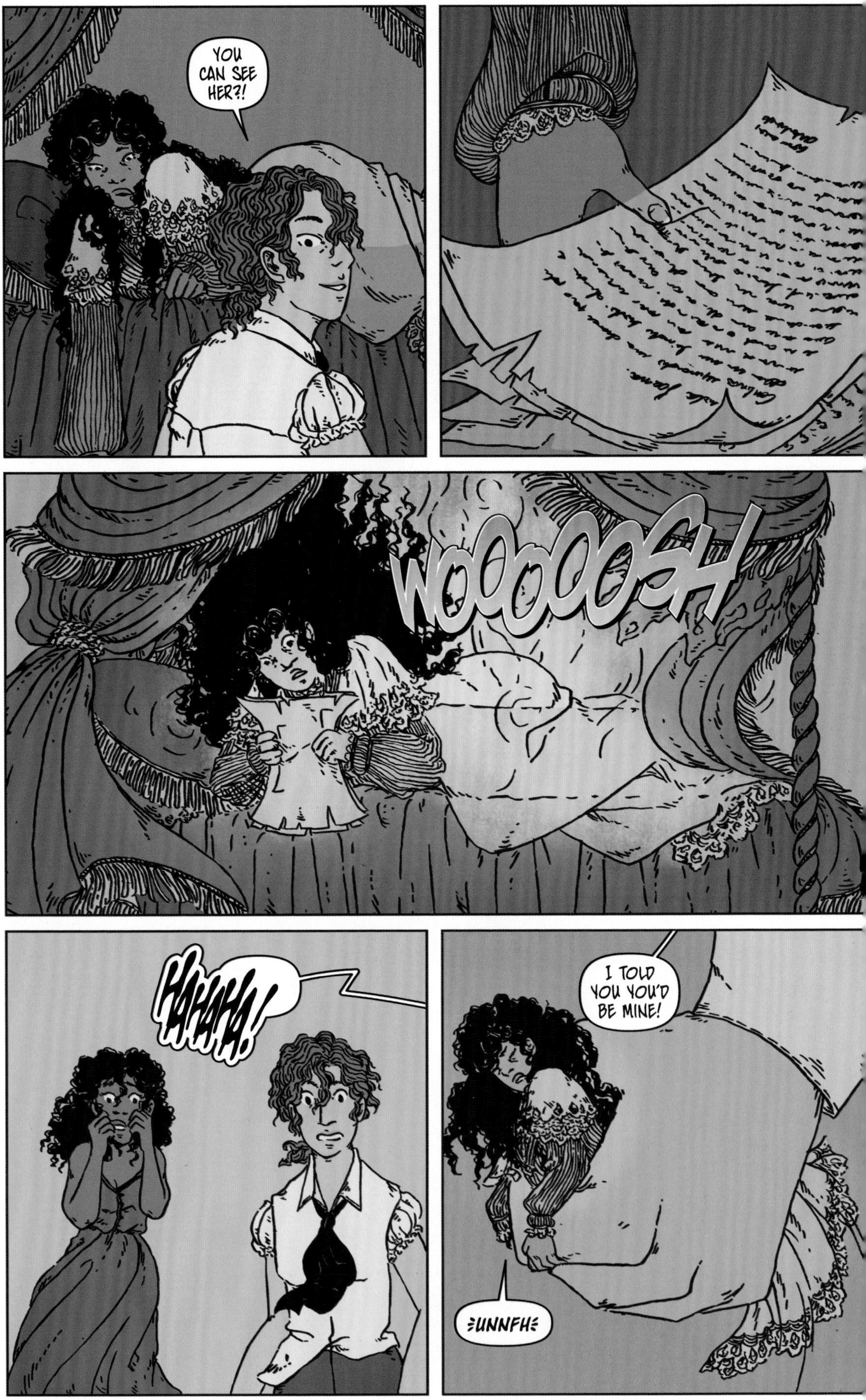

YOU CAN SEE HER?!
WOOOOOSH
HAHAHA!
I TOLD YOU YOU'D BE MINE!
UNNFH

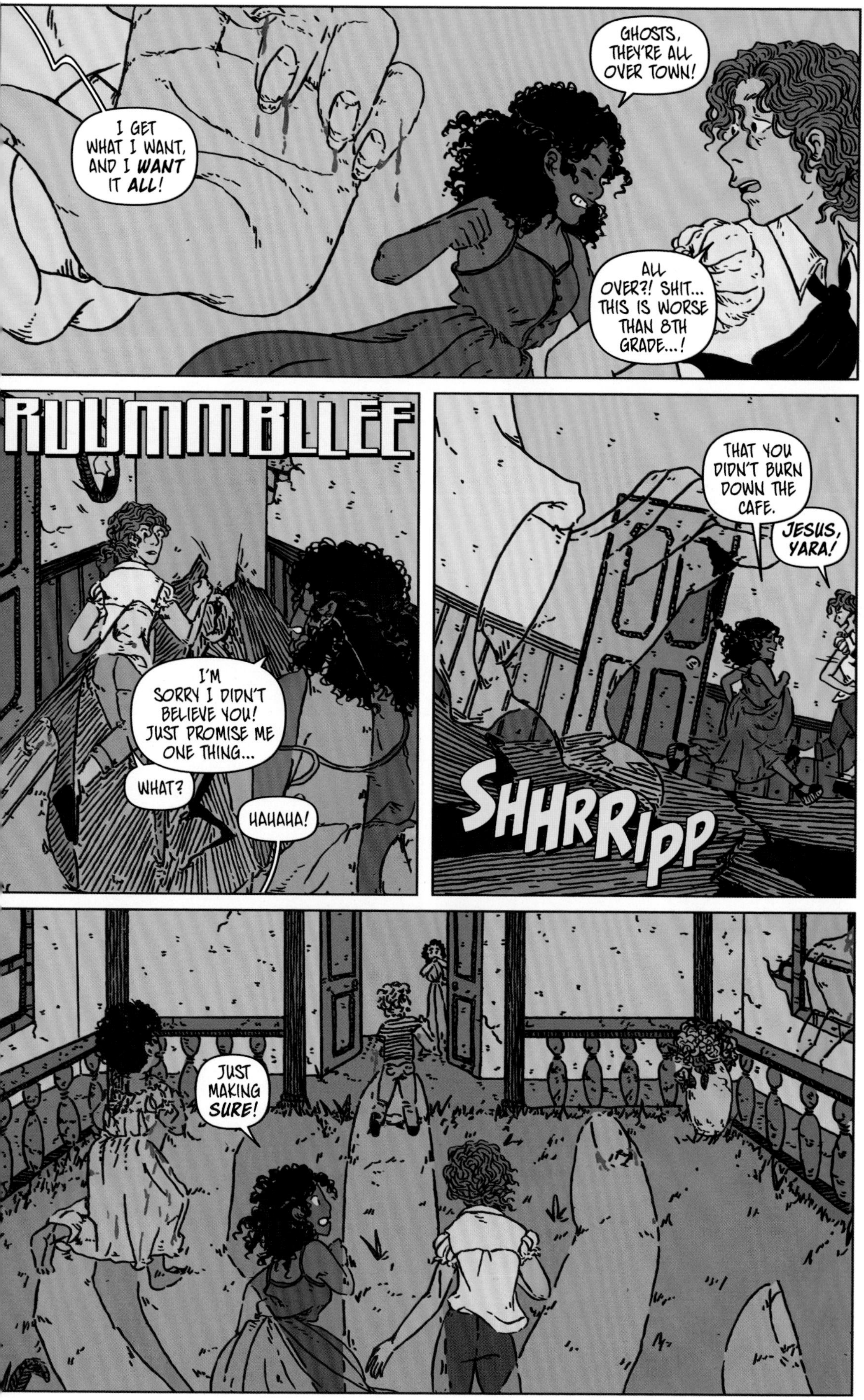
I GET WHAT I WANT, AND I WANT IT ALL!
GHOSTS, THEY'RE ALL OVER TOWN!
ALL OVER?! SHIT... THIS IS WORSE THAN 8TH GRADE...!
RUUMMBLLEE
I'M SORRY I DIDN'T BELIEVE YOU! JUST PROMISE ME ONE THING...
WHAT?
HAHAHA!
THAT YOU DIDN'T BURN DOWN THE CAFE.
JESUS, YARA!
SHHRRIPP
JUST MAKING SURE!

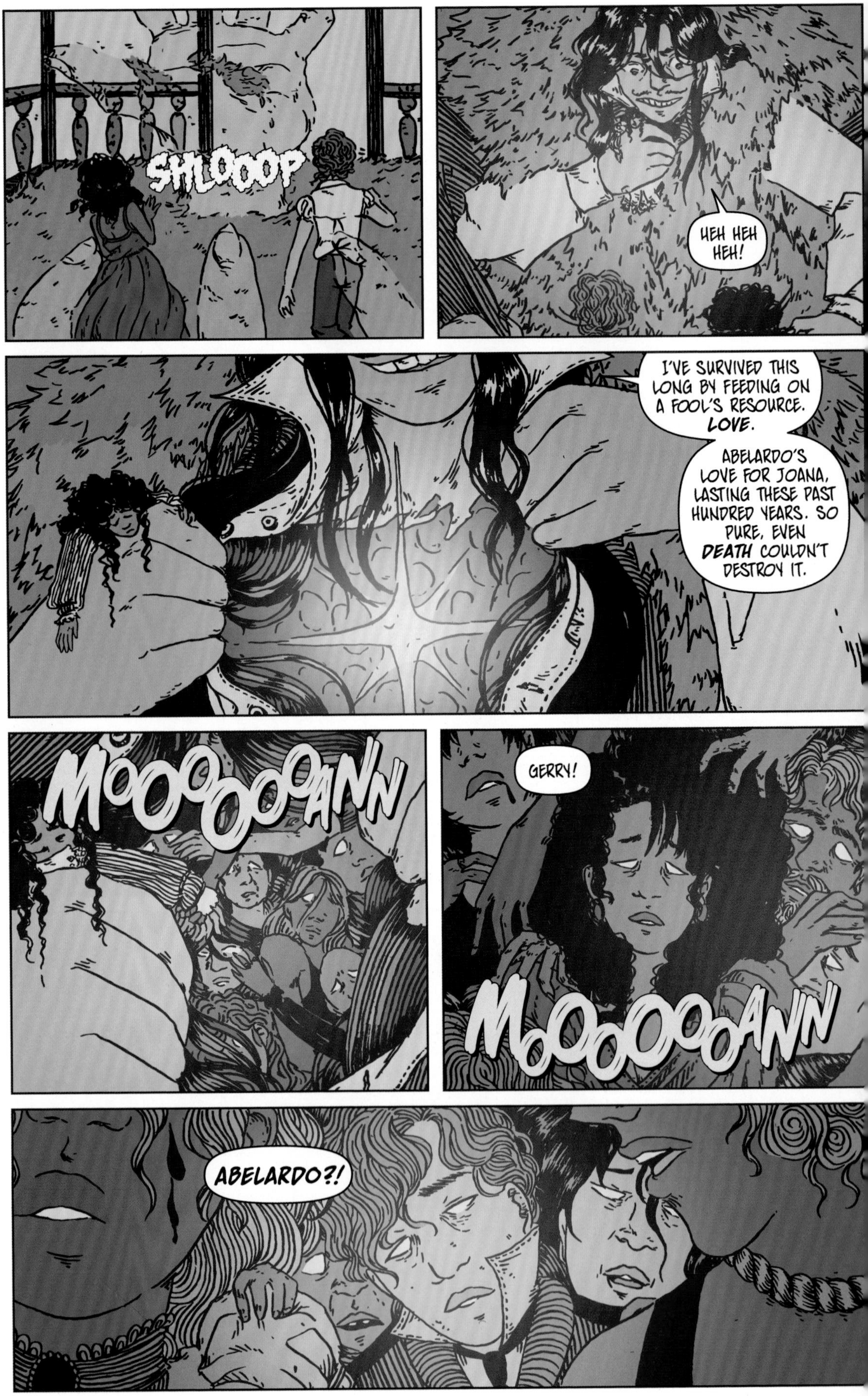
SHLOOOP
HEH HEH HEH!
I'VE SURVIVED THIS LONG BY FEEDING ON A FOOL'S RESOURCE. LOVE.
ABELARDO'S LOVE FOR JOANA, LASTING THESE PAST HUNDRED YEARS. SO PURE, EVEN DEATH COULDN'T DESTROY IT.
MOOOOOOANN
GERRY!
MOOOOOOANN
ABELARDO?!

WHEN WE DIED, DURING THE FIRE...

MY LIFE, GONE. I LOST *EVERYTHING*... EXCEPT MY HUNGER...

...THAT, TOO, WAS FADING FAST. I BEGAN TO FORGET WHO I WAS.

THEN FOR THE FIRST TIME, I SAW. THAT LOVE IS THE ONLY THING THAT LASTS.

LOVE LASTS *FOREVER!*

I MADE ABELARDO WRITE DOWN HIS MEMORIES OF JOANA. SO THAT HE'D REMEMBER. HIS LONGING FUELED BOTH OF US.

HIS WERE THE LETTERS YOU FOUND IN THE CAFE BASEMENT.

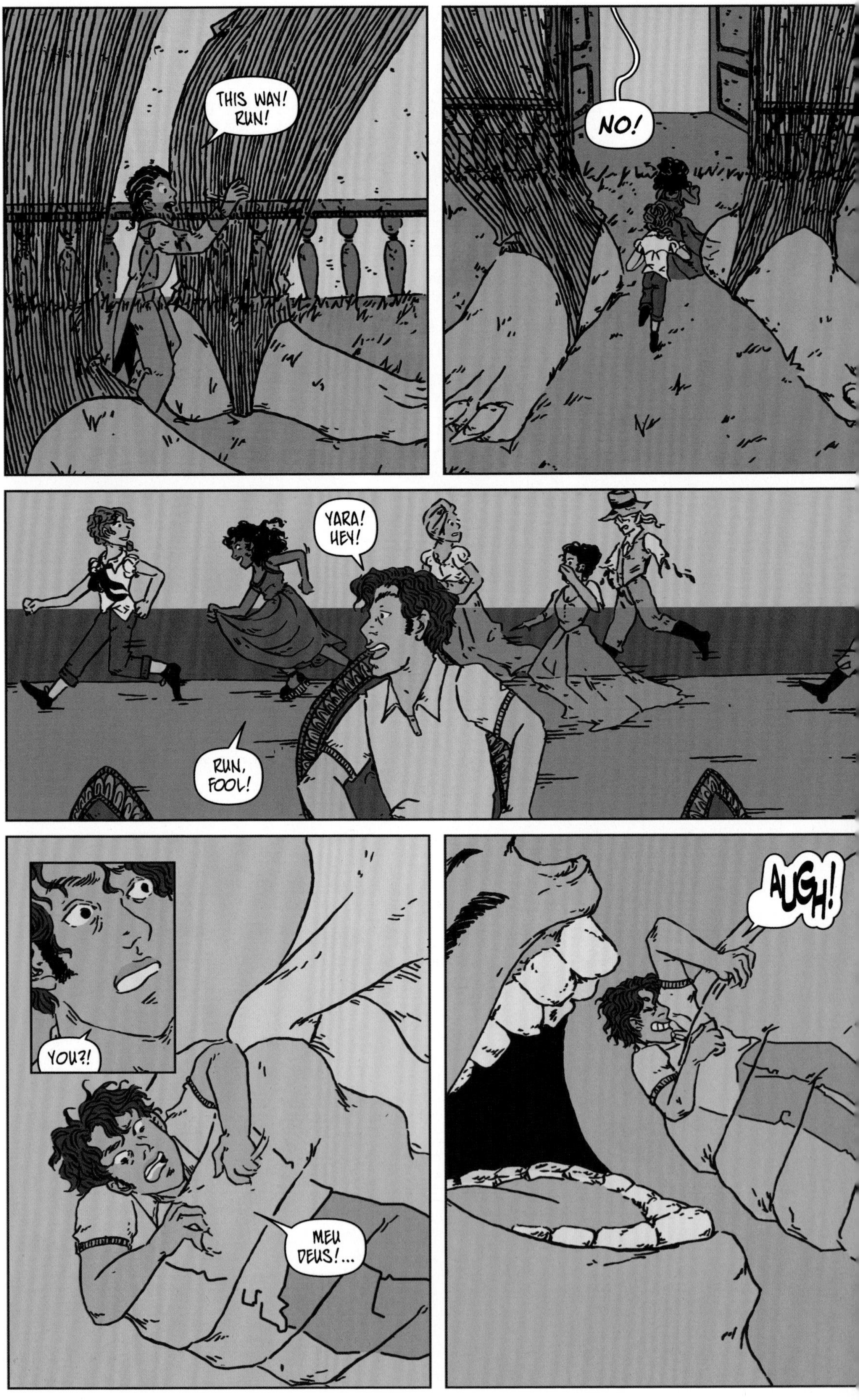
THIS WAY! RUN!
NO!
YARA! HEY!
RUN, FOOL!
YOU?!
MEU DEUS!...
AUGH!

ESME!

WE CAN TALK AFTER WE OUTRUN THAT VAMPIRE GHOST.

NO. I'M NOT RUNNING ANYMORE.

WHAT ARE YOU DOING?! HE'S GONNA EAT YOU!

ESME, THIS IS MY HOME.

OUR HOME. I'M GONNA FIGHT FOR IT. FIGHT FOR US.

STOP BEING DRAMATIC!

WHOOOAA!

RUUMMBLLEE

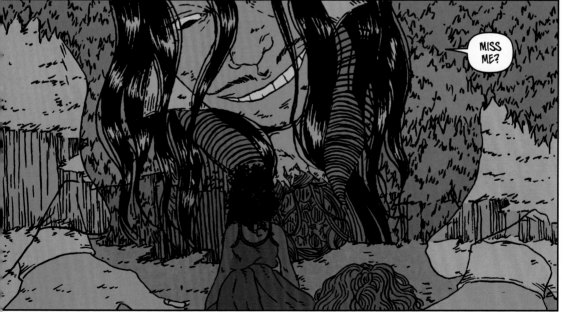

MISS ME?

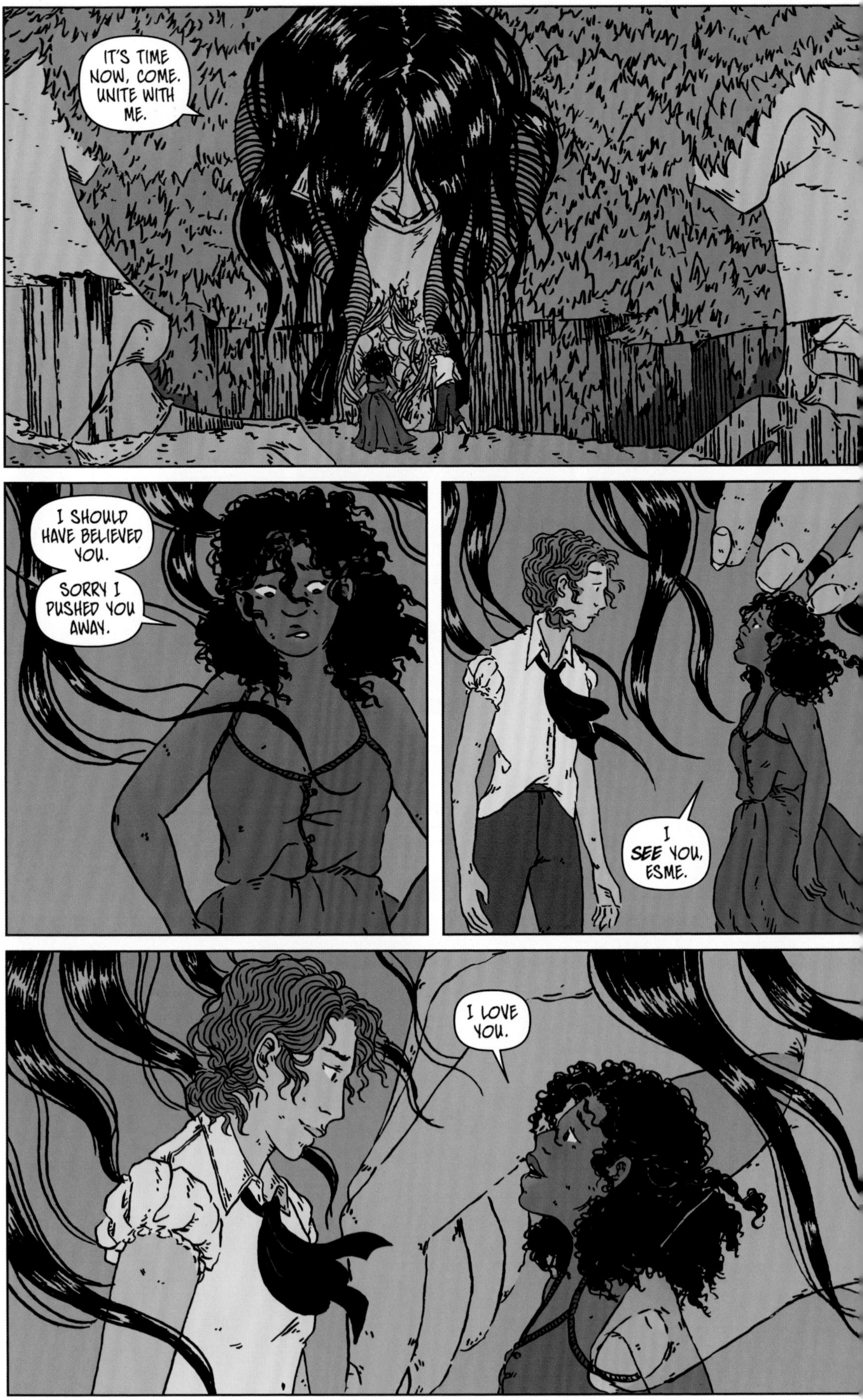
IT'S TIME NOW, COME. UNITE WITH ME.
I SHOULD HAVE BELIEVED YOU.
SORRY I PUSHED YOU AWAY.
I SEE YOU, ESME.
I LOVE YOU.

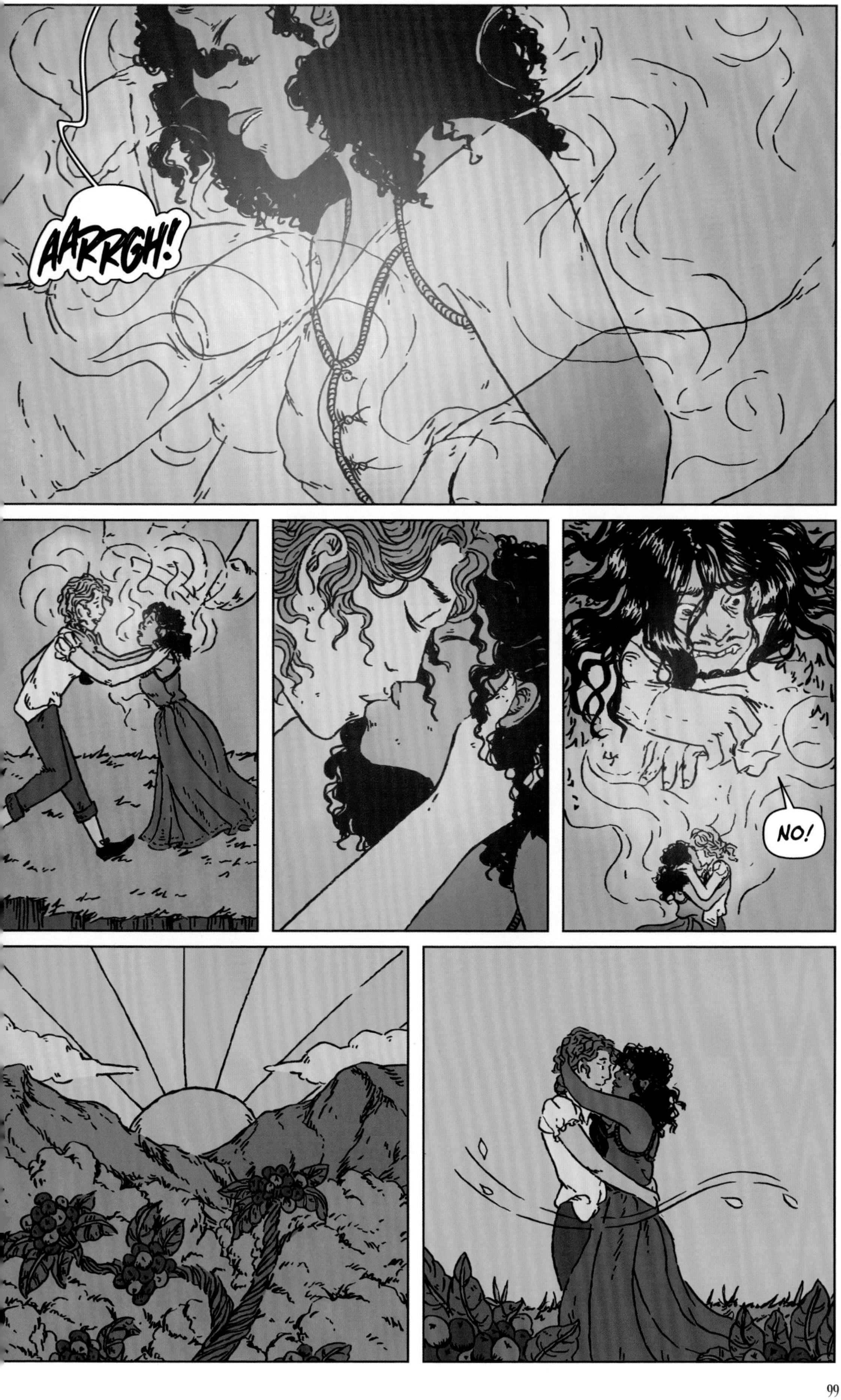
AARRGH!
NO!

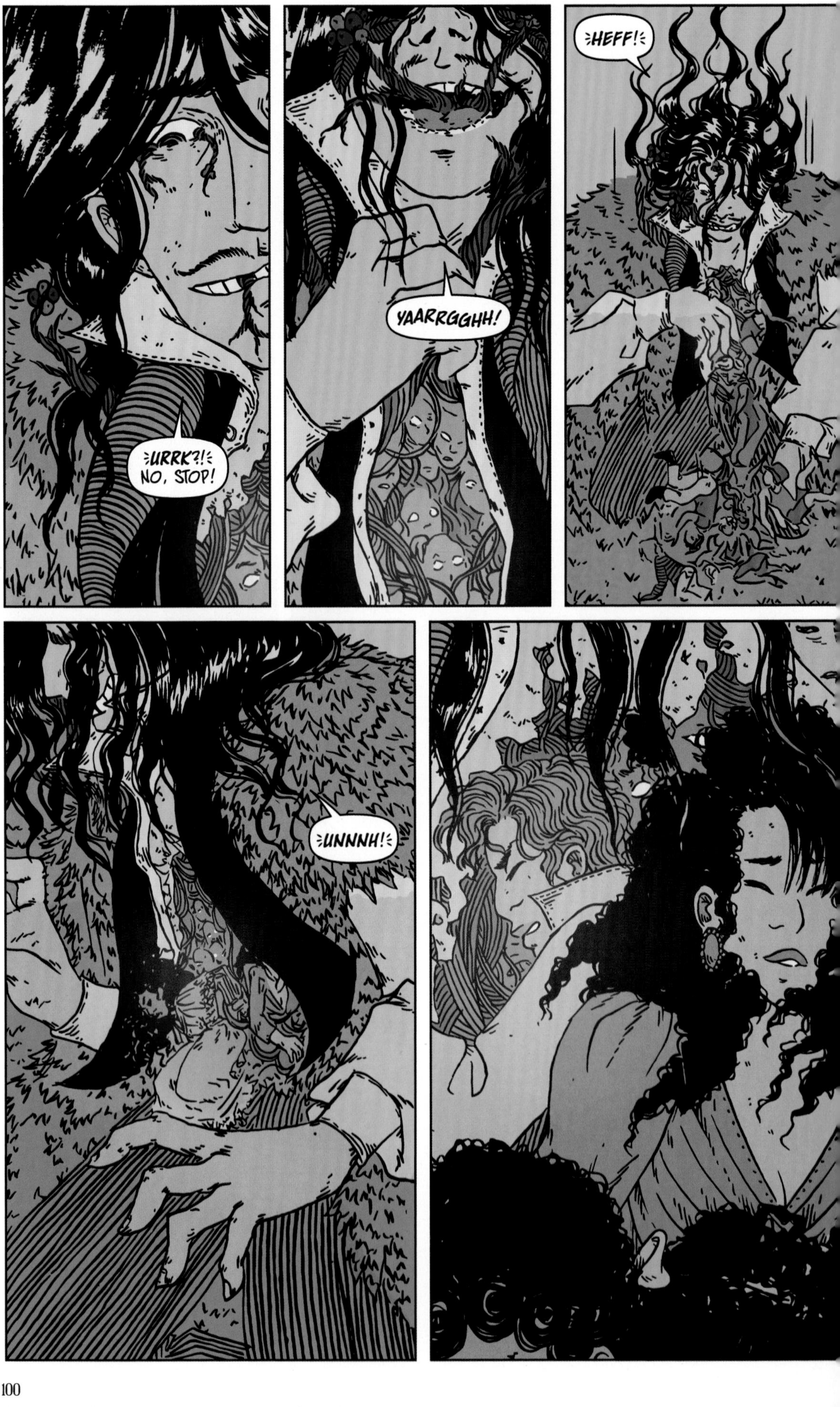
URRK?! NO, STOP!
YAARRGGHH!
HEFF!
UNNNH!

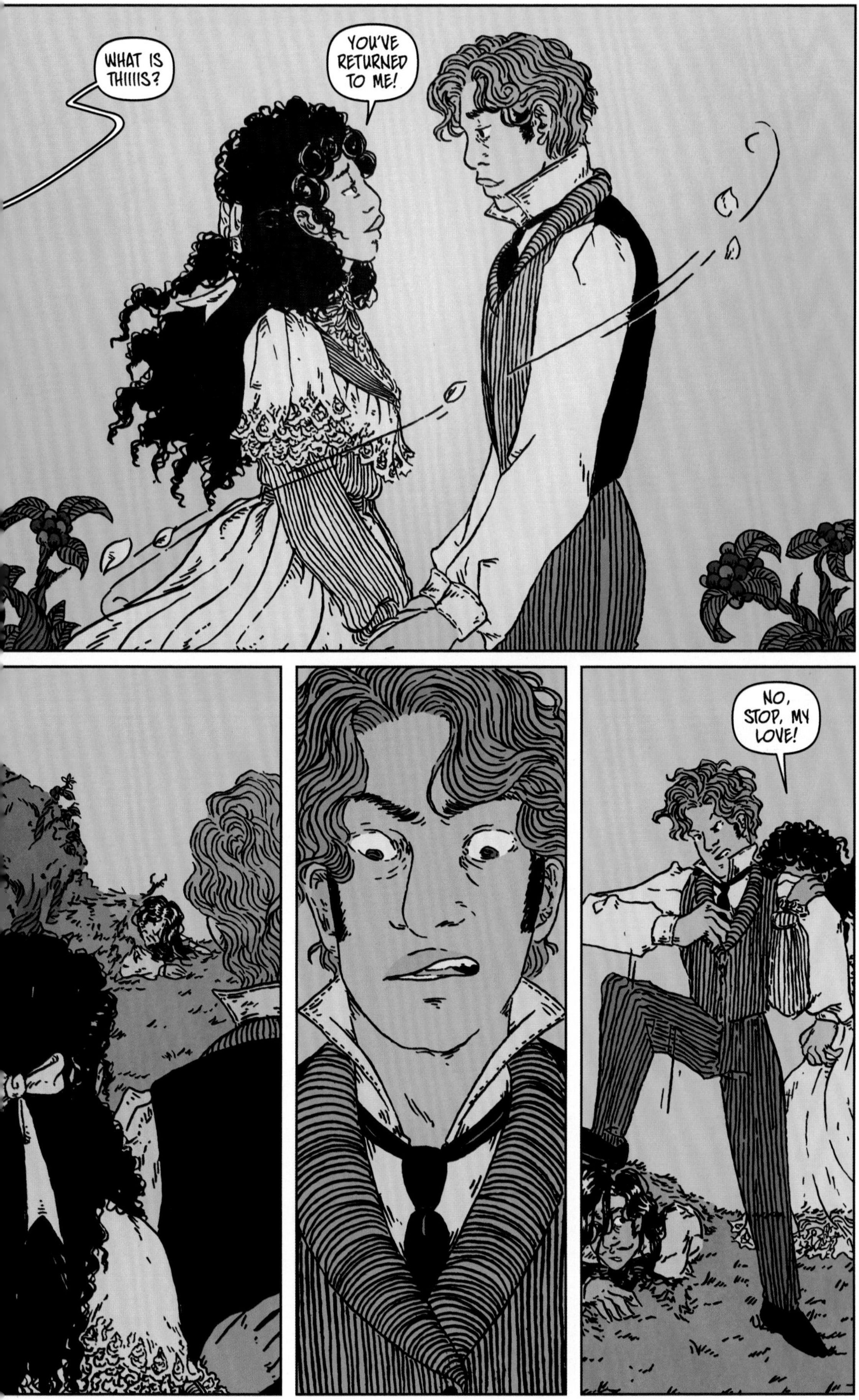
WHAT IS THIIIIS?
YOU'VE RETURNED TO ME!
NO, STOP, MY LOVE!

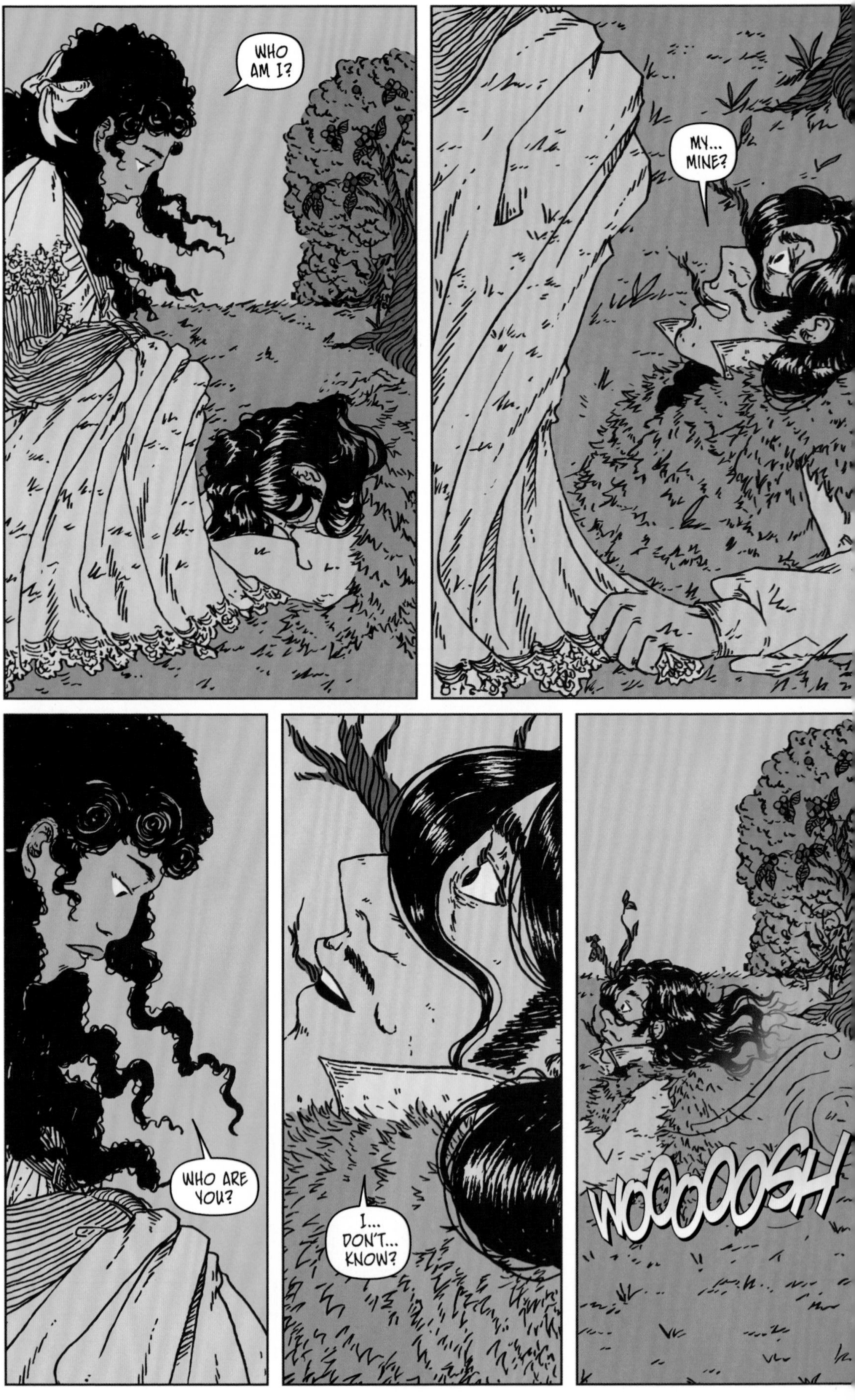
WHO AM I?
MY... MINE?
WHO ARE YOU?
I... DON'T... KNOW?
WOOOOOSH

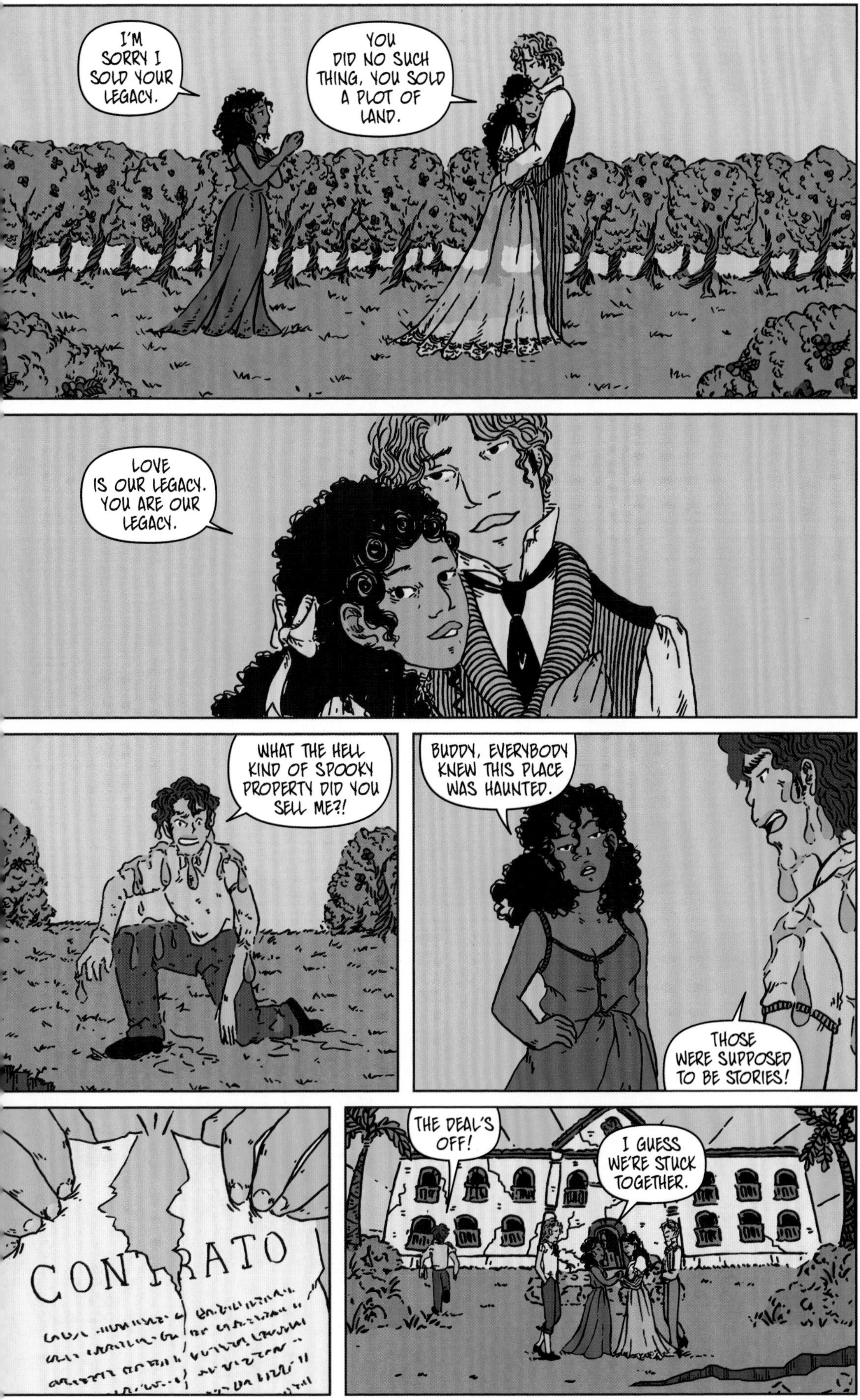
I'M SORRY I SOLD YOUR LEGACY.
YOU DID NO SUCH THING, YOU SOLD A PLOT OF LAND.
LOVE IS OUR LEGACY. YOU ARE OUR LEGACY.
WHAT THE HELL KIND OF SPOOKY PROPERTY DID YOU SELL ME?!
BUDDY, EVERYBODY KNEW THIS PLACE WAS HAUNTED.
THOSE WERE SUPPOSED TO BE STORIES!
CONTRATO
THE DEAL'S OFF!
I GUESS WE'RE STUCK TOGETHER.

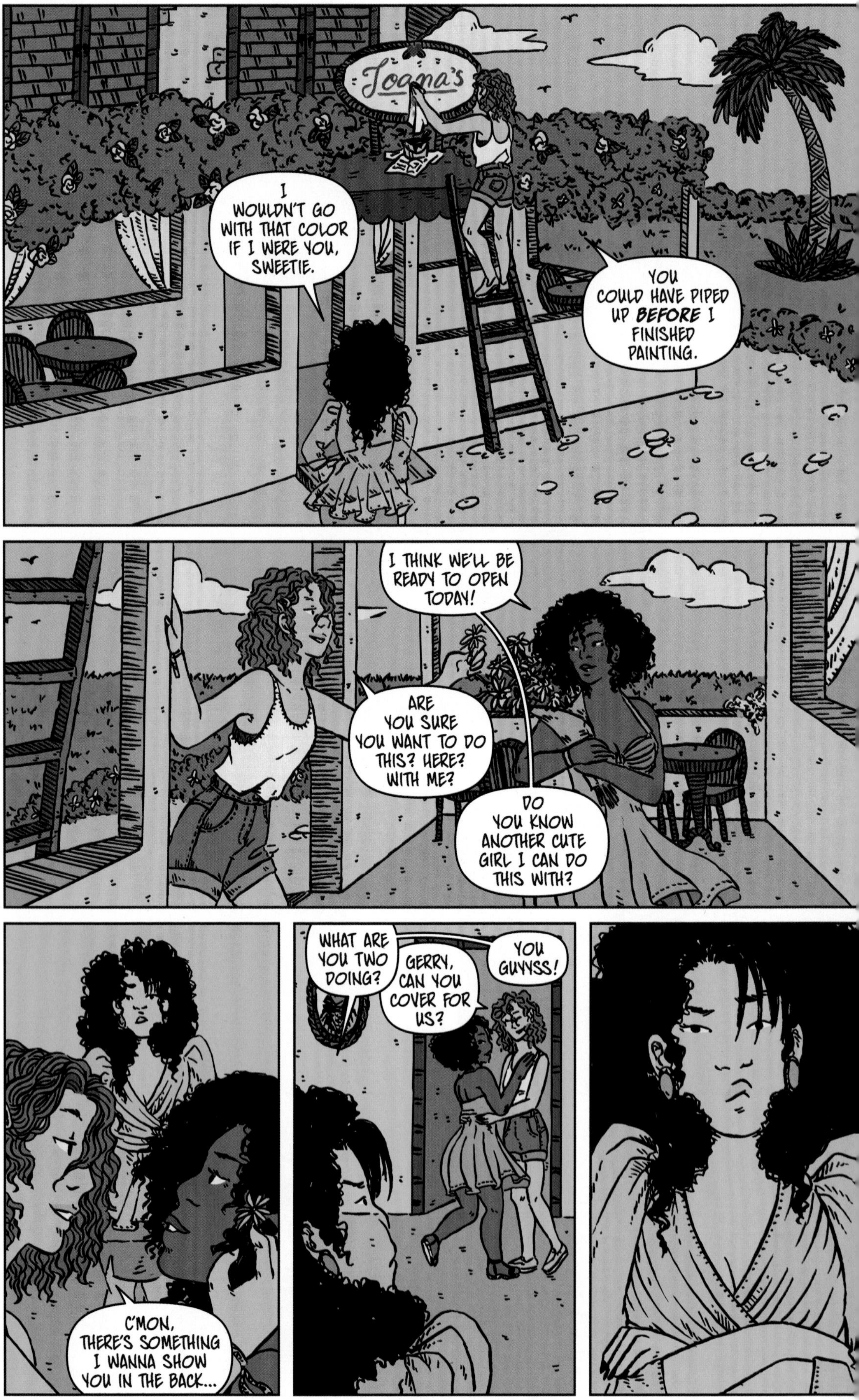
Joana's
I WOULDN'T GO WITH THAT COLOR IF I WERE YOU, SWEETIE.
YOU COULD HAVE PIPED UP **BEFORE** I FINISHED PAINTING.
I THINK WE'LL BE READY TO OPEN TODAY!
ARE YOU SURE YOU WANT TO DO THIS? HERE? WITH ME?
DO YOU KNOW ANOTHER CUTE GIRL I CAN DO THIS WITH?
C'MON, THERE'S SOMETHING I WANNA SHOW YOU IN THE BACK...
WHAT ARE YOU TWO DOING?
YOU GUYYSS!
GERRY, CAN YOU COVER FOR US?

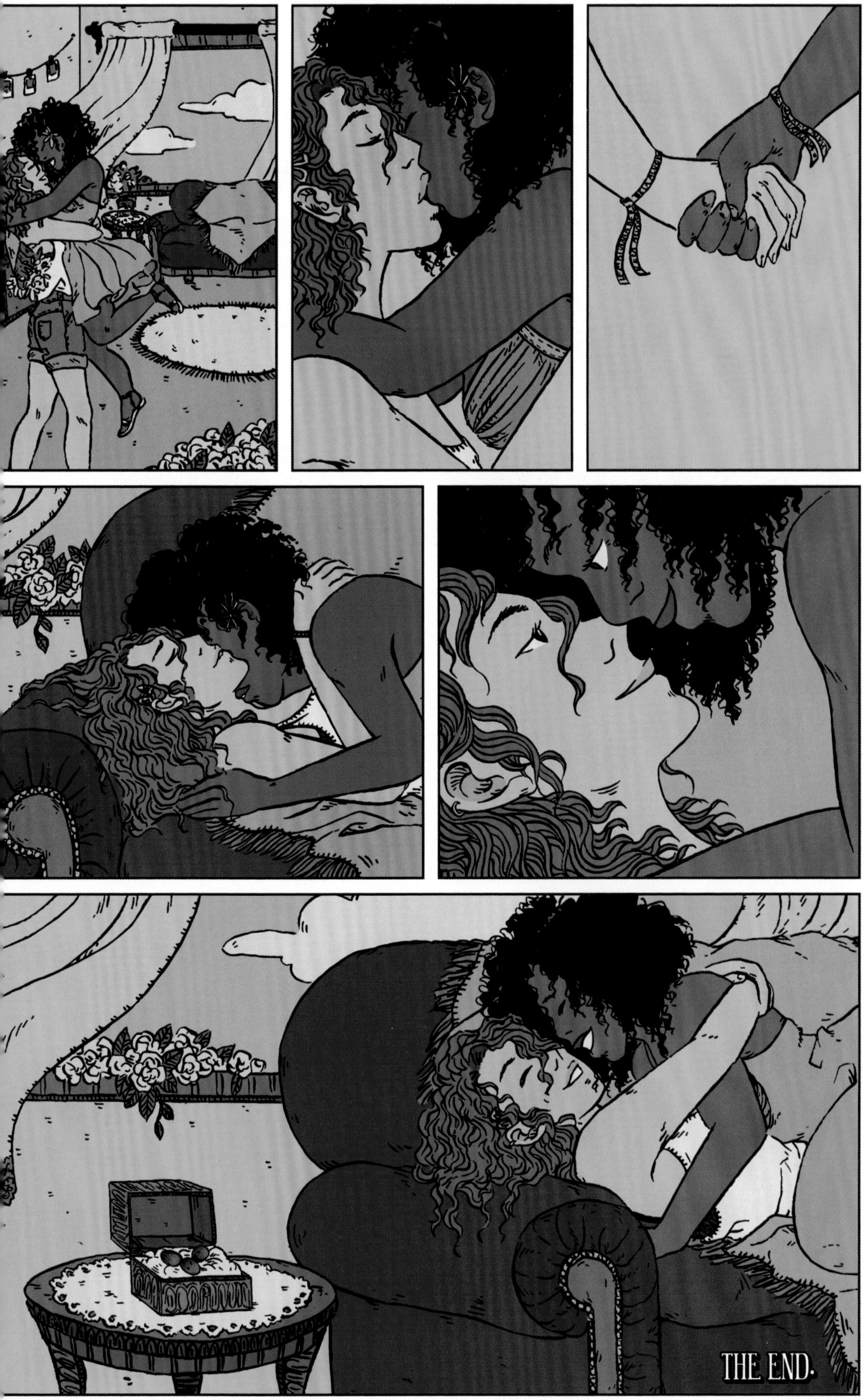
THE END.

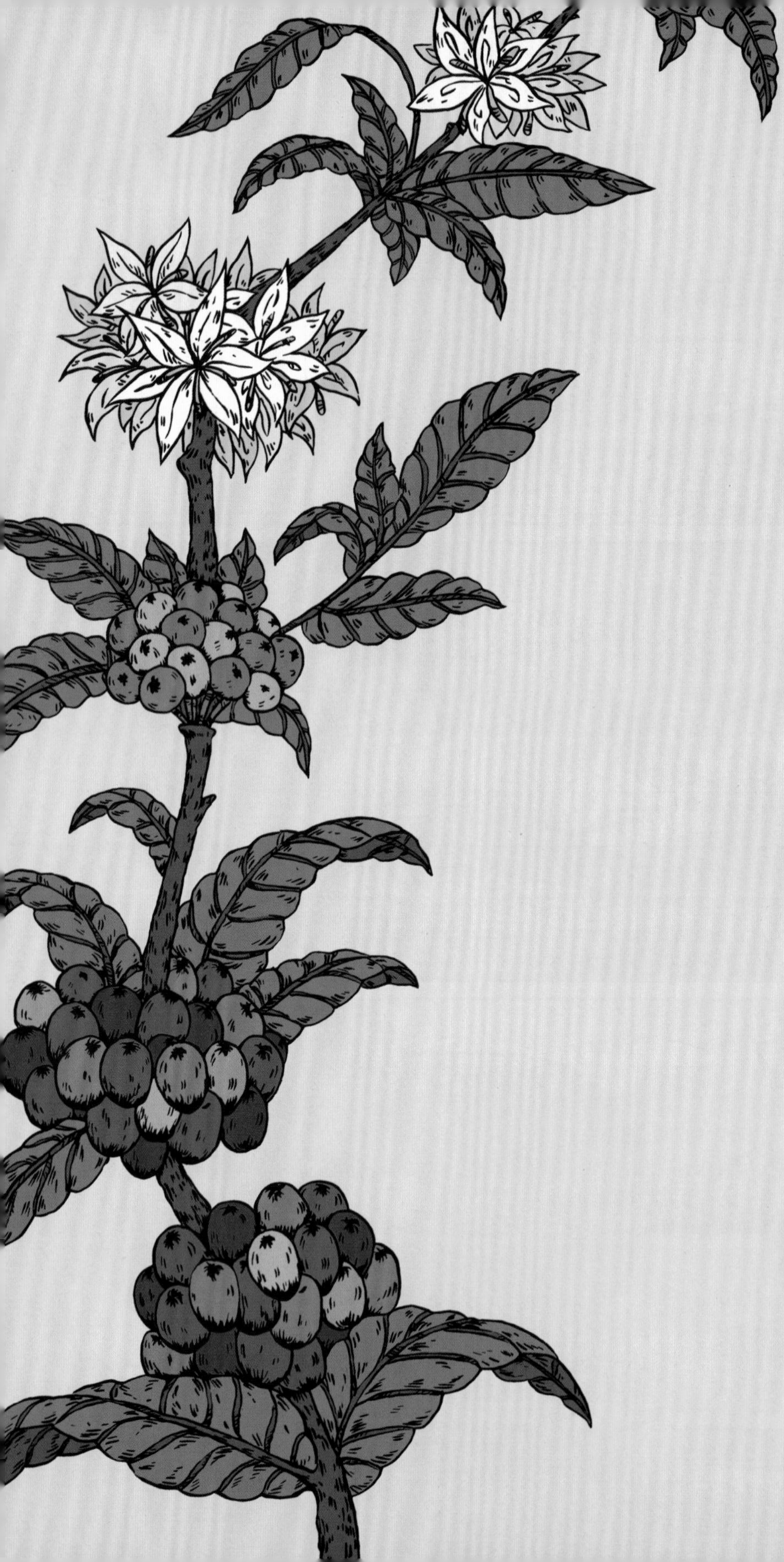

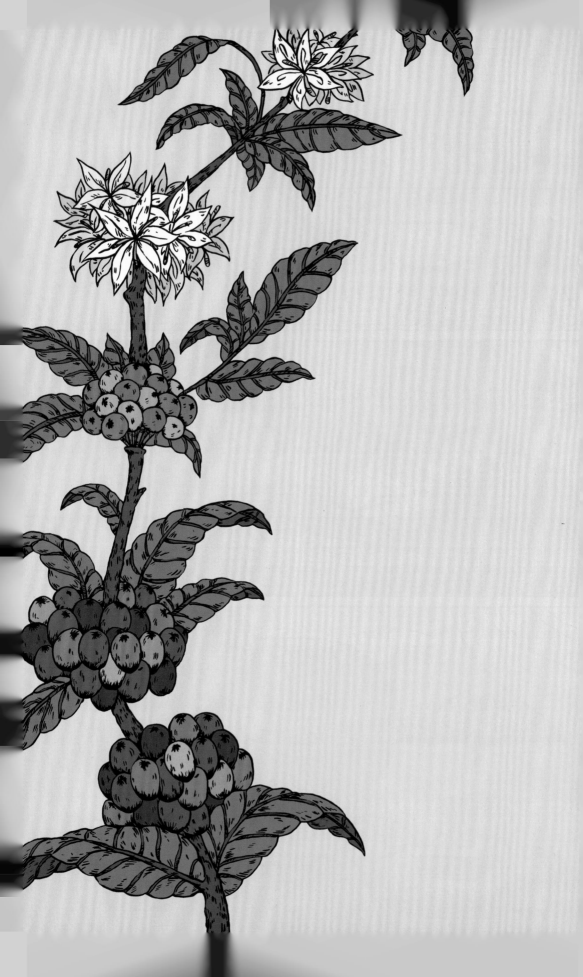

THE
CULTURAL & VISUAL
REFERENCES OF
CREMA

Artist Dante Luiz explored different aspects of Brazilian culture and aesthetics to develop the rich visual identity of *Crema*. From imagining an original scenario for the story to adding elements of telenovelas to the narrative, the ambiance of the graphic novel is both fictional and historical, magical and real. Below, we spotlight a few of the references used in the process.

1. SETTING

Bela Alvorada is not a real town; it was created solely for *Crema* and was inspired by historical cities from the state of Minas Gerais for their untouched Portuguese colonial architecture. The decision to place the story in a small colonial town was made due to the fact that most English-speaking fiction depicts Brazil only through urban settings and beaches. Because one of the major themes of the narrative is how the past is still alive, it's represented here by baroque houses and churches in a modern world.

There are also references to Coffee Era farms from the state of São Paulo in the work. The name Bela Alvorada (beautiful dawn) was crafted to feel believable, referencing Belo Horizonte (beautiful horizon), the real capital of the same region.

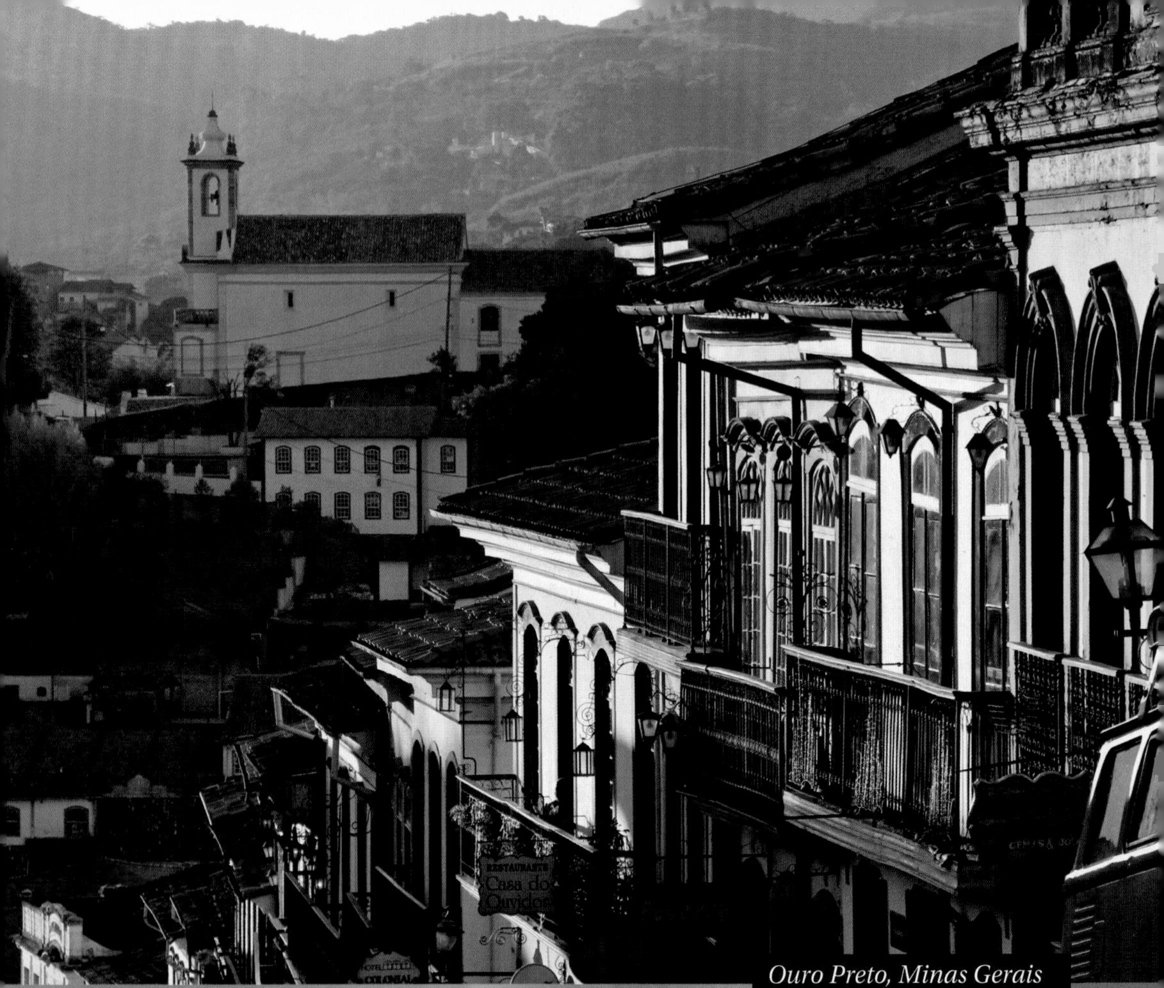
RESTAURANTE
Casa do

Ouro Preto, Minas Gerais

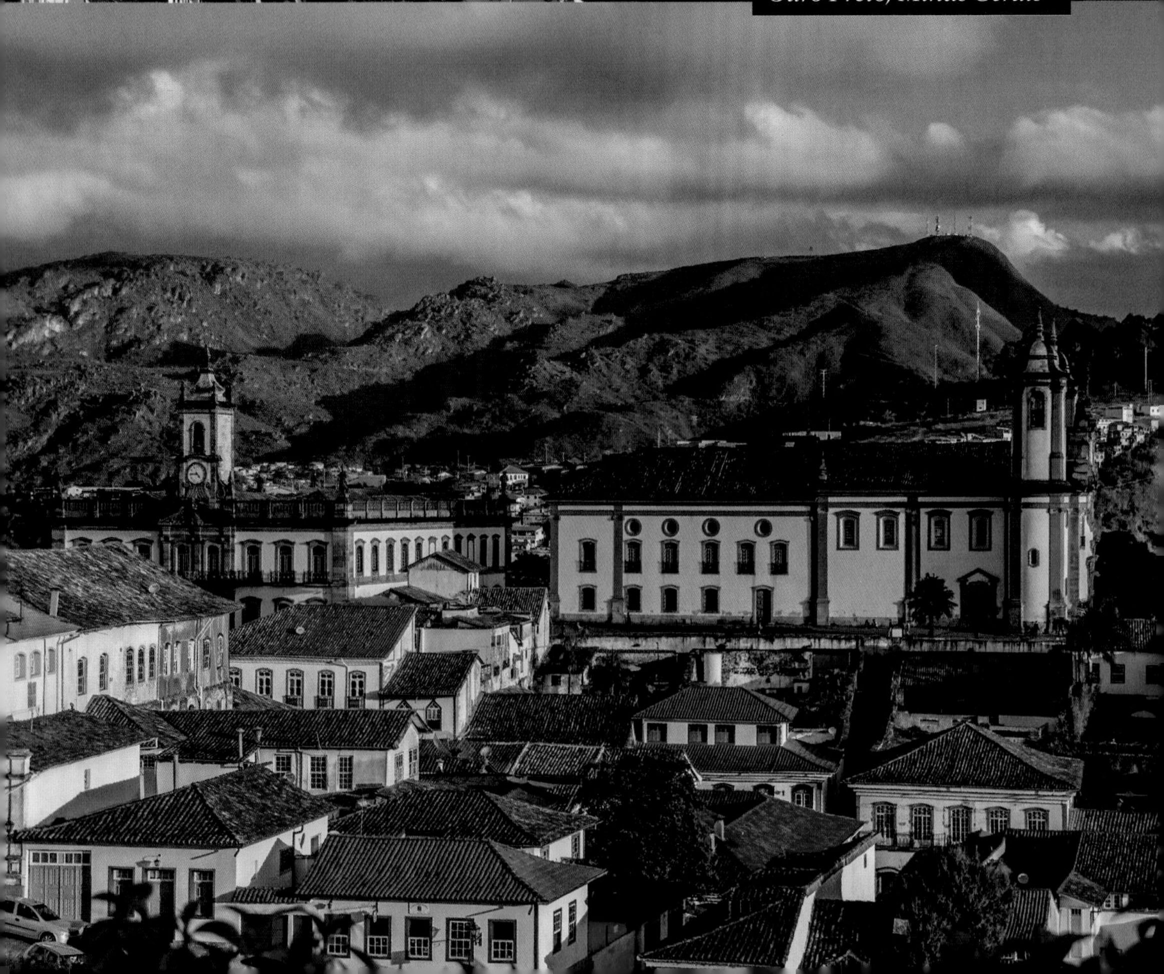

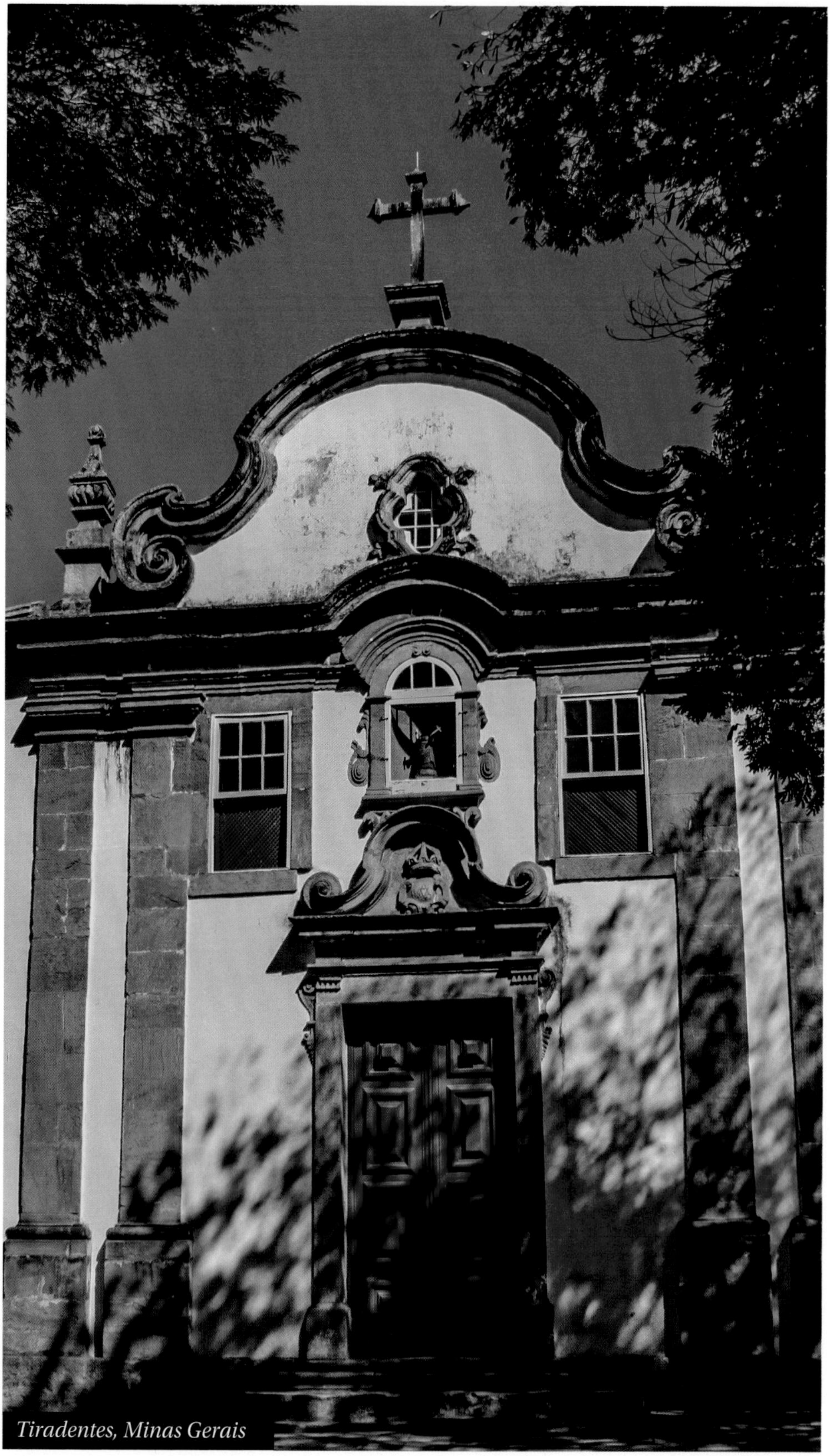
Tiradentes, Minas Gerais

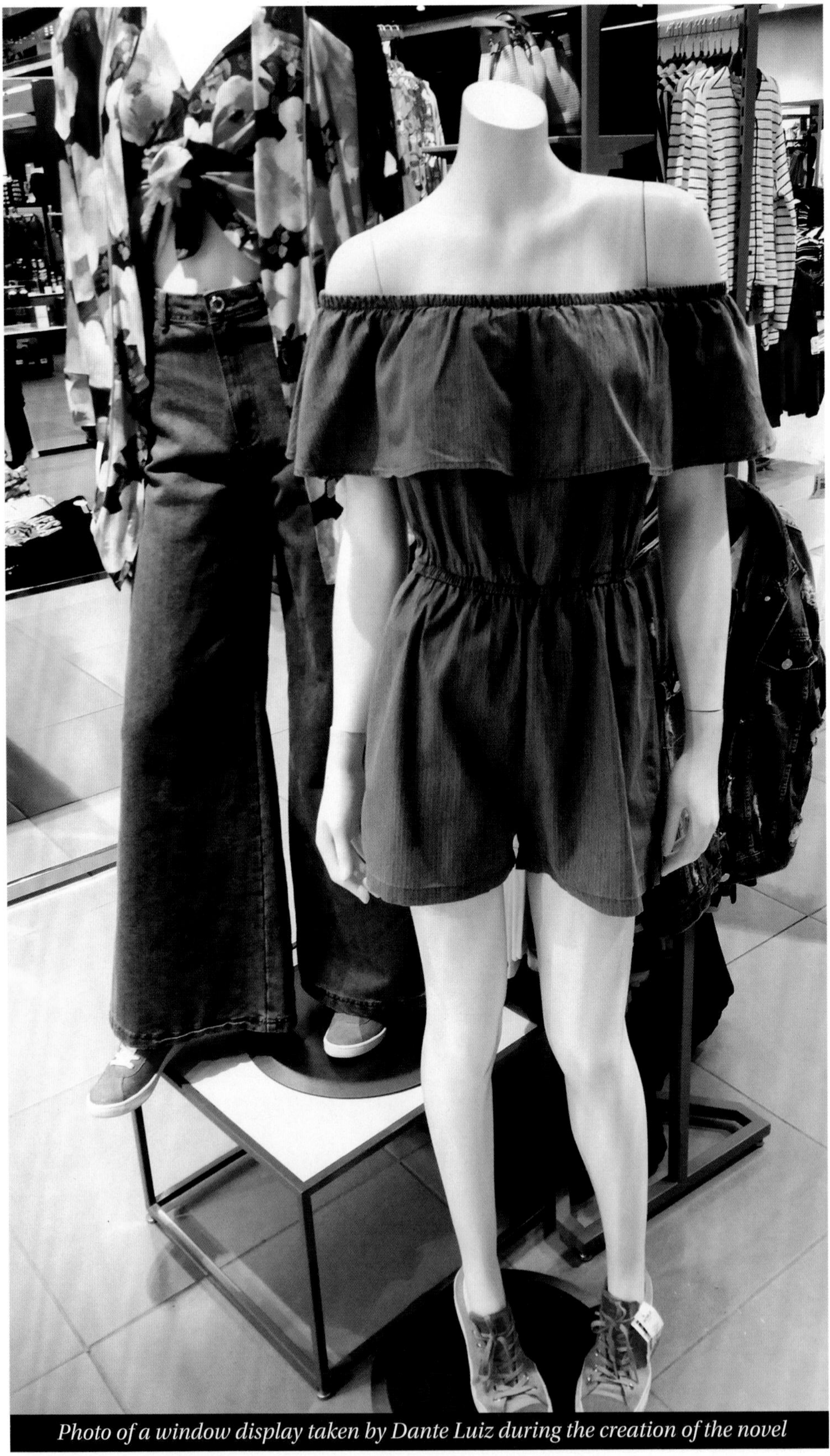

Photo of a window display taken by Dante Luiz during the creation of the novel

2. YARA & FASHION

She may be the young heiress of a century-old empire, but Yara's style mirrors what is found on the streets of Brazil and in everyday department stores across the country: cool, fresh, and affordable. Her clothes reflect her confident personality, and her style starts influencing Esme as well in the second part of the graphic novel.

3. COSTUME DESIGN

Although the ghost story line happens during the belle époque, the costumes and visuals of the flashbacks were not created to be an accurate representation of historical fashion but rather a stylized version inspired by Brazilian telenovelas from 1970 to 1990. Television shows from those decades used to recycle previous costumes to save time and money, creating a specific kind of anachronistic imagery now common in most historical fiction in Brazil. This style was also reproduced in *Crema*, with inspiration taken from such works as *Xica da Silva* (1996), *Marquesa de Santos* (1984), and, more recently, *Lado a lado* (2012).

THE PROCESS OF CREATING CREMA

PAGE 33 (five panels)

PANEL 1

Now they're entering Yara's home. Yara leads Esme (by the hand) across the living room. There are packed boxes everywhere.

> YARA
> They think it was a gas leak. I knew I shouldn't have left those guys alone...

PANEL 2

> YARA
> You're ok though, right?.
> (cont)
> C'mon, let's get you out of those smokey clothes.
> I'll draw you a bath.

PANEL 3

Yara sits on the edge of the tub, her hand in the water, but she's looking over her shoulder at Esme: Standing in the doorway fumbling with her top.

PANEL 4

Yara helping Esme remove her top.

YARA

Here, let me help.

PANEL 5

Closer. Intimately, Yara's nose hovering over Esme's bare shoulder.

YARA

Just breathe.

PAGE 34

PANEL 1

Esme now very assertively approaching Yara. Taking Yara's top off.

PANEL 2

Esme's eyes open, eagerly. Like a tiger's.

PANEL 3

They kiss.

PANEL 4-(however many you need)

They begin to make love in the bathroom. Pressed up against wall tiles, fogged reflections in the mirror, etc.

PAGE 35

Dante, for love making sequences, I'm going to switch over to "Marvel Method". Stating the page objective, but leaving it up to you to decide how we achieve it. Number of panels, sequence of action, all up to you.

MARVEL METHOD

Yara leads Esme to her bedroom. Yara's room should be in contrast to Esme's. Big, and well appointed. It's the place of a wealthy person. The lovemaking continues here on Yara's big bed.

The lovemaking should build in passion and intensity over the next two pages. Make it, engaging, hungry, erotic but shy away from showing genitalia.

PAGE 36

MARVEL METHOD

The love scene escalates reaching its crescendo at the end of the page.

Stage 1: Script

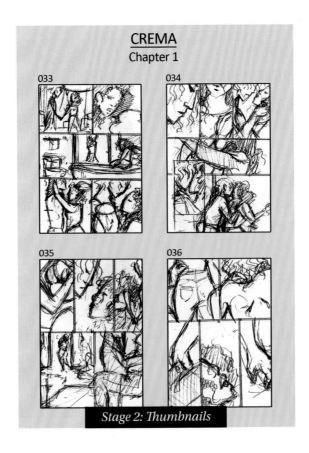

Stage 2: Thumbnails

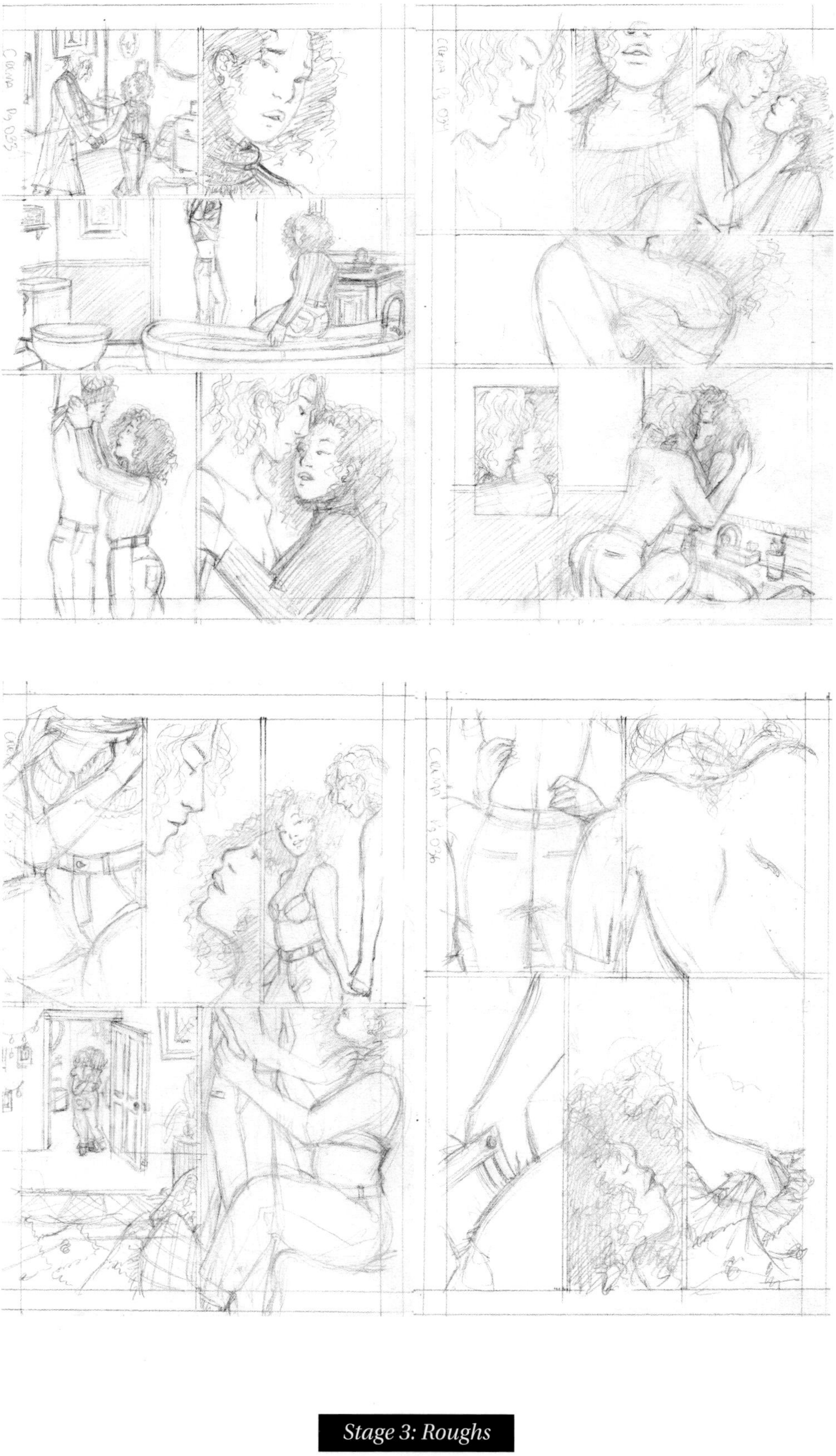

Stage 3: Roughs

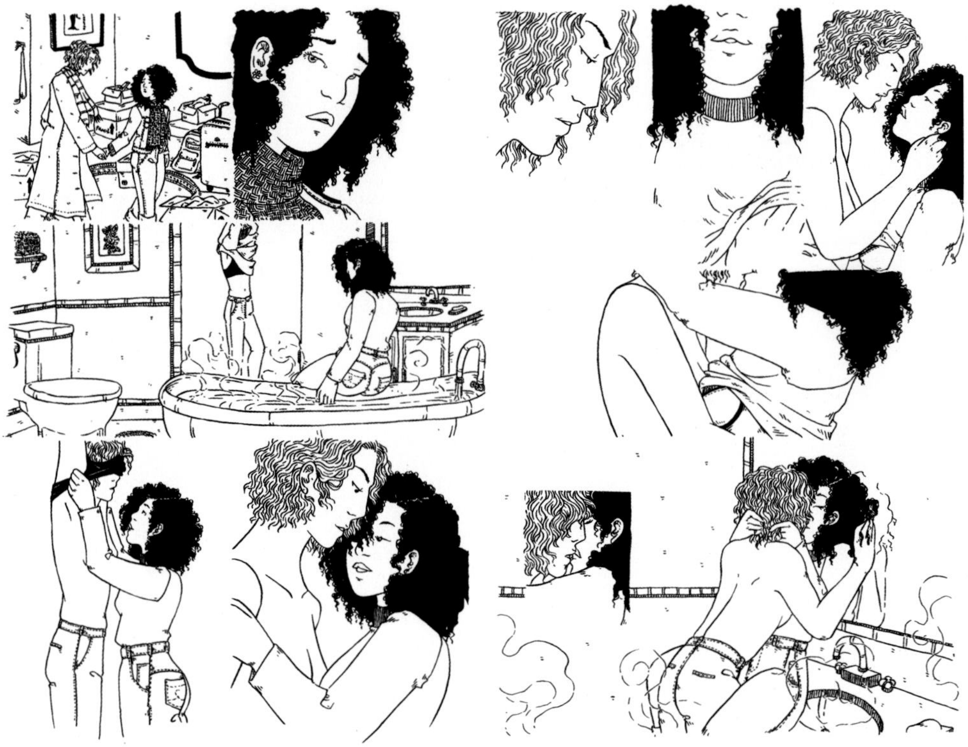

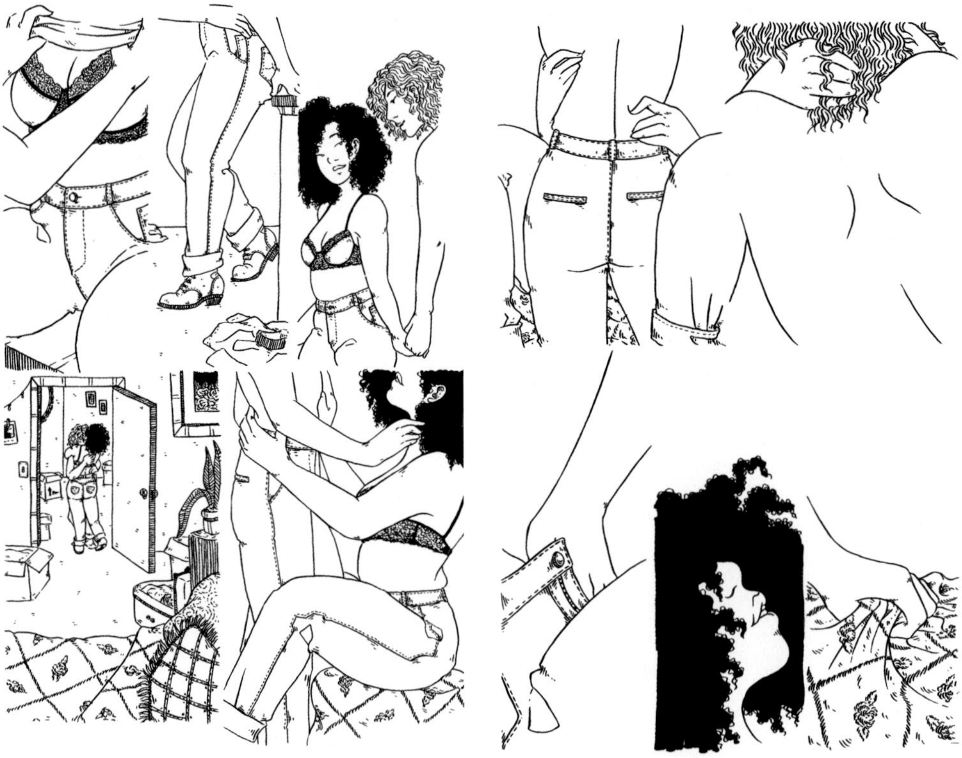

Stage 4: Inks

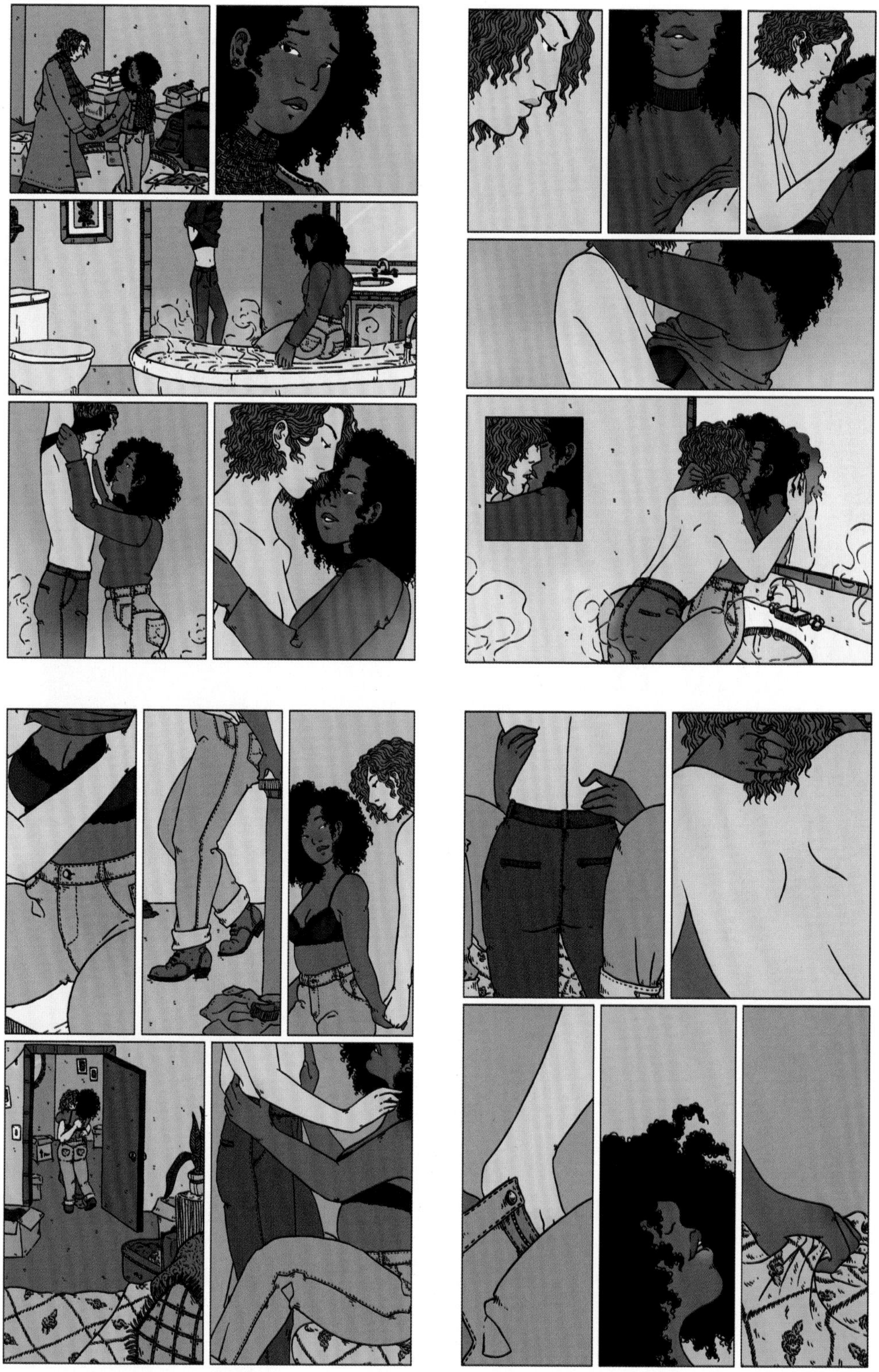

Stage 5: Colors

CHARACTER SKETCHES

BY DANTE LUIZ

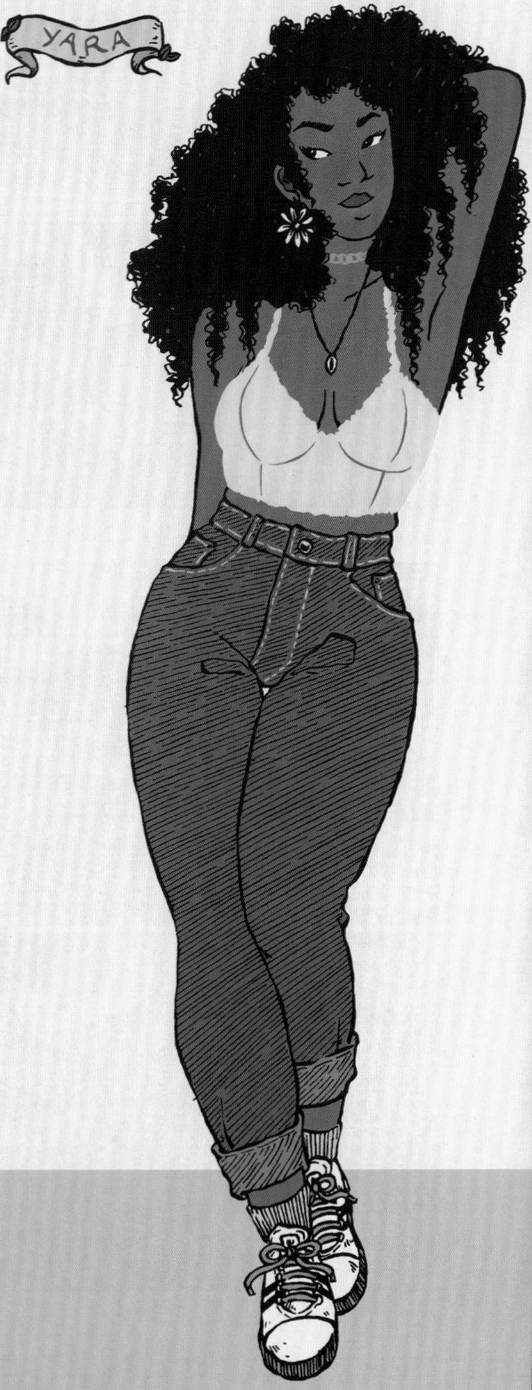
YARA

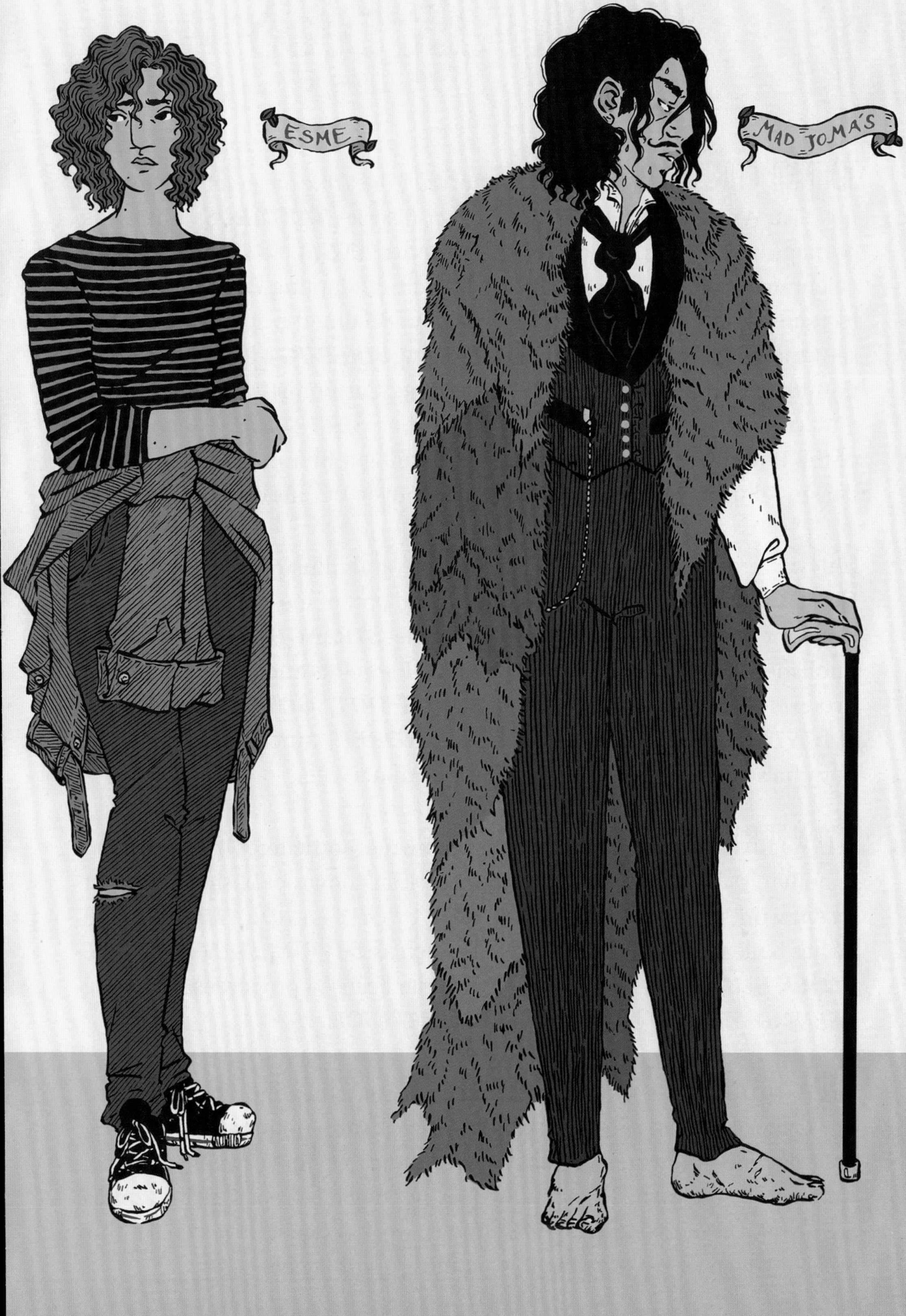
ESME
MAD JOMAS

CREATOR BIOS

JOHNNIE CHRISTMAS is a number-one *New York Times* best-selling graphic novelist. Writer of the Image Comics sci-fi series *TARTARUS*, Johnnie is perhaps best known for cocreating the series *ANGEL CATBIRD* with the celebrated writer Margaret Atwood, as well as adapting William Gibson's lost screenplay for *ALIEN 3* into a critically acclaimed graphic novel of the same name. His credits also include creating *FIREBUG*—for which he was nominated for the Joe Shuster Outstanding Cartoonist Award in 2019—and cocreating the pre-apocalyptic thriller *SHELTERED*. A graduate of the Pratt Institute in Brooklyn, NY, earning a BFA in communication design / illustration, Johnnie makes Vancouver, BC, his home.

DANTE LUIZ is a comic artist, editor, and illustrator from Brazil. He's a two-time Prism Awards nominee and part of the 2020 Hugo-finalist team for the speculative fiction magazine *STRANGE HORIZONS*. He publishes adult romance comics at Filthy Figments and has participated in several anthologies, such as *SHOUT OUT*, *GOTHIC TALES OF HAUNTED LOVE*, and *WAYWARD KINDRED*, among others. Right now, he's quarantined in Porto Alegre with his wife.

RYAN FERRIER is a Canadian comic book writer and letterer, having worked in both roles with every major North American comics publisher. His most recent work includes *I CAN SELL YOU A BODY* and *DEATH ORB*, and he has built acclaim with original titles such as *D4VE*, *CRIMINY*, *KENNEL BLOCK BLUES*, and several of your favorite licensed properties, including *TEENAGE MUTANT NINJA TURTLES* and *G.I. JOE*.

ATLA HRAFNEY is an Icelandic comics writer and editor who's worked on Eisner, Broken Frontier, and Xeric Award–nominated projects. As a day job she works at Hiveworks Comics as part of their editorial staff, and by night she . . . actually does her day job, because time zones are awful. On occasion she finds time to work on neat projects like this one, and even writes her own forthcoming graphic novels.